PENGU.. . _ _

DATELINE ISLAMABAD

Amit Baruah is *The Hindu*'s Diplomatic Correspondent and Senior Assistant Editor. In his twenty-one years as a journalist, he has covered a wide range of issues, including Jammu & Kashmir, the conflict in Punjab and matters of internal security.

Baruah worked as the newspaper's Special Correspondent in Colombo (1995-1997), Islamabad (1997-2000) and South-East Asia/Pacific Correspondent based in Singapore (2000-02).

In 2000, Baruah was awarded the Prem Bhatia Award for excellence in journalism. The citation for the award read: 'He has shown courage and objectivity during his assignment in Pakistan; and his coverage of such major events as Kargil, the Indian Airlines hijacking to Kandahar and the Musharraf coup was regarded as outstanding.'

In 2002, Amit Baruah returned to New Delhi where he lives with his wife and two children.

Dateline Islamabad

Amit Baruah

PENGUIN BOOKS

PENGUIN BOOKS
Published by the Penguin Group
Penguin Books India Pvt. Ltd, 11 Community Centre, Panchsheel Park,
New Delhi 110 017, India
Penguin Group (USA) Inc., 375 Hudson Street, New York, New York 10014, USA
Penguin Group (Canada), 90 Eglinton Avenue East, Suite 700, Toronto,
Ontario, M4P 2Y3, Canada (a division of Pearson Penguin Canada Inc.)
Penguin Books Ltd, 80 Strand, London WC2R 0RL, England
Penguin Ireland, 25 St Stephen's Green, Dublin 2, Ireland
(a division of Penguin Books Ltd)
Penguin Group (Australia), 250 Camberwell Road, Camberwell,
Victoria 3124, Australia (a division of Pearson Australia Group Pty Ltd)
Penguin Group (NZ), 67 Apollo Drive, Rosedale, North Shore 0632,
New Zealand (a division of Pearson New Zealand Ltd)
Penguin Group (South Africa) (Pty) Ltd, 24 Sturdee Avenue, Rosebank,
Johannesburg 2196, South Africa

Penguin Books Ltd, Registered Offices: 80 Strand, London WC2R 0RL, England

First published by Penguin Books India 2007

Copyright © Amit Baruah 2007

10 9 8 7 6 5 4 3 2 1

ISBN-13: 9780143102465   ISBN-10: 014310246X

Typeset in *Sabon Roman* by SŪRYA, New Delhi
Printed at Chaman Offset Printers, New Delhi

For

Minu, Anushka and Antara—
who made it all possible

Contents

❖

Preface   ix
Introduction: Arrival in the Sharif Era   xi

1. Great People, Paranoid State   1

2. India and Pakistan—Talking At Each Other   16

3. Nawaz Sharif vs Sajjad Ali Shah   36

4. Sharif, Karamat and Musharraf   56

5. Going Nuclear   75

6. Vajpayee in Lahore   101

7. From Lahore to Kargil   124

8. The Fallout from Kargil   153

9. The March of the 111 Brigade   178

10. Musharraf, India and Kandahar   197

11. Can Musharraf Reverse the Zia Legacy?   219

12. India and Pakistan: Looking to the Future   242

     Notes   261

Preface

❖

THIS IS A journalistic account of the events I reported from Islamabad between April 1997 and June 2000 for *The Hindu* and *Frontline*. It's an effort to show how difficult the job of a foreign correspondent is in a hostile nation.

In this, I have tried to be as honest and candid, but have held back personal details. There is a reason behind my reticence here. Naming names could impact negatively on my many friends and acquaintances still living and working in Pakistan.

This book could not have been written without the insights of my Pakistani friends. Of course, the impressions of life in Islamabad are all my own, but I was benefited enormously by my conversations and interactions with so many Pakistanis.

My friends in the Indian High Commission in Islamabad were invaluable to our existence in Pakistan— both at the personal and professional levels. But again, I prefer that they remain anonymous.

This account is, I believe, the first that provides an

insight into an Indian reporter's many personal struggles in Pakistan. Despite all the personal and professional difficulties that one faced, my Pakistan assignment was both exciting and enriching.

Having spent a total of eighteen years working with *The Hindu*, what I am today has largely been shaped by that newspaper. I am grateful to *The Hindu*'s Editor-in-Chief N. Ram, who pioneered investigative journalism in India, for permission to write this book.

I would like to thank *The Hindu*'s Editor N.Ravi and then Executive Editor Malini Parthasarthy for posting me in Pakistan. My interest in that country was kindled for the first time in December 1989 when *The Hindu*'s then Editor G. Kasturi sent me to Srinagar on a reporting assignment.

I'm also grateful to Nandini Mehta (earlier with Penguin and now Features Editor in *Outlook* magazine) for believing that the book was a good idea and going through the manuscript with a toothcomb. Prita Maitra of Penguin, who took over from Nandini, was both diligent and full of encouragement.

This book could not have been written without the unstinted support of my wife, Minu, who bore life in Pakistan with a grin. My daughters Anushka, and Antara, born in Islamabad, made for wonderful distractions.

New Delhi   **Amit Baruah**
15 June 2005

Introduction:
Arrival in the Sharif Era

❖

FOR ANY INDIAN reporter, Pakistan is the biggest story. I got mine at the end of 1996 when, after my having spent two-and-a-half eventful years as *The Hindu*'s correspondent in Sri Lanka, my office asked me to move to Islamabad.

It was an assignment that was at once challenging and intimidating. I was going to be setting foot on 'enemy' territory. My Colombo experience as a foreign correspondent would prove invaluable in navigating the daily challenges life and work would pose in Islamabad.

The posting to Pakistan evoked considerable interest amongst friends and acquaintances in Colombo. There was some distress too. An Indian diplomat's wife was quite direct about her concerns.

She told me over lunch at our Queens Terrace house: 'Just don't go.' And, she didn't stop with me. My wife, Minu, was her next target. The same message was conveyed to her as well.

I was a little surprised that the news had prompted so

extreme a reaction. But, then, India–Pakistan relations hadn't ever been great and the legacy of hatred and mistrust was a long one.

My flight out from Delhi to Islamabad, via Lahore, was on Saturday, 12 April 1997. Sipping beer and eating the Saturday afternoon biryani at the Press Club of India, I wasn't entirely sure I would make it to Islamabad that day.

The reason: the Air Traffic Controllers (ATC) were on strike and flights in and out of the country stood cancelled. But, not leaving anything to chance, my bags were already packed and waiting at home.

Suddenly, a friend got a call saying that the ATC strike had been called off. I rushed home from the club, picked up my luggage and made my way to the Indira Gandhi International Airport in time for the flight.

Minu and my daughter, seven-month-old Anushka, were to remain in Delhi till I was able to sort things out for their stay in Islamabad. Our household things had already been dispatched from Colombo by ship and the plan was for Minu and Anushka to join me after some weeks, when presumably, all would be in readiness at our new home.

We had been given an entry visa at the Pakistani High Commission in Colombo. After filling in all kinds of forms and supplying no less than fifteen photos each of Minu and I, we had joked that our pictures would be up in all the police stations of Islamabad.

For the first time in my life, I had to fill up a 'religion' column in the visa form. Much against our agnostic leanings my [nominally Jain!] wife and I wrote 'Hindu'.

'Hindu' was to ensure that there would be no problem in buying and drinking alcohol in an officially alcohol-free nation. In order to ensure that the visa would come through smoothly, we also entered 'housewife' in the 'profession' column in Minu's visa form despite the fact that she had been a journalist for as long as I had. Journalists from India were not the most welcome of their species in Pakistan.

There was, we were aware, no chance of Minu being able to write for an Indian newspaper or magazine from Islamabad. The Pakistani authorities did not surprise us on this score. Minu didn't write a single story in Pakistan.

When I reached Islamabad late in the evening, in heavy rain, a lone Pakistani motorcycle-borne intelligence operative tailed my taxi to the hotel.

I was booked to stay at the Best Western Hotel, which I later discovered was in the middle of nowhere—far from what would be the centre of my work in Islamabad.

It was not as if I was entering Pakistan 'blind'. Sunil Narula, a close friend had been posted in Islamabad as *The Times of India*'s correspondent in 1992–93, and Kesava Menon, *The Hindu*'s first correspondent in Islamabad in the 1990s, had freely shared their experiences and assessments with me.

After staying at the Best Western for a couple of days, I moved to the VIP Guest House near House 5, Street 39, F-6/1, which would shortly become, after some repairs, both home and office.

Moving about in Islamabad was not easy. There were no taxi stands you could telephone to call a cab, and one had to walk all the way to the supermarket to catch a 'yellow taxi'. To save time, I bought a bicycle. This I would employ to transport me to the supermarket, where I would chain it and then take off in a taxi. My bike, I may add, was never lifted.

What was convenient to me, however, was inconvenient to Pakistani intelligence. The motorcycle behind me had to follow at cycle pace. Even in the empty streets of Islamabad, where the presence of intelligence men was a given, especially the F-6/1 sector where many Indian High Commission staffers live, it was an absurd sight—a motorbike tailing a bicycle.

I worked from home. One room in our spacious two-floor bungalow, rented by *The Hindu*, was my office. A laptop, a fax machine, a printer, a mobile phone and an internet connection made up my arrangements.

Getting through to my editorial headquarters in Madras (it wasn't Chennai at the time), or to Delhi by telephone, was a perennial problem.

Email, one came to realize, was the best option to file news reports, but even this failed on occasion. The fax was often my back-up. On occasion, I faxed reports to colleagues in Singapore, London and Bahrain and requested them to send those on to Madras.

Even installing a fax machine posed a problem. After purchasing one, the technician who came to instal it almost never made it to the office because Pakistani intelligence questioned him about what great gadget the new Indian correspondent was setting up in his house. Pakistan, it dawned on me, was going to be one big challenge.

Social contact was limited. Few Pakistanis—friendly as they were—would openly fraternize with me. In their place, I, too, would have stayed away from Indians. Who wanted to be asked uncomfortable questions, visited at home and in the office by interrogators?

Whatever you said or wrote, Pakistani intelligence agencies were clear on one thing: all Indians posted to Pakistan were actual or potential agents working for India's external intelligence agency, the Research & Analysis Wing (RAW). Nothing would convince them to the contrary.

From the early part of April to the end of May, when Minu and Anushka arrived from Delhi, it was a period of combing Islamabad. What one could buy where; what arrangements had to be made so that my infant daughter would be comfortable.

All in all, I discovered, Islamabad is a nice, sleepy, picturesque town. Situated at the foot of the Margalla Hills, it is divided into residential sectors—E, F, G, I— with the neatness that is the hallmark of a planned city.

The address '1, Islamabad' belonged to none other than Field Marshal Ayub Khan, during whose tenure in the 1960s Pakistan's capital was shifted from Karachi to Islamabad. In the heart of the city, this private residence was being used by Pakistan's foreign minister, Gohar Ayub Khan, the son of Ayub Khan.

Accreditation, I thought, was a must the moment I landed. Press Information Department (PID) officials were always pleasant and cheerful, although I suspect each of them would have to account for what was said and discussed with me in their offices.

When I told a Pakistani journalist friend about having successfully obtained my PID card, he said: '*Aapko* accreditation *ki kya zaroorat hai*, accreditation *aap ke saath chalta hai* (Why do you need a formal accreditation card, your accreditation [the intelligence operatives] moves around with you).'

Even while waiting to meet a senior PID official, and seated in his PA's room, the intelligence official (whom we called Taklu; Minu and I had names for each of the dozen-odd men who chased us through the streets of Islamabad), to my discomfiture, walked in.

It was to be the first of many occasions this was to happen. Whether paying the telephone bill or at the doctor's, the shadow was always there. This was an integral part of our lives outside our home in Islamabad. On the rare occasion when the intelligence personnel went missing temporarily, we feared something had gone wrong.

When I went to chase up a visa with the directorate-general of external publicity, part of the ministry of information, an escort was sent with me from the reception area. The office was in the Cabinet Block (something like the South and North Block complexes in Delhi), adjacent to the Aiwan-e-Sadar, the presidential residence. I was, clearly, a security risk to the Government of Pakistan.

Early on, it struck me that the presence of the intelligence operative was intended to intimidate and coerce. There was no effort at tailing you discreetly; at a traffic light the motorcycles, which always had weird and patently false number plates, would halt immediately behind my taxi, later on, my car.

Getting a driving licence was easy enough. If you had a valid driving licence for another country, you were qualified for a Pakistani one. I had two—one Indian and the other Sri Lankan.

In August 1997, just before India's Independence Day, I got a car. It was a Margalla, the Pakistani equivalent of a Suzuki Esteem in India. With that, life became much easier and, by this time, I was reasonably familiar with the broad contours of the city.

But like everything in Pakistan, the car story had a twist to it. Since I'd bought the car from a local dealer, he handled the registration as well. When the car came, it had a normal black-and-white number plate and I drove it around for some time.

And then, I came to realize, the Pakistani intelligence agencies' paranoia about Indians, was for real. How would they know, otherwise, who was behind the wheel of a car, a Pakistani or an Indian? Don't we look alike?

Ah, but our number plates don't. Or aren't meant to. One morning, a car drove up to the house and an officious-looking gentleman came to the door with an envelope in hand. I was being called by the chief of the Islamabad vehicle registry department as there was an 'error' in the number plate accorded to me.

I was waved into the director's office in Sector F-8 Markaz (Centre) and offered tea. I knew something was afoot. As there had been a mistake in registering the car, I was told, new number plates would have to be affixed.

It was the magic number '27' (used to identify all Indians living in Islamabad; the Indian High Commissioner's car, for instance, is 27 CD 1) which was missing from my plate. While it is true that foreign journalists are given yellow number plates—with the number of the mission placed in front—all Indians clearly required further distinction.

The kindly gentleman said they would have to correct the registration book. I agreed, aware that objection must have come from those who tailed me since the black-and-white number plate must have caused them occasionally to lose track of their quarry.

Coming out of the registry, I had another surprise waiting for me. The new number plates were already being installed on my car—gratis the Government of Pakistan. Finally, I was properly 'dressed'—wherever I went, the Indian tag went with me.

The other bizarre feature of our visa was that you could exit Pakistan only three times during its one-year validity period. Since one exit had to be kept for an emergency at all times, one was permitted effectively two exits from Pakistan in a year. There were times—lasting a couple of months—when we had no visa at all. This was because 'renewal' took time. (These gaps are still very visible in my passport.)

In the interim, I would be given a letter by the ministry of information that my visa case was being processed. For Indian correspondents (and presumably some other foreign journalists), the information ministry acted more like a 'post office'; forwarding our letters to the intelligence establishment.

It was during Benazir Bhutto's second term as Prime Minister that the all-Pakistan, multiple-entry visa was reduced to the three-city, three-exit status. Also, correspondents working for *The Times of India* and *Hindustan Times* were sent back by Benazir's government in order to ensure that Indian journalists did not have too great an advantage over Pakistanis in terms of numbers.

Picking up the cue, India chose not to renew the visa of the Radio Pakistan man in New Delhi and the compliment was returned when the All India Radio correspondent had to leave Islamabad. From a five-three situation in favour of Indian journalists, it was two-two.

That left *The Hindu* and the Press Trust of India (PTI) in Islamabad, and, in my time, *Jang* (Pakistan's leading Urdu daily) and the Associated Press of Pakistan (APP, the official wire service) in Delhi.

Despite numerous efforts by leading Indian newspapers and television channels to post correspondents in Pakistan, this situation persists till date, with one minor difference: the *Jang* slot has now been allotted to Radio Pakistan.

To move out of Islamabad and head for Lahore or Karachi, we had to 'inform' the minstry of information forty-eight hours in advance. This would ensure that the moment we landed in Lahore or Karachi, appropriate arrangements would have been made to tail us.

It was a system of 'informing on yourself'.

Other than visiting Lahore and Karachi, my only journeys out of Islamabad were a day-trip to Murree, in

June 1997, for the India-Pakistan foreign secretary talks, and a look-in on Taxila, an hour's drive from Islamabad. The first was work, the other was intended simply to take my in-laws (who had visited us before the birth of our second daughter, Antara, in December 1998) on an excursion. I had applied weeks in advance in anticipation of the Taxila *yatra*. Nothing was heard; I kept calling the India officer in the information ministry. It was still being processed, I was told. Finally, I gave up.

But, Pakistan is always full of surprises. On the day we had intended for the trip, a Press Information Department (PID) officer landed up at home with the letter of permission in hand. Of course, I had to get the endorsement done on the passports, but, in the end, we got to see historic Taxila!

But knowing that the system was reluctant to afford us any extra facilities, we never tried too hard to go anywhere. Minu's and my dreams of travelling to Mohenjodaro and Harappa remained dreams. When our diplomat and Pakistani friends spoke of going up to exotic locations in Swat, we could only listen. There was no question of our going to any of these places.

My first trip out of Islamabad was to Karachi in July 1997. One hundred and ninety-two Indian fishermen were being repatriated after long periods of detention in Pakistan. This was one of the agreements reached during the meeting between Prime Ministers Inder Kumar Gujral and Nawaz Sharif earlier that year in Male.

Shahid Khan, my PTI colleague, and I both went down from Islamabad to cover the release of the Indian fishermen. Thanks to the local Bohras, who have links with their community members in India, the fisherfolk had been given a new set of clothes (which they were wearing) and a box of sweets as they boarded the Indian Airlines flight to Karachi.

Karachi, for an Indian bound to the limits of Islamabad, was a huge sprawling city. It was massive; many people felt it was like Mumbai or Kolkata. It certainly felt like a friendlier city than Islamabad. That visit to Karachi yielded several enduring friendships, especially with Pakistani journalists, which have continued to this day.

It was a brief visit, but it led me to the Karachi Press Club, the starting point of protest marches and demonstrations. Inside the club were a bunch of most hospitable journalists, many of whom, in the evening, would saunter into the deep recesses of the club for a beer.

On 24 April 1997, soon after I arrived, nine persons were killed in sectarian violence in the Pakistani Punjab. It was a story that would be repeated over and over again. For one not familiar with these matters, the 'separate' worshipping in Shia imambargahs and Sunni masjids was a telling commentary. Also, during most of my stay in Pakistan, key places of worship had a heavy police guard during Friday prayers.

It takes a foreign correspondent a few months to get familiar with the issues in the country of his posting. In a place like Pakistan, where first-hand access to information is always limited, the written word becomes terribly important.

Whether it is the principal newspapers, weeklies, monthlies, books, you have to read them all—cover to cover. It gives you an information base that is key to understanding the politics of the country. For me, the *Dawn* newspaper was like *The Hindu*, solid and reliable. Its anti-India rhetoric was limited, used only on occasion. Soon, I developed my favourites: reading *Dawn* columnists such as Ayaz Amir, Mazdak (later revealed as Irfan Hussain) and Ardeshir Cowasjee was an integral part of my life.

The Friday Times, a weekly edited by Najam Sethi (who would be picked up by Prime Minister Nawaz Sharif's henchmen in the Intelligence Bureau from Lahore for his forthright views), was another favourite.

The News always gave you the 'establishment view'. Some of its regular front-page writers were 'fed' by the powers that be. Different sections of the Pakistani media together presented the 'whole picture' if you bothered to look.

One Pakistani journalist went to the extent of saying that only those cleared by the 'agencies' could write on the front page! While it may be true in the case of one or two newspapers, this doesn't do justice to the independence of a majority of Pakistani reporters, especially when it comes to issues of domestic politics.

The Herald, a *Dawn* publication, and *Newsline*, both serious, investigative monthly magazines, were the other bits that fitted into my press jigsaw. The BBC's Urdu news bulletins in the evening were a good source of information. Several outstanding Pakistani journalists could always be relied upon to provide both facts and perspective.

Today, in Pakistan, with the advent of private news channels, the job of the foreign correspondent has become easier. All you sometimes need is a tip-off. Not only do you get spot news, you also get a wide variety of views that goes missing on Pakistan (State) Television.

For a reporter used to getting his information directly, and coming from a place like Colombo where *The Hindu*'s access has always been great, it was frustrating to get information in driblets—or after some time had elapsed.

Even then, an Indian reporter was better off than an Indian diplomat. We could go for press conferences (as and when we got to know about them), cover proceedings of Parliament (while it existed during my tenure), go to the Supreme Court (which provided good copy) and get the odd interview with Pakistani ministers or officials willing to meet you.

I never hesitated to ask questions. If you wanted information or confirmation, asking was important. And if you didn't ask, only you were the loser. If the question went unanswered, there was 'information' in that too.

Meeting well-informed diplomats was a must. I could bounce off information, check whether my analysis of a particular event or situation was the same as theirs. Some clued-in Western diplomats would often share nuggets of information with one.

On 27 May, I rushed out of the house as a series of 'explosions' was heard. I then tried my hand at calling the police and an ambulance unit to ask what had happened. Nothing was known till late that afternoon. Minu and Anushka had just arrived in Islamabad and I found the 'blasts' scary.

That same evening the Pakistani Air Force announced that an Indian MiG-25R reconnaissance aircraft had violated Pakistani air space and caused a series of sonic booms over the city. There was no way to confirm the report.

Many months later, an Indian official did confirm that the Pakistani contention was true. The Indian Air Force (IAF) did send its MiG-25R aircraft on photography missions from time to time. The Pakistanis, I was told, could do nothing about that aircraft as it flew at a height of 60,000 feet. There was nothing in the Pakistani Air Force arsenal (not even the F-16) that could come anywhere close to the height at which the MiG-25R flew. The 'sonic booms', I was told, were just to irritate.

In any case, those were 'pre-nuclear bomb' days and the IAF could get away with such things. Officially, the stance was one of denial, but 'unofficial' confirmation about the 27 May 'explosions' was available to me months after the event had taken place. Circumstantially, too, this has to be true. Because, on the 'ground', nothing happened on 27 May. All my Pakistani reporter friends had given up investigating by late morning and told me nothing had happened in the whole of Islamabad. So my belated 'source' information has to be true.

On the domestic front, I could see that Nawaz Sharif was on the ascendant, having taken back from the President the power to dismiss an elected government. This Punjabi PM, who took office in that position for the second time in 1997, had been dismissed by President Ghulam Ishaq Khan back in 1993.

Proud of proclaiming that he had been elected with a 'heavy mandate', Sharif was a whimsical person who cared little about the lives of ordinary Pakistanis. Picked by the military in the 1980s to be the chief minister of the Punjab province, Sharif was trying to assert himself as his own man. The PM was not just trying to protect his flanks; he would soon show himself up as a leader with severe autocratic tendencies.

As Chapter 3 will show, Sharif almost lost his chair following a period of protracted confrontation with Chief Justice Sajjad Ali Shah and President Farooq Leghari. Sharif managed to see off both Shah and Leghari, but sullied his image by getting his goons to attack the Supreme Court itself in November 1997. It was a body blow to Pakistani democracy and the rule of law.

After entering into dialogue with India (see Chapter 2), the prime minister would soon reel under the impact of India's May 1998 nuclear tests and Pakistan's own retaliatory tests later in the same month. As I argue in Chapter 4, the Indian and Pakistani nuclear tests sent bilateral relations into a new and dangerous downward spiral. Rhetoric levels were high and the world viewed both India and Pakistan as irresponsible nations.

Emboldened by his ability to see off President Leghari and Chief Justice Shah, the prime minister came to believe that he was untouchable; that his power was supreme.

In October 1998, Sharif sacked Jehangir Karamat as chief of army staff for publicly airing his views on the state of governance in Pakistan (Chapter 5). And, then he committed a fatal error. The prime minister appointed Pervez Musharraf as the new army chief.

The new general would oust the prime minister from office in exactly a year (Chapter 9). Unlike Karamat, Musharraf would not heed the prime minister's diktat. He staged a successful coup with the full support of the army as an institution.

I have also examined the role of the army in Pakistan's politics and power structure (Chapter 5) while looking at its jehadi approach towards India in Chapter 11.

Musharraf's adventurism in Kargil and the involvement are examined in detail in Chapters 7 and 8 while Prime Minister Atal Bihari Vajpayee's trip to Lahore, which produced a 'false dawn' in bilateral relations, takes up Chapter 6.

Looking beyond immediate events, in the concluding chapter, I argue that India–Pakistan relations have never been better and seem to be moving in a positive direction.

Through all this, I have looked at the role of the United States, a country which has come to stay as a powerful third party in the politics of the subcontinent, enjoying enormous influence and clout both over Pakistan and India.

1

Great People, Paranoid State

❖

AS I SAID in my introduction, it was an escorted existence, always under the scanner. Minu and I were never 'alone' in Pakistan. We always had a minder: a motorcycle-borne intelligence operative following us each time we left home and keeping a close watch on all who entered the house.

Whether we were going to a press conference, a dinner, school, a bookshop or even the neighbourhood market, the minder was always close at hand. We counted a series of at least ten different people watching us in our three-plus years of stay in Islamabad.

A vast network of Intelligence Bureau (IB) and the Inter-Services Intelligence (ISI) Directorate operatives kept a watch on all Indian nationals. We joined the 'favoured' Indians on whom strict surveillance was maintained.

A lone man tailing an Indian national in Islamabad was a common sight. Often, if other Indians were invited to our house, a pack of motorcyclists and their machines were stationed right outside. It was evident to all our neighbours—the Indians were partying.

In my twenty-year career as a reporter, there's little doubt in my mind that Assignment Islamabad is the toughest I have handled—both on the job and off it. With time and distance, I can also say that it was extremely rewarding.

In every which way, life was a challenge, but never dull.

Outside of the Indian High Commission (and of my family, of course), there were just two Indian correspondents and a couple of Indian Airlines personnel resident in Karachi and Lahore, on assignment, in the whole of Pakistan.

Our three-entries-a-year visa didn't extend to Rawalpindi, Islamabad's twin city. It was simply for Islamabad, Lahore and Karachi. The last two cities were added on because all the flights to India are from Lahore or from Karachi.

There are no direct flights between the capital cities of India and Pakistan.

The visa regime was strictly implemented. I realized just how stringent it was within only a few months of going to Islamabad. We had gone for an evening drive to the Margalla Hills on Anushka's first birthday in September 1997 when the motorcyclist tailing us suddenly overtook our car and informed us that we were outside city limits and in violation of our visa.

We never once got to Rawalpindi. It was out of bounds for us. Rawalpindi may be a stone's throw away from Islamabad, but for us it could have been as far as Kabul. Of course, the Islamabad airport (or the Chaklala air base) was in Rawalpindi and we had, perforce, to land or take off from there during our rationed visits to India.

The same 'courtesy' was extended by the Government of India to the two Pakistani correspondents based in New Delhi—they could travel only to Mumbai and Kolkata. Such reciprocity suited both governments; neither wanted nosy journalists to have too much freedom to travel and write stories.

Islamabad is an easy city to live in. With a resident population of less than a million, the city is essentially a city of bureaucrats. Surrounded by villages, the Islamabad parliamentary constituency at the time was a largely rural one.

In Islamabad, or even in Lahore, you don't see in-your-face poverty like in Indian cities. There are few beggars and no people sleeping on the roads as you see in Delhi and Kolkata. There are *katchi abadi*s in Islamabad, where a lot of daily-wagers live—tiny houses behind walls—but you still can't call them slums.

The disparities were, however, still striking. While Islamabad city had piped gas for household use, nearby villages like Noorpur Shahan, just behind the prime minister's grand official residence, had no such facilities and people trekked to the foothills of the Margallas to gather firewood.

Even in the limited interaction we had, it was clear there was a vast army of school dropouts out there looking for jobs. Many of them, with little purpose in life, used to hang around local mosques. And yet, Islamabad had fantastic old bookshops, with all kinds of books available.

Islamabad was a city of contradictions. The rich lived well. Houses were sprawling, although smaller than those in Lahore and Karachi. But like in Lahore or Karachi, the elite had a great life in Islamabad. Big houses, big cars and a retinue of domestic servants marked the elite. And, in order to have the right type of elite connections, at least one member of the family had links with the military. This was essential; like an insurance policy.

Tailing an Indian in a small city like Islamabad with its wide roads and easy-flowing traffic wasn't difficult. But it could be a nightmare in a city like Karachi. During a visit to the teeming coastal city, I once saw that two motorbikes—with four riders in all—were chasing my taxi. Obviously, in a huge city like Karachi, local intelligence wasn't taking any chances of missing me.

I was out in the market looking to buy a mobile phone, which was said to be cheaper in Karachi than in Islamabad. After visiting several shops, I finally returned to the first to buy the phone I'd seen there. I immediately realized that there had been major dramatics there since my first visit: some of the shopkeepers had manhandled the plainclothes intelligence men tailing me.

Before I could buy my phone, I had to answer a simple question. Who was I? From my clothes and speech, I could have passed off as a Karachiwallah. When I told them I was from India, the shop attendants relaxed. It appeared that the intelligence men had missed me and had interrogated them over my whereabouts. But they were mostly amused by the whole episode and quoted a good price for the phone I bought.

For special, marked-out persons, say, the naval advisor posted in the Indian High Commission, military intelligence personnel could also be deployed on a round-the-clock basis. At the time we lived in Pakistan, the navy was the only force that had its headquarters in Islamabad.

Interestingly, the Pakistanis felt a particular fascination

for the naval adviser in the Indian High Commission. In the late 1980s, an Indian naval adviser was 'honey-trapped' by Pakistani intelligence. He had fallen for the allure of a Pakistani woman who turned out to be an intelligence operative. I was told that the two were photographed together, after which the Pakistanis began putting the squeeze on him. It was a classic intelligence operation. When pressure was put on him to produce information, the naval adviser rushed to Delhi (leaving his family in Islamabad) and told all to his chief. That act saved him from prosecution, but his service career came to an end.

Since then, the naval adviser was one of the 'most-watched' officials in the Indian High Commission in the hope that another officer might be trapped. Even after late-night parties ending at 2 a.m. and beyond, at the height of Islamabad's chilling winters, the motorcyclist was always there—waiting to follow the man from the Indian Navy home.

There are many stories that circulate about intelligence men and Indian nationals. Some are downright unpleasant and some quite funny. These stories are part and parcel of every Indian's life in Pakistan.

Take this one for instance. A particular Indian diplomat was a fitness freak and would take off every evening into the spectacular walking tracks winding through the Margalla Hills (his diplomatic status allowing him a privilege denied me). His 'follower', clearly not in the fitness camp, would huff and puff his way dutifully up the hills but gave up after a few days. 'I'll just wait for you here,' he finally told the Indian diplomat at the foot of the walking track.

I maintained a no-initiation-of-contact policy with the intelligence men. The nastier the individual tailing you, the greater the intrusion into your private space. There were some who entered the shop with you, standing next to you as you purchased a book, or whatever, and others who maintained a more discreet distance, waiting outside while you finished making your purchases.

But some degree of contact was inevitable. On one occasion, Anushka had to be taken for an X-ray to the state-run Pakistan Institute of Medical Sciences (PIMS) in the emergency section. For some reason, Minu and I were that day tailed by a black-tinted Toyota with three or four men inside. As we spoke to the doctors inside the casualty wing, the intelligence men barged in. '*Kya hua? Baby theek to hai* (What happened? Is Baby okay)?' they asked anxiously. Yes, I assured them, all was well. They returned to their vehicle, waited outside till the X-ray was done and tailed us back home.

One of my chores was accompanying Minu to the Sunday bazaar (earlier known as the 'Jumma' bazaar as Friday was previously the weekly holiday in Pakistan) to buy vegetables. Sometimes, the intelligence guys waited outside, on other occasions they would follow me in.

As we walked around one Sunday, I thought I was seeing things. One of the chaps who had been tailing us was sitting in the *mandi*, selling lemons. I told Minu that perhaps I had finally begun to lose my mind. And then, I thought, maybe Pakistani intelligence was planting people in the mandi to keep a watch on what kind of vegetables and fruits Indians were buying.

The next Sunday, the intelligence man turned *nimbu*-seller was still there. I could bear it no longer. I went up to him and asked him about this 'second' job. 'What to do, sahab, my salary is not enough. When my brother isn't around to do the job, I have to supplement my family income by doing this.' It was the truth, for I subsequently saw the brother at the same spot.

On other occasions, I wondered whether staying on in Pakistan was worth the personal cost it extracted. A time came when the absence of a valid visa came to haunt us. Minu's father, staying in Delhi, wasn't well. I was desperate that she visit him and began making the rounds of the directorate-general of external publicity, part of the Pakistani information ministry, impressing upon the officials the need for the visas to be issued.

Delay, as I was aware, was part and parcel of official harassment. Almost all the information ministry officials were helpful, but there was little they could do. Basically, they acted like a clearing house, sending our requests to the powers-that-be: the intelligence establishment. Decisions were not in their hands, but they were singularly pleasant and hospitable.

Although the officials said Minu could go and get her passport stamped at the Pakistan High Commission in New Delhi, it was too much of a risk to take. Antara was just six months old. Minu's visa finally came through in September 1999—after nearly three months of my pursuing it. She left immediately for New Delhi and returned after a week. She'd been just in time. Three days later, Minu's father passed away and we were on our way back to Delhi.

It was 28 September. We had no tickets, no bookings. On reaching Islamabad airport, we managed to catch the Fokker flight to Lahore, normally only forty-five minutes away, to catch a connecting flight to New Delhi. En route to Lahore, I asked the airhostess to find out from the captain what time we would land. I also told her the reason why it was absolutely essential for us to make it in time for the New Delhi flight.

The captain reacted promptly. He radioed our names ahead to Lahore and handed over controls to his deputy for landing. When we got off the flight, he was waiting for us on the tarmac to usher us through. While Minu and Anushka waited for the baggage, he rushed me to the international terminal to buy our tickets for the New Delhi flight. He then came back to the domestic terminal and, on finding that the luggage had not yet arrived, went personally to the aircraft and wheeled the bags to us. He rushed us through immigration and ensured that we caught the flight, which had been waiting only for us. We were humbled.

I wish I had asked him his name.

I was stumped on other occasions too. On the morning of our return to Islamabad in the first week of October 1999, the doorbell rang. The gate at the end of our drive was closed. Outside stood one of our regular minders. I walked to the gate, puzzled. This was most unusual; 'calls' were a strict no-no. What was up? 'I'm very sorry about your father-in-law passing away,' the man called out. 'I came only to pay my condolences.' I opened the gate and thanked him. That was all.

The experience of my father-in-law's death and the days preceding it demonstrated the frustration that we felt at our existence. But this simple gesture of such extraordinary spontaneity shone through the absolute grief we felt at the time.

Our domestic help in Pakistan were like family to us. Much to the surprise of Indians and Pakistanis alike, we would routinely leave Anushka (and later, Antara) with their Bibi. My children were never happier, and never better cared for, than when they were with Bibi.

There were experiences, too, that left us fuming and humiliated. We'd been invited for dinner to a Pakistani friend's house. Minu and I were sitting inside when one of the other guests told the host: 'Why are there so many policemen outside your house? They are asking for you.'

The host had to go outside and speak to the intelligence men, who told him that their boss, a superintendent of police, wanted to talk to him about his Indian guests. The call was made, the dinner continued, our host was cool. But Minu, I could tell, was very upset.

She felt humiliated that such inquiries could be made about us when all we were doing was attending a social event. But for the Pakistani establishment, we remained suspect till the day we left Pakistan.

Anushka, who was then two, and who went to playschool in Islamabad, couldn't have a normal equation with her Pakistani classmates. She couldn't meet kids out of school and received very few birthday invitations. One of her well-known Pakistani classmates in Treehouse, the playschool she attended, was the granddaughter of Abdul Qadeer Khan, then a national hero for making the nuclear bomb for his country.

The school itself was fantastic, and we never felt uncomfortable about leaving her in the care of what were wonderfully caring teachers. But everyone knew that Anushka was Indian. (At the time, I don't think Anushka knew she was any such thing!)

All this was part of our normal life.

The only time I felt a direct threat was a little after the May 1998 nuclear tests. Indian High Commission officials invited my PTI colleague Shahid Khan and me to the chancery. We were told that 'information' had been received by the mission that the Harkat-ul-Mujahideen, a Pakistani terrorist group operating in Jammu & Kashmir, was planning to kidnap an Indian journalist in Pakistan and use the victim to bargain for the freedom of some of their members detained in India.

Since Shahid and I were the only Indian journalists based in Pakistan, it didn't need a Sherlock Holmes to tell us that the 'information' implied a threat to the two of us. I could also see that High Commission officials were not prepared to discount the information they had received. One of them painted a rather drastic picture: 'Suppose you are pulled into a vehicle while shopping and then taken across the border into Afghanistan—there's little we can do when you cross into Taliban-controlled territory.'

At home I informed Minu about what the High Commission officials had said. She was stunned. 'I don't want to stay here any longer,' she told me. 'Let's go home.'

I tried to reason with her—such information was often baseless—and told her we would take precautions. She asked what we could possibly do. Limit our movements for a while and be extra careful about where we went, I told her. Minu was far from convinced. For several days after that, till we left for India, I would make sure that Minu knew where I was going and always locked the car doors, particularly at red lights.

As things turned out, nothing happened to Shahid nor to me. Down the road, I felt there could be a link between this piece of information and the Kandahar hijacking of December 1999 to free the 'journalist' and fire-spewing Pakistani cleric, Masood Azhar, who had spent several years in a Jammu jail before being released in return for the freedom of passengers aboard the hijacked Indian Airlines flight IC-814.

The pressure to release Azhar was coming from all sides—from organizations as diverse as jehadi outfits to groups representing Pakistani editors and newspaper employees. Both editors' guilds and newspaper employees' federations had passed resolutions calling for Azhar's release.

As is well known, Azhar had even been writing for a

Karachi-based jehadi journal (*Sada-e-Mujahid*) linked to the Harkat-ul-Mujahideen in Karachi from inside his jail cell in Jammu. How he managed this, obviously, is a question only the jail officials in Jammu can answer.

With such articles under his belt, Azhar qualified as a 'journalist'. And, since he was an important man in jehadi circles in Pakistan, it would have made tactical sense to pick up an Indian journalist and hold him till Azhar was released.

The idea that Shahid and I could actually have been possible targets really only hit me after the Kandahar event. It was evident that the hijacking, essentially, was all about freeing Azhar.

It must be said that my experience with Pakistani intelligence was benign compared to what some of my Pakistani peers went through. A Lahore-based journalist who played a leading role in inviting Indian parliamentarians to Islamabad in February 1999 had his spanking-new Suzuki car burnt to cinders while it was still standing in his driveway. He had displeased some powerful people.

Another gutsy Pakistani woman journalist's pet dog was poisoned. The lady, who initially didn't know how her pet had died, was informed of it while being beaten by lathis during a demonstration she'd joined defending the freedom of the press. '*Sali ko aise maro, jaise hamne iske kutte ko mara tha* (Beat her up, like we fixed her dog),' she heard her assailants tell each other.

After our initial discomfort, we took the intelligence men in our stride. It was part of the assignment. The only three places where we could go and they couldn't were the

Indian High Commission, the American Club inside the American Embassy and the United Nations' Club.

At the United Nations' Club you could feel relatively normal—you could, for instance, sit at the bar. Or have a pizza and a swim at the American Club, away from the eyes of Pakistani intelligence.

Pakistanis, of course, could not become members of the American Club. As I discovered, many Pakistanis love their drink and have sufficient ways and means to get the booze delivered to their doorstep. When I asked a Pakistani friend how supplies were arranged, he said, 'Just call a mobile number and your supplies will be delivered to you. All you need is money.'

Equally, there were many people who abhorred alcohol. Zulfiqar Ali Bhutto, who enjoyed his drink, nevertheless banned alcohol in the 1970s in a bid to curry favour with the religious right. But many of my friends in Lahore told me that Indian whisky was easily available, brought across the border by smugglers.

Our social life was restricted; a lot of the socializing we did was with other Indians. But over time, we developed some very close Pakistani friends as well. Ironically, the people we liked the most we met the least because they could get into serious trouble with the intelligence agencies. And some of them *did* get into trouble for meeting us.

In 1997, when I landed in Islamabad, scholar-activist Eqbal Ahmed was one of those who maintained an open house. He wasn't intimidated by intelligence operatives. I enjoyed his hospitality on several occasions.

Eqbal, who divided his time between Pakistan and the United States, took a passionate interest in India–Pakistan matters. His concern for the fate of the Kashmiris was genuine, as was his search for a solution to the enduring dispute over Jammu & Kashmir. My association with him was all too brief; he passed away in May 1999. But, even those fleeting encounters were more than worth the dangers they posed.

Eqbal wrote a regular column for both *Dawn* and the Cairo-based *Al-Ahram* and was a colourful personality. The scholar, who worked with the anti-colonialist Franz Fannon, in Algeria, specialized in West Asian affairs and international relations in general.

Soon after his death, *Dawn* wrote, 'In Eqbal's death, Pakistan has lost possibly its most prescient observer of society and politics.' I couldn't agree more.

My life revolved around a number of Pakistani journalist friends who must remain nameless in this account. They were the ones who livened my life, who were sharply critical of their government, almost always of India, but yet had a degree of empathy and concern that I found admirable.

One of my dreams was to travel to Dera Ghazi Khan, my maternal grandfather's home; the other to Quetta in Baluchistan, where a massive earthquake had killed two of my maternal uncles. It was not to be.

If there were personal problems, professional life was even worse. As a reporter, one couldn't just take a car or catch a flight to report from the site of an incident. The only two cities I could visit were Lahore and Karachi and for this, as I said, advance notice had to be given.

But the reporter in me always lamented the lack of opportunities to travel out into the country and see and report what I saw.

On 6 May 1998, the bishop of Faisalabad, John Joseph, shot himself dead outside the court of the additional sessions judge, Sahiwal, in protest against Pakistan's blasphemy laws.[1] I couldn't travel to report the funeral and the fallout.

It came as a shock to me that a bishop could take his own life. I realized that his action was a desperate attempt to focus attention on the threats that minorities in Pakistan faced.

The blasphemy laws[2] have long been used to settle scores against Pakistani minorities. However, the bishop's action did have some impact because Ayub Masih, a Christian charged under the blasphemy laws and sentenced to death in 1998, was finally acquitted by the Supreme Court in 2002.

Ayub Masih was let off by the Supreme Court; but others facing the wrath of the blasphemy laws haven't been so lucky. According to the Pakistani National Commission for Justice and Peace, some 647 persons have been charged with blasphemy since 1988. Twenty persons accused under these laws were murdered, the non-governmental group said in 2004.

During the Kargil conflict of 1999, all international presspersons, barring the two Indians, were taken to the spot where the wreckage of an Indian Air Force aircraft was found. The PTI man and I, of course, didn't fit into the international category, so we weren't invited. Given the situation, it wasn't surprising that we weren't taken, but it was still annoying.

The most frustrating occurrence was when the Kandahar hijacking took place in December 1999. United Nations' aircraft were going to and from Islamabad and Kandahar, but I was not allowed to enter Afghanistan from Pakistan. I still rue the fact that I couldn't report from the ground in Kandahar, from where many of my Pakistani journalist friends were reporting. It's one of my enduring regrets.

Though these memories still rankle, I was thrilled when I got to speak, at the end of July 1997, to one of my idols, the qawwali maestro Nusrat Fateh Ali Khan. I telephoned Nusrat in Lahore to seek an interview with him. He came on the phone line readily. I introduced myself as the correspondent in Pakistan of *The Hindu*, and to my delight, Nusrat immediately agreed to be interviewed.

When could I go to Lahore, he asked me. 'It would take me a minimum of forty-eight hours,' I told him. 'No, no, I can meet you if you come tomorrow,' he said, adding, 'I'm leaving for London the day after'.

We fixed to meet after he returned from London, something that never happened as he passed away on 16 August. It was a personal loss to me, even though I had never met the great man.

Soon after his death, I wrote in *Frontline*:

> Nusrat Fateh Ali Khan returned *qawwali* to the world. He made it popular again not just in Pakistan and India, the home of the traditional *qawwali*, but in the United States, the United Kingdom, Japan and other countries. He performed in over forty countries and recorded more than 150 albums and sold millions of copies worldwide.
>
> He took the *qawwali*—the devotional music of the Sufis—out of the South Asian milieu, added pep and verve, and placed it on the world's music map. The *qawwali Shahenshah*'s death on August 16 [1997] in a London hospital following a cardiac arrest triggered by kidney and liver failure was an occasion of grief for millions.

2

India and Pakistan—
Talking At Each Other

As a matter of fact, it is to India's advantage that Pakistan be a secure and prosperous State with which we can develop close and friendly relations. If today by any chance I were offered the reunion of India and Pakistan, I would decline it for obvious reasons. I do not want to carry the burden of Pakistan's great problems. I have enough of my own. Any closer association must come out of a normal process and in a friendly way which does not end Pakistan as a State, but makes it an equal part of a larger union in which several countries might be associated.

—Jawaharlal Nehru, speaking at a special
convocation of Allahabad University,
13 December 1947

PRE-PREPAREDNESS IS A sure recipe for success in talks between India and Pakistan. If you want to produce an agreement at a scheduled round of discussions, you must hammer out its basic contours in advance. A bit like heating a ready meal in a microwave and just dishing it out.

Since 1997, when I began following India–Pakistan relations, this formula has worked well. And, where it was not employed, like at the Agra summit in July 2001, the discussions ended in failure.

Failure, largely, is the story of India–Pakistan relations. Agreements that were never implemented; good intentions that were never taken forward. The list is long—as long as the list of suspicions harboured about each other by the two establishments.

To secure an agreement of sufficient dimension between New Delhi and Islamabad, advance negotiation is indispensable. And, for advance negotiations to take place, a degree of trust and a desire to move forward are prerequisites. The media glare that is directed at each high-level meeting between India and Pakistan adds to the need for advance preparation.

This formula has been applied successfully to four crucial meetings between India and Pakistan: the June 1997 composite dialogue agreement, the February 1999 Lahore declaration, the November 2003 ceasefire accord and the Musharraf–Vajpayee January 2004 joint statement.

Although Lahore itself produced key agreements, India showed little understanding of the dynamics of the Pakistani establishment, failing to recognize the Pak army as a player in Pakistani politics. Atal Bihari Vajpayee's Lahore visit served to raise expectations—but belied the hopes the people of the subcontinent placed on it.

Of course, it's easier for Pakistan to comprehend the

workings of the Indian establishment, than for India to understand the construct of powers between a Pakistani Army chief and a civilian prime minister. And yet, for India, that understanding is crucial. Crucial, too, for Pakistan to come to terms with coalition politics in India, the pulls and pressures within political allies, the influence wielded, for instance, by the Rashtriya Swayamsevak Sangh (RSS), on the Bharatiya Janata Party (BJP).

When I arrived in Islamabad in 1997, a new process of dialogue was just about commencing between the two countries, after the hiatus that had followed seven rounds of talks at the level of foreign secretaries between July 1990 and January 1994.

Traditional wisdom has it that India and Pakistan were quite close to reaching an agreement on Siachen and the resolution of the boundary dispute over Sir Creek in the early 1990s, but nothing tangible finally emerged from it all. Pakistani and Indian officials have given me conflicting accounts of the talks (as was to be expected), but both felt that while agreement was close, especially on Siachen, it didn't happen.

A 'non-paper', or off-the-record document putting forward government policy, presented by India to Pakistan on 24 January 1994, pointed out that during the sixth round of talks at the foreign secretary level in 1992, a broad understanding had been reached on disengagement and redeployment, monitoring, and maintenance of peace and an implementation schedule in Siachen. A final agreement, of course, is still waiting to be signed.

In contrast, some progress in relations between India and Pakistan had been achieved during the period Rajiv Gandhi and Benazir Bhutto were in power. The Agreement on Prohibition of Attack against Nuclear Installations and Facilities signed in December 1988 was a case in point.

In December 1989, Rajiv travelled to Islamabad to attend the fourth South-Asian Association for Regional Cooperation (SAARC) summit. It was during this visit that the agreement on non-attack of nuclear installations was signed. Following this agreement, the two countries started to exchange a list of their nuclear installations every year on 31 December.

Again, in July 1989, Rajiv Gandhi paid a two-day visit to Islamabad, the first 'bilateral' visit—a trip to a SAARC summit wasn't officially counted as bilateral, even though a key agreement had been signed—since his grandfather, Jawaharlal Nehru, visited Karachi to sign the Indus Waters Treaty back in 1960.

There was no core issue of Kashmir that was preventing agreement at the end of the 1980s between India and Pakistan on other, equally important issues. Non-attack on nuclear installations was a major agreement between the two countries.

An editorial in the Lahore-based *Friday Times* weekly revealed how peripheral the 'core issue' on Kashmir was for Pakistan at one stage: 'Indeed, the fact remains that, despite having agreed to effectively cold-storage Kashmir at Shimla in the early 1970s, Islamabad launched a policy of fingering New Delhi in Indian Punjab in 1984, which prompted the Indians to think of hitting back in 1984 and 1987...

'In 1988, democracy was ushered into Pakistan and Benazir Bhutto arrived on the scene. There was a significant change in Pakistan's stand immediately... it did not argue that Kashmir was a "core" issue without whose resolution the building blocks of peace could not be first built. Indeed, it went ahead and negotiated the draft of a settlement with India on Siachen...'[1]

The editorial said that after the Kashmir problem

'spontaneously erupted' in 1989, Islamabad changed tack and whipped the issue out from cold storage and began to press its case with great vigour. Arguing that the Nawaz Sharif regime in 1991 deepened covert and overt assistance to Kashmir, it added that Pakistan now insisted that Kashmir was the 'core' issue in any dialogue with India.

According to senior Indian officials, Benazir Bhutto and Rajiv Gandhi had developed an equation despite their differences on Kashmir. The security establishment in Pakistan held a grudge against Benazir for supplying information about the terrorist network operating in the Indian Punjab.

Notable successes achieved by the Indian security forces in Punjab were attributed by the Pakistanis to the information supplied to India at the behest of Benazir. Clearly, both Rajiv and Benazir, both members of leading political families of the subcontinent, were new to politics.

However, being young and willing doesn't always work. Rajiv was in the midst of the bruising Bofors scandal and consequently facing waning popularity. Benazir herself remained prisoner to the limits laid down by President Ghulam Ishaq Khan and the army chief Mirza Aslam Beg.

Benazir's foreign minister, Sahibzada Yaqub Khan, was a pillar of the permanent Pakistani establishment, one that was built by the Pakistani Army with key civilians acting as props and spokespersons. This establishment didn't give Benazir a chance when it came to India, being far from pleased at her efforts at making friends with India under Rajiv.

Talks at the level of foreign secretaries in the early 1990s did inch along with Shahryar Khan and Muchkund Dubey signing agreements on Advance Notice on Military Exercises, Manoeuvres and Troop Movements and

Prevention of Air Space Violation, and for Permitting Overflight and Landings of Military Aircraft in April 1991.

In January 1994, the talks collapsed. A joint statement said at the time, 'The talks recognized all aspects of the Jammu & Kashmir problem. Both sides recognized that there are basic divergences... the two sides will consult each other on the question of further talks on the foreign secretary or other level.'

It took the return of Nawaz Sharif as prime minister, with Inder Kumar Gujral as his counterpart in India, to kick-start the process of talks again. In March and April 1997, the foreign secretaries and foreign ministers of India and Pakistan met, setting the stage for a 12 May 1997 meeting between Sharif and Gujral, on the sidelines of the SAARC summit in Male.

As the late Sri Lankan foreign minister, Lakshman Kadirgamar, had once pointed out, whatever else SAARC may have achieved or not achieved, SAARC meetings had, usually, provided an opportunity for Indian and Pakistani leaders to meet on issues of mutual concern.

In the second week of June 1997, it was announced that the two foreign secretaries would meet in Islamabad from 19 to 23 June, pursuant to the decision taken by Gujral and Sharif in Male.

It was apparent from the 'sealed lips' of Indian diplomats that something major was on the cards. With the benefit of hindsight, one can say that they wanted to ensure that an agreement being worked on would actually be signed between the two countries.

Foreign secretary Salman Haidar and his Pakistani counterpart Shamshad Ahmed met with their delegations at Punjab House in Islamabad. In a move without precedent, the spokesman for the Pakistani foreign ministry,

Tariq Altaf (who died in a tragic road accident when he was Pakistan's high commissioner to Canada several years later) was appointed the 'joint spokesman' for the talks.

At the time of the talks, Indian and Pakistani reporters were in the dark about how the 23 June agreement had been reached. During all the briefings, authorities on both sides deliberately misled us into believing that 'hard issues' would be tackled, when actual agreement had already been reached. Sustained, quiet diplomatic efforts between the two sides had done the trick.

An Indian diplomat would in fact later tell me that when the venue of the talks shifted to the nearby hill station of Muree for a day, a much talked-about photo of the two foreign secretaries poring over documents actually only pictured them reading statements that they would read out at a press conference the next day.

But I have to admit that while no reporter likes to be misled, confidentiality is all important when it comes to issues between India and Pakistan. That is one lesson I learnt from the 23 June agreement: if India and Pakistan are to move forward, the formal talks are often a charade—backroom work and confidentiality is the key to success.

And, this cuts across all levels. Whether it is with foreign secretaries or national security advisers, or even joint secretaries, India and Pakistan don't manage to achieve much in the absence of what I may be permitted to call a 'pre-agreement'.

In June 1997, India and Pakistan agreed to address all outstanding issues of concern to both sides, which included peace and security (including confidence-building measures), Jammu & Kashmir, Siachen, the Wular barrage/Tulbul navigation project, Sir Creek, terrorism, drug-trafficking, economic and commercial cooperation as well as promotion of friendly exchanges.[2]

They agreed to 'set up a mechanism, including working groups at appropriate levels, to address all these issues in an integrated manner'. Apart from discussing peace and security, and Kashmir, the foreign secretaries would also oversee the progress made in discussing other issues as well.

Addressing the press in Islamabad, Salman Haidar revealed that four days of intensive discussions in the Pakistani capital were part of the process initiated in Delhi in keeping 'with the directions' given by the two prime ministers.

'It is our purpose that the dialogue leads to establishment of trust, friendship and cooperation between the two countries,' Haidar said, concurring that the mechanism for dialogue included the creation of working groups.

The dust was yet to settle on the 23 June statement, when the Indian compulsions on Jammu & Kashmir surfaced. India did not want to be seen agreeing to a 'working group' on Kashmir at a time when the Pakistani press was speaking of the creation of a working group on Kashmir.

'We have an established position on this subject [J&K]. There is no dispute on our part of Kashmir in the sense of a disputed area. Our concerns relate to Pakistan-occupied Kashmir, infiltration and support to terrorism,' Haidar said in New Delhi on 25 June,[3] puncturing the 'trust and cooperation' line.

In the tit-for-tat relationship that is the hallmark of India–Pakistan ties, the Pakistan Foreign Office spokesman immediately called Haidar's remarks propaganda. 'We would, however, wish to reiterate that the internationally-recognized position is that Jammu & Kashmir is a disputed territory, the future of which is to be determined through a reference to the people in terms of the United Nations Security Council resolutions,' he added, restating the well-known Pakistani position.

Clearly, the process was not off to a good start. Traditional positions had taken centre stage, and India and Pakistan were making the usual statements from their respective capitals once the four days of talks ended in Islamabad.

However, for the first time since the Shimla Agreement of 1972, India and Pakistan had agreed to discuss J&K as an issue between themselves. Indian officials rejected the idea that New Delhi had agreed to a working group on Kashmir, pointing out that the mechanism included 'working groups'.

These officials told me later that India and Pakistan had, indeed, been discussing a draft on how to discuss outstanding issues for quite some time. They revealed that a draft of the agreement had been shown to all major political parties in the capital, including the then-in-Opposition BJP. The Gujral-led government wanted to make the process inclusive and the BJP to be on board the process.

Indian and Pakistani realities are very different. And for a journalist trying to report on them honestly, it's a constant challenge to marry them together. As I came to realize, this would be a constant and very difficult part of my Islamabad assignment.

All along, it was clear that the Pakistanis didn't really want a bilateral dialogue with India. They wanted only to use the mechanism of the bilateral dialogue to 'expose' India and bring in a third party to resolve the Kashmir dispute for them.

Time and again, Pakistani ministers and spokesmen alleged that India was not serious about addressing the dispute; it meant only to continue the status quo on Kashmir. The only way out, they felt, was to find the third party, which, in most cases, meant the United States of America. Lip service was paid to the UN, but Pakistan wanted America to simply push India into an agreement on Kashmir.

Soon, the differences on the working group for Kashmir came to dominate bilateral discourse. After taking a step forward, the Indians and Pakistanis were stuck, and neither side wanted to oblige the other by ceding anything.

On 4 August, India proposed the next round of talks between foreign secretaries, but there were doubts till the very end that the talks would take place at all.

Finally, in September, Shamshad Ahmed travelled to Delhi for talks with his new Indian counterpart, K. Raghunath. At the end of the talks, both said they had 'adjourned' their meeting, saying further consultation was required.[4]

If the statement was not enough indication of an impasse, Ahmed, during a brief stopover in Lahore, on his way back from Delhi, lashed out at India for 'resiling' from the 23 June agreement.

The Pakistani foreign secretary claimed that the 'other side had resiled from the agreement set out in the Islamabad joint statement' and that there were differences of opinion on 'operationalizing' the mechanism on Kashmir.

That was the last dialogue that took place at the level of foreign secretaries during the time the Gujral government was in power. A paradigm shift was soon to take place in India–Pakistan relations as a BJP-led government took power in the country.

The BJP, a party that had maintained a hawkish posture towards Pakistan all along, had gone to the extent of declaring in its political programme that it would turn

India into a nuclear weapons' state. This would have
obvious implications for Pakistan and India–Pakistan
relations as well.

A downward slide in bilateral ties was a consequence
of the Indian nuclear tests of May 1998, followed, of
course, by Pakistan's own nuclear tests. At the same time,
the Western world was furious—more with India and less
with Pakistan—because New Delhi had taken the first
step.

As can be imagined, tension was high in the wake of
the nuclear tests. However, the tenth SAARC summit in
Colombo in July 1998 offered yet another opportunity for
the leaders of India and Pakistan to be present at the same
venue.

On 14 June, quite out of the blue, Prime Minister Atal
Bihari Vajpayee wrote to Nawaz Sharif suggesting a
meeting on the sidelines of the SAARC summit in Colombo.
The offer was accepted by the Pakistanis, but it was a
belligerent Sharif who met with Vajpayee in Colombo—
the nuclear tests of May 1998 still very fresh in the minds
of South Asians and the rest of the world. At the end of
the discussions, Sharif described the results of the talks as
'zero'.[5]

Soon after the talks, Pakistan-based terrorist groups
struck in the Indian state of Himachal Pradesh, killing
thirty-four construction workers on 3 August in one
incident, and slaughtering twenty-four villagers, including
fourteen children, in a remote Kashmiri village in the
second.[6] It was a difficult time.

Finally, the breakthrough on the dialogue front came
in September 1998, when Sharif and Vajpayee met on the
sidelines of the United Nations General Assembly in New
York and allowed the resumption of the bilateral dialogue
between the foreign secretaries of the two countries.

To kickstart the talks, the Vajpayee government made a significant concession to the Pakistanis. It was, possibly, the first indication that with the nuclear tests behind them, the Vajpayee government was not going to stick to the straight and narrow when it came to dealing with Pakistan.

The strictly bilateral route, preferred by successive governments in New Delhi, was not going to bind Mr Vajpayee and his associates.

Accepting a very Pakistani formulation, Vajpayee concurred with Sharif that the peaceful settlement of all outstanding issues, including Jammu & Kashmir, was essential for creating an environment of peace and security in the entire region.

For the first time ever, India had accepted there was a link between a resolution of the Kashmir issue and peace in South Asia. It was a formulation that displeased many Indian diplomats who had been involved in the negotiation process with Pakistan.

The foreign secretaries agreed in New York to operationalize the 23 June 1997 mechanism by holding talks at their level separately on peace and security and Kashmir, and the rest of the six issues at the level of the officials concerned.

'... all the issues shall be addressed substantively and specifically through the agreed mechanism in an integrated manner,' the foreign secretaries decided, with talks on peace and security and Jammu & Kashmir scheduled for October 1998 in Islamabad. The other six issues were to be discussed in the first half of November 1998 in New Delhi.

According to the New York agreement, during each round of the 'two-plus-six' dialogue, separate meetings would take place on peace and security and Kashmir in order to accommodate Pakistani requirements.

Islamabad had been insisting that Kashmir could not be placed on par with other issues such as Sir Creek and the Wular barrage. For Pakistan, Kashmir had to be accorded primacy of place in any dialogue with India.

The Pakistanis feared that progress would take place on other issues, but not on the core issue of Jammu & Kashmir, which, in Pakistan's view, would be contrary to its national interest.

If officialdom in Pakistan was to be believed, Pakistan's whole being was linked to Kashmir and its ability to prise this area from the control of India. Also, at this time, Pakistan felt that the international community was still receptive to its concerns on Kashmir and 'violations of human rights' there.

Any observer of the Pakistani scene would be aware that a thin elite comprising serving and retired generals, intelligence bosses, key journalists, select ministers, politicians and bureaucrats manufactured the 'consensus' on Kashmir.

This group, which was the permanent establishment itself, enjoyed a hallowed status within the portals of power. At every meeting and press conference, selected journalists would ask: how can we trade with India when Kashmiris are being killed by Indian security forces? In short, it was indicated that there could be no normality in relations with India until Kashmir was resolved on Pakistan's terms.

Whether it was Nawaz Sharif's information minster, Mushahid Hussain, or key writers in Pakistan's leading newspapers (*Dawn*, *The Friday Times* and some writers in *The News* being honourable exceptions), the programmed peddling of the Pakistani point of view on Kashmir was part of the daily dose of propaganda.

Pakistan Television, of course, was the worst offender—

almost every news bulletin began with how many Kashmiris had been 'martyred' at the hands of Indian security forces in Kashmir.

In October 1998, Indian foreign secretary K. Raghunath arrived at the head of a largish Indian delegation. The Pakistani game plan at the time was reasonably simple: turn the focus back on Kashmir and try to ensure that India doesn't go ahead with strengthening its nuclear and conventional military capability. Towards this goal, they proposed a strategic restraint regime, which, moreover, was not restricted to nuclear arms, but extended to conventional weapons as well.

As part of this regime, Shamshad Ahmed called for the prevention of a nuclear and missile race, an accord on risk-reduction measures, avoidance of nuclear conflict, a moratorium on further nuclear tests by both countries, non-induction of air- and sea-based missile systems and a nuclear doctrine of minimum deterrence.[7]

Raghunath didn't mince any words on the issue of terrorism. He said that if Islamabad desisted from supporting terrorists operating in Jammu & Kashmir, this would act as a major confidence-building measure in the bilateral relationship.

At the talks, India proposed a no-first-use of nuclear weapons, extending the hotline between the directors-general of military operations of the two countries to divisional and sector commanders, giving advance notice before testing missiles with a range of 200 km, extending the existing accord on non-attack of nuclear installations to population and economic centres, renewed an invitation to the Pakistani Army Chief to visit India and proposed exchange of officers between National Defence Colleges.

Also, India suggested that the two countries exchange views on security concepts and nuclear doctrines, work out nuclear and conventional confidence-building measures, increase information exchange in the nuclear field to facilitate greater transparency and set up a consultative machinery to review and implement CBMs.[8]

On 18 October, the closing day of the talks, the cold war that had marked the talks came under full public gaze at a joint press conference addressed by Ahmed and Raghunath.

The Indian foreign secretary favoured the easy to the difficult approach as far as discussing contentious issues, but Ahmed maintained that in order to get into 'fourth gear', you had to engage the first one first. Kashmir was the difficult problem; the other issues were easier to tackle, the foreign secretary argued.

'It does not generally help in international relations to frontload a process with problems that are unduly complicated. This is basic common sense,' Raghunath pointed out.

For his part, Ahmed held firm on the 'Kashmir-first' approach that had stood in the way of serious negotiations between the two countries. 'Realism [in dialogue with India] requires the acceptance of objective realities as they exist and not as we choose to accept them selectively...' Ahmed stated.

The mandatory joint statement of 18 October blandly read: 'The meeting on 17 October discussed Jammu and Kashmir. The two sides reiterated their respective positions.'

Mercifully, the public disagreements over Kashmir did not end the process of the dialogue.

For one round to be complete, talks on the other six issues, Siachen, the Wular barrage/Tulbul navigation project, Sir Creek, terrorism and drug-trafficking, economic and commercial cooperation and promotion of friendly exchanges would now take place in New Delhi from 5 to 13 November 1998.

It was gradually becoming clear to me that no real progress was possible at the level of talks between foreign secretaries. Their job was not to give an inch in the discussions. Even if the political leadership had signalled some degree of softness (difficult for the Indian government at a time when jehadi activities continued unabated), the bureaucracy would find ways and means to sabotage the process.

Down the line, most officials I encountered, even when they were personally realistic and wanting a rapprochement with the other side, had a job to do and that was to defend the national interest as laid down by the respective establishments. There was not much room for manoeuvre here.

It would be unfair, however, to blame diplomats alone. Often, politicians took a stand on Monday, twisted it around on Tuesday, and finally denied taking it altogether on Wednesday.

Prime Minister Nawaz Sharif, who had come to power on an election manifesto that promised better relations with India, hadn't taken the trouble to build a consensus within his Cabinet on the issue. Ministers continued to shoot their mouths off on Kashmir and related issues; the nuclearization of the subcontinent meant hawks were the flavour of the season.

The dramatic events of Lahore, and then Kargil in mid-1999, were to follow. Sharif's relationship with the army, too, was undergoing a dramatic shift. At a time when the jehadi honeymoon both in Afghanistan and Kashmir was continuing between the terrorists and the Pakistani establishment, hoping for better relations with India was, perhaps, somewhat of a pipedream.

The Lahore agreements, signed between Vajpayee and Sharif in February 1999, like the June 1997 statement, had been negotiated in advance, with the Indian prime minister's close confidant, Brajesh Mishra, arriving in Lahore to negotiate details with the Pakistani side. The Lahore process (dealt with in Chapter 6), may have been shortlived, but, yet again, proved that advance contacts had worked.

After Kargil and the October 1999 coup, India–Pakistan relations were not much more than a daily exchange of abuse between New Delhi and Islamabad. And then came an invitation in May 2001 from Vajpayee to Chief Executive Pervez Musharraf to visit India at his convenience. To the Pakistanis, it was a complete surprise.

A large number of unilateral measures were announced by New Delhi in advance of Musharraf's arrival in July 2001, including instructions to the Indian director-general of military operations (DGMO) to visit Pakistan to strengthen 'processes for peace' along the Line of Control (LoC).

All these proposals, from what I could gather, were made to the press first and, through it, reached the Pakistanis. As can be expected, they were not impressed. There were no high-level advance negotiations of the kind needed to ensure success or, at least, the absence of failure.

After months of trading abuse and refusing to talk to Pakistan till it ended cross-border terrorism, India had clearly put Pakistan on its guard. Prime Minister Vajpayee told the Indian Parliament on 16 August 2001 that India's 'old agenda' was on the table. 'And then, in the middle of the discussions [in Agra], we prepared a small agenda and sent it to them,' Vajpayee said.

Speaking in Hindi, the Prime Minister remarked:

Ham samajhte the ki Taj Mahal ki chhaya mein baith kar, Taj Mahal ki prishtbhumi mein jab baat hogi to phir baat aisi hogi jo bhavishya ke liye milkar kaam karne ka rasta nikalegi, lekin aisa hua nahin (We thought that in the shadow and with the backdrop of the Taj Mahal, we would chart a strategy for the future, but this did not happen).

Clearly, the expectation was misplaced. India had failed to read Musharraf. The general was not about to sign away his national position just because the Indian side had invited him to sit in the shadow of the Taj Mahal.

External affairs minister Jaswant Singh revealed in Parliament just how badly the talks were structured, when he revealed that Pakistani officials refused even to sit down to negotiate on a joint statement on 15 July in Agra.

Singh said in the Lok Sabha on 6 August:

The officials from the Pakistan side would just not sit down with our officials because they had no directions; they had no instructions and they had no document. It was after the banquet was over—by now we had reached 11 o'clock at night on the 15th—finally, at 2 o'clock at night, Pakistan officials said they were ready to sit with us... there was only half a day left.

The officials... worked till 4.30 am [on 16 July] jointly. The possible outline was prepared... there were a number of square brackets [areas of disagreement]... that document was referred to the heads of government on the morning of the 16th.

Agra was the scene of a diplomatic disaster between India and Pakistan. The talks failed on the twin issues of Jammu & Kashmir and cross-border terrorism. The cost of the failure was high; India and Pakistan had missed a chance to kiss and make up.

None other than Vajpayee's national security adviser,

Brajesh Mishra, said in April 2005 that he was not consulted about the invitation to Musharraf in 2001, and that he would have had reservations about it if he had been.

After Vajpayee's change of heart in April 2003 and his 'hand-of-friendship' speech in Srinagar, back-channel contacts between Mishra and Tariq Aziz, secretary of the Pakistani National Security Council began. Mishra is himself on record pointing out the importance of those back channels.

In October 2003, India made a dozen confidence-enhancing proposals to Pakistan, including running a cross-LoC bus from Srinagar to Muzaffarabad and reopening the Khokrapar–Munabao rail link, closed since the 1965 war.

On 23 November, Prime Minister Mir Zafarullah Khan Jamali made a surprise announcement: Pakistan was ready to implement a ceasefire along the LoC on Id, 26 November. A day later, India proposed that this ceasefire should be extended to the Actual Ground Position Line in Siachen.

A terse statement, announcing the ceasefire, was made in New Delhi on 25 November. It said:

> The directors-general of military operations of India and Pakistan, in the course of their weekly conversation, today agreed to observe a ceasefire with effect from midnight tonight along the international border, LoC and Actual Ground Position Line (AGPL) in Jammu & Kashmir.

In three days, through public offers and counter-offers in Islamabad and New Delhi, the two countries suddenly 'resolved' a problem involving decades of mindless firing along the Line of Control, leading to countless military and civilian casualties.

If only it were so simple!

Many months later, I was to learn that the ceasefire and the sequencing of offers had been settled during a meeting in early November 2003 between Brajesh Mishra and Tariq Aziz in Dubai. Quiet back-channelling had again produced tangible results.

I commented in a piece in *The Hindu* just days after the ceasefire agreement:

> Keen observers of the India-Pakistan scene cannot but overlook the ease with which India and Pakistan agreed to the Id-ul-Fitr ceasefire. These things don't just happen, they are made possible by behind-the-scenes diplomacy.[9]

At the time, I had no firm details about the advance meeting between Mishra and Aziz. But the back channel was, clearly, at work. Again, in January 2004, India and Pakistan clinched a major agreement due to the pre-arranged efforts between Mishra and Tariq Aziz that took into account New Delhi's concerns on cross-border terrorism and led to the resumption of dialogue between the two nations.

Arising from this, my proposition is a simple one: in an atmosphere of suspicion, advance contacts ensure that agreement is possible when the leaders of India and Pakistan meet.

In their absence, televised failures like Agra in July of 2001 are waiting to happen.

3

Nawaz Sharif vs Sajjad Ali Shah

❖

Please let me do my work, let me plan for the future, let me mobilize the economy. I have no time to lose. I do not want to get involved in [a] confrontation of egos and wills. Everything I have belongs to my country and is for my country.

—Nawaz Sharif, addressing Pakistan's National Assembly on 31 October 1997

DEMOCRACY HAS NEVER really put down strong roots in Pakistan, in the absence of an independent judiciary. Judges there have been committed more to legalizing the dictatorships of successive military rulers, rather than enforcing the rule of law, thereby preventing the judiciary from developing as an institution.

And, it's not just military dictators who have taken

recourse to intimidating the judiciary, or packing the higher courts with judges of their choice. Civilian rulers have taken the same route.

But a few months after I arrived in Pakistan, it began to look like the Supreme Court, headed by Chief Justice (CJ) Sajjad Ali Shah, was beginning to show some spunk. For instance, it had begun hearing a petition that the ISI Directorate had been funnelling funds to political parties to enable them to rig elections.

Nawaz Sharif never understood the principle behind the separation of powers; all he wanted was to harness greater power for himself. With his vast parliamentary majority, the prime minister began to feel that there was nothing he could do wrong and none could challenge his authority.

Sharif was, after all, a creature of the military establishment. He had come to power (for the second time) with a rousing majority (on the lines of Rajiv Gandhi's victory in 1984) that permitted him to make constitutional changes.

Pakistani analyst Hamid Yusuf, in his *Pakistan—A Study of Political Developments 1947-97*, has argued that Sharif's rise to the job of prime minister was meteoric. After a period of probation as a provincial minister in Punjab during Zia-ul-Haq's military rule, Sharif became chief minister of Punjab in the party-less polls of 1985. According to Yusuf, Nawaz Sharif inherited a major commercial empire (with modest beginnings), causing the future prime minister to acquire the mindset, too, of a businessman.

Having been forced by the army, under pressure from then chief Abdul Waheed Kakar, to resign as PM in 1993—a fellow victim being President Ghulam Ishaq Khan—Sharif felt that he had to do everything to ensure there was no threat to power and position in his second term in that post.

The Sharif clan was based in Raiwind, near Lahore, and it was widely believed that the PM took orders from 'Abbaji', his religious-minded father. Younger brother Shahbaz Sharif was chief minister of Punjab province.

Certainly, the PM was no team-player. He relied on only select ministers—and, of course, his friend and 'Ehtesab' (Accountability) Bureau chief, Saifur Rehman who, it was also believed, ran the Intelligence Bureau. Whether it was in information, the judiciary, or even the army, Sharif felt he was strong enough to bulldoze others into accepting him as the sole power centre.

But, as Sharif would soon discover, CJ Sajjad Ali Shah was far from a pushover. He had his own ideas and believed, rightly, that the actions of the executive could be questioned in a court of law.

As I observed for myself in court, Shah was a strong personality and wasn't about to bend to the command of the Sharif government. Shah wanted to act as a check on the power of Nawaz Sharif. His instincts were right, but Shah's actions, before being removed from office, verged on the desperate.

Sharif, of course, had come to believe that a grand conspiracy was at work between President Farooq Leghari and Chief Justice Shah to oust him from office. Countermeasures, he consequently decided, were a must.

One of Sharif's first acts after taking office in 1997 was to get Parliament to repeal two of the President's key powers (to dissolve the National Assembly and to appoint the service chiefs) by passing the thirteenth amendment to the Pakistani Constitution.

While the move was applauded abroad, Pakistani scholars and analysts were divided on its merits. Outside

Pakistan, the principle of separation of powers is widely recognized as a fundamental pillar of democracy. But given the morphed nature of democracy in Pakistan, this strict separation of powers wasn't rooted in reality, considering the immense clout that the army enjoyed. And, now, Sharif wanted to push the judiciary and the army into the roles of supplicants.

Within the country, many believed that the balance of power between the Pakistani 'troika'—the President, the prime minister and the army chief—had been fundamentally altered by the passing of the thirteenth amendment.

Nawaz Sharif wanted to ensure that no one would challenge his authority. If the Constitution needed to be amended, so be it. Parliamentary business could be suspended, and amendments passed without discussion, on the strength of his brute majority. The prime minister was a great believer in obviating the need for debate.

But the one man who stood in Sharif's way was the Sindhi CJ Sajjad Ali Shah.

Sharif had a bizarre desire for 'speedy justice'. Terrorists, criminals and murderers, the prime minister felt, were getting away with their sins, and the layered tiers of justice (through the process of appeal, for instance) stood in the way of this 'wish' of his. Day in and day out in his speeches, he laboured on about the ills of justice delayed. In an address to the nation on 11 June 1997 he said: '...what is the use of...[the] law which fails to provide protection and security against terrorists, dacoits and perpetrators of terror in our society?'

Underlining his concept of the vast gulf that separated the leader and the led, the prime minister said, 'I am determined to lead my people to a secure, prosperous and honourable life. I had even taken steps to enact laws seeking an early end to violence and cruelty in society.

'But the Chief Justice of Pakistan assured me that the judiciary can deliver justice within the parameters of the existing legal and judicial system ... people even die before their cases in the courts are decided; they sell all their properties in the pursuit of an elusive justice ... if the courts could ensure speedy and timely justice, a large number of our problems could be resolved,' Sharif said in one of several speeches on the same theme.

On 13 August 1997, the National Assembly and the Senate passed the Anti-Terrorism Act, which allowed for the 'arrest, without warrant' of any person who had committed an act of terrorism, or 'against whom a reasonable suspicion exists that he has committed, or is about to commit, any such act or offence'.

The punishment for such acts? 'If such [terrorist] act has resulted in the death of any person, [the guilty will] be punished with death,' the Act said, making it clear that the logic applied here was 'an eye for an eye'. In other cases, the minimum sentence would be seven years.

The establishment of special courts under the Act laid the arena for a major dispute between Sharif and Sajjad Ali Shah. Soon after the Anti-Terrorism Act was passed, the Chief Justice stated that the law itself was justiciable and the court would rule on its legality.

In a statement on the Anti-Terrorist Act, the Human Rights Commission of Pakistan (HRCP) said, 'The government is unable to recognize what has been elementary to all the rest: that it is not deficiencies of the law but failures of the law-and-order machinery, which, next to political factors, have been most responsible for the spread of terrorism in the country.'

'The government has made a curious golden [independence] jubilee present to the nation,' the HRCP added. 'It's ... [the] Anti-Terrorist Act, 1997, [it] is designed to strike terror in the hearts of common citizens far more than it is likely to petrify the terrorists or would-be terrorists.'

And then, the gloves came off. On 21 August 1997, the Sharif government reduced the sanctioned strength of Supreme Court judges from seventeen to twelve.

This came a day after, press reports said, the Chief Justice had recommended the elevation of five judges to the Supreme Court to fill the existing vacancies. The drama had begun in earnest.

I'd never guessed that the Pakistani Supreme Court would soon become my regular port of call. My trips to the Court became a daily routine. The hideous building that housed it, on Constitution Avenue, was quite close to Parliament, with its high glass roof stretching skyward, seemingly without end. I have little doubt that the Supreme Court is the ugliest building in otherwise picturesque Islamabad. Court No. 1, presided over by the Chief Justice, occupied the space directly below the daunting ceiling. It would soon become a battlefield for a no-holds-barred clash between the judiciary and the executive.

And, I, as an Indian reporter, would soon be listening to chapter and verse from Indian case law. Here, there was no bar on things Indian.

Two other players were involved in this tamasha— President Farooq Leghari and the army chief, Jehangir Karamat. With the President having lost the power to dismiss an elected government, the presidency was a weakened institution.

Leghari, who had ambitions of his own, could not give marching orders to Sharif as he had done to PM Benazir Bhutto in 1996. The 'troika' of President, army chief and prime minister, which had governed Pakistan since 1988, was missing a limb. And the missing limb was the President.

It came to be the actions of the low-profile Karamat that were crucial in the days ahead. On his part, the army chief in Pakistan had never drawn his powers of dismissal from the Constitution. The Pakistani Constitution gave him no such role. His power lay in the uniform he wore. It marked him out as an unfettered and supreme being; in the past, both prime minister and President feared the power of the chief of the army staff.

In the meantime, the courtroom drama was continuing in earnest. On 16 September, Attorney-General Chaudhry Farooq informed a bench of the Supreme Court that the federal government had withdrawn the presidential order reducing the strength of the Supreme Court.

It seemed the crisis was over; that the matter had been resolved. But like many other things in Pakistan, it was a deceptive calm.

On 9 October, Chief Justice Shah left Pakistan for an 'Umra' pilgrimage to Saudi Arabia. The judge next in line, Ajmal Mian, was sworn in, by Pakistani custom, as acting Chief Justice on the same day. The very next day, Ajmal Mian made it publicly known that Shah had not consulted his 'brother judges' while recommending the elevation of five judges to the Supreme Court.

As Mian convened a meeting of all the judges of the Supreme Court, Shah rushed back from Saudi Arabia and shunted off some leading lights of the Court to Quetta, Karachi and Lahore. Shah believed that by dispatching the ringleaders of the brewing revolt, he would be able to secure his position with the support of his loyalists.

But distance, as the Chief Justice would come to realize, didn't really make a difference. The Supreme Court would not be allowed to stand in the way of Sharif's grandiose plans.

Although it tried hard enough. Opening another front

against the government, the Supreme Court on 29 October stayed the operation of the anti-defection law passed on 1 July 1997 by Parliament. The anti-defection law, or the fourteenth amendment to the 1973 Constitution, was a mechanism to ensure that Sharif's parliamentary flock did not desert him. The Chief Justice had struck back.

Immediately, Sharif convened a meeting of the Pakistan Muslim League (Nawaz), or PML (N) party, and its allied legislators, all pretence at nicety was dropped. The prime minister told reporters that the Supreme Court stay was illegal and unconstitutional and that it had given a fresh lease of life to 'lotaism', the colourful term used by Pakistanis to describe the politics of defection and horse-trading.

This statement was to become the basis of a contempt-of-court petition against Sharif, which would lead to the prime minister being summoned to the highest court in the land to answer personally the charges levelled against him. It was politics absolutely unprecedented.

That same night (mystifyingly, most incidents of importance in Pakistan tended to occur late at night) Parliament passed a resolution stating that it was supreme—the ultimate authority in governance. Leading figures associated with the ruling party attacked the power of the Chief Justice and the Supreme Court on the floor of the National Assembly.

On 30 October, the Supreme Court also asked the President to notify the appointment of five judges to the Court as per the recommendation of the Chief Justice on 20 August.

Earlier, the press had reported a meeting between the army chief, the President, the prime minister and the Chief Justice and said that a 'settlement' had been reached between these gentlemen.

In open court, Justice Shah announced that no such 'settlement' had been reached. In this battle, he may have had an ally in Leghari, but the President could not be of much help unless he was rearmed with the powers of dismissal—powers taken away by the thirteenth amendment.

It was fascinating to witness so closely the battle between Sharif and Shah, 'Parliament versus the Judiciary'. Hordes of reporters flocked to the Supreme Court to watch the drama. The press was sanctioned special seats on the left and right of Court No. 1 and I, along with the legal correspondents of leading Pakistani papers, was one of those who sat through the proceedings.

There was absolutely no hesitation in quoting Indian case law. Whether it was a judgment of the Allahabad High Court, or a verdict of the Supreme Court of India, Pakistani lawyers had it all pat. Many of their juniors and munshis could be seen carrying fat, leather-bound volumes of records of Indian judgments pronounced in the past.

If it was the Supreme Court in the day, it was the National Assembly at night. By late afternoon, the duel ended at the Supreme Court, and then the gauntlet would be picked up by Parliament.

On 30 October, Sharif wrote to President Leghari asking for thirty days to prepare and file a review petition against the stay order granted by the Supreme Court in the anti-defection case. 'No reasons have been given by the Court. Notice of these petitions was only issued this morning and the hearing was also fixed at 11.30 a.m. this morning ...' Sharif said in his letter to the President.

In the general face-off, it was Sharif who seemed to blink first when he announced that the government had decided to accept the Chief Justice's recommendation on the elevation of five judges to the Supreme Court on 31 October.

It appeared that the crisis was going to blow over. But that was simply a mirage—'Mian Sahib' had been persuaded by some of his associates that a settlement with Sajjad Ali Shah was still possible.

But the Chief Justice had other ideas about imposing his own supremacy. On 3 November, the Supreme Court issued notices to Sharif and several other parliamentarians in a 'contempt case' relating to remarks made about the judiciary on 29 and 30 October.

At the centre of the storm was the term I introduced you to earlier: 'lotaism' (defected legislators were known as 'lotas'), the equivalent of 'Aya Ram, Gaya Ram' in India. Sharif was accused of stating that the politics of 'lotaism' had been given a fresh lease of life by the Chief Justice.

On 12 November, a Supreme Court bench summoned Nawaz Sharif and the other parliamentarians to appear before it on 17 November. It was an unprecedented situation in Pakistan: the prime minister of the country being hauled up for contempt by the Supreme Court of the land.

Soon after the notices were issued, speculation began in earnest. Would the prime minister agree to appear before the Supreme Court? Wasn't the government 'working on' other judges? Would the PM apologize unconditionally—and end the controversy once and for all?

A day before Sharif was to appear, I met a senior Indian High Commission official. Did I think Sharif would apologize? he wondered. Yes, I did, I replied.

After all, wasn't it the dharma of politicians the world over to cling to power, somehow, some way? Wasn't a mere apology a small price to pay to continue holding the reins?

But the official had a different take. Sharif, by his reckoning, would not apologize. Why? I asked. And, then I was bowled by a googly. '*Moochch ka sawal hai* (It's a matter of losing face)', he told me, adding that in his assessment Sharif would not bend before the Chief Justice and his Supreme Court.

The official was proved right. He had read the situation correctly, and I hadn't.

Sharif appeared in what was virtually a victory procession on 17 November in the Supreme Court. (Sajjad Ali Shah and four of his 'brother judges' had refused to exempt him from a personal appearance.) Since the show was a big draw, one had to be up at the crack of dawn to enter Court No. 1 early enough to get a ringside view of the action.

A brief statement by Sharif was read out by his lawyer. There was no hint of apology in it. 'Of late,' it said, 'efforts were made to do away with the curse of changing political loyalties ... I received various opinions and interpretations about constitutional powers. And when news reporters put questions to me seeking an explanation of the matter, I cautiously gave them brief answers.'

As reporters hung on to every word, Sharif's statement went on to blandly allude to the esteem in which he held the judiciary. 'However,' it continued, in a more defiant manner, 'I am obligated to express my views on the consequences of a court ruling in the light of varying opinions'.

It was, he said, 'unfortunate' if, in the performance of his duty towards these obligations, any of his statements had been deemed by any learned judge to be in contempt of court. 'Please allow me to repeat that I have upheld the honour of the Supreme Court by appearing before it in person.'

Sharif was saying that his appearance was a matter of choice, not compulsion. It was he who had 'upheld the honour' of the Supreme Court. It had nothing to do with the rule of law and obeying the order of the highest court of Pakistan.

Would the Chief Justice now drop the case? Nothing of the sort. A grim-faced Shah and colleagues decided to soldier on.

On the day itself, the National Assembly passed a bill to amend the 1976 Contempt of Court Act. The bill provided that an 'intra-court' appeal be allowed against any show-cause notice or order passed by a Supreme Court bench in any case, including a pending matter, to a 'larger bench of all the remaining available judges of the [Supreme Court] within the country'.

It was a bill that was intended to save Sharif's skin alone. And, it was becoming clear, the remaining judges of the Supreme Court were becoming sympathetic to the prime minister and would soon question the actions of their Chief Justice. The amendment to the Contempt Act would allow the other judges an entry into the case against Sharif.

The prime minister now opened another front—against President Leghari. On 20 November, Sharif decided to begin impeachment proceedings against the President, believing that the delay in Leghari giving his assent to the Contempt of Court (Amendment) Bill, was deliberate. It was also decided that a breach of privilege motion would be brought against the Chief Justice for alleged contempt of the House.

In the meantime, the Supreme Court had adjourned the contempt petition against the prime minister and his colleagues till 28 November. Many Pakistani reporters told me at the time about how key associates of Sharif went to Supreme Court benches with suitcases full of money; stories that obviously could not be verified.

My personal diary entry for 27 November reads: 'Chief Justice heckled in court.' The next day's simply says: 'SC stormed by Nawaz supporters.'

As I was parking my car outside the Supreme Court building that morning, I remember a uniformed Islamabad policeman coming up to me to put forward the thoughtful suggestion that I station it at a healthy distance from the main gate of the Court.

I took him at his word and parked far away—almost as far as the Pakistani Foreign Office. As events were to demonstrate, the policeman had done me a huge favour. Sharif's supporters had planned protests outside the Supreme Court—and they turned out to be ugly ones.

As the Court assembled, it was clear that even those of Sharif's supporters who were inside were restive. Soon after the proceedings commenced, a senior ruling-party member of the National Assembly, a co-accused in the case, trooped out of Court No. 1 with prior permission from the Chief Justice.

Did this person carry a message to the ruling-party supporters outside? One will never know.

As the hearing continued, two reporters—Fakhrur Rehman of the Turkish daily, *Zaman*, and Zahid Hussain of the Pakistani monthly, *Newsline*, burst into the courtroom shouting: 'They have come to arrest you!'

In the heat of the moment, the two reporters had blurted out what first came to their minds, seeing the organized group outside making its way into the Court premises unhindered by the police. What they had meant to say was that the goons were on their way to beat up the Chief Justice, but what came out was that 'they' had come to 'arrest' Sajjad Ali Shah. The Chief Justice and his other judges quickly withdrew from the court to their chambers, but only in the nick of time.

Hordes of Sharif's supporters came bursting into Court No. 1, shouting slogans and hurling abuse. They were in a vile mood; determined to 'fix' the Court and Chief Justice that had dared challenge the writ of their leader Nawaz Sharif.

Frankly, I feared for myself—the only Indian in the courtroom. My friends told me to wait quietly in a corner for the whole thing to blow over. I followed their advice both in letter and spirit; I had no plans to become a victim of Sharif's goons.

They were clearly an angry lot. I believe that, by their whistle-blowing act, Fakhrur Rehman and Zahid Hussain had saved the Chief Justice and his supporters from actual violence on their persons. And from the expressions on their faces, the goons' inability to lay hands on Chief Justice Shah had doubled their anger and frustration. A sound thrashing was the least of what seemed to be on their minds.

After a couple of hours—which seemed like years— we were able to leave the court. I didn't ask any questions, but Pakistani friends pointed out to me, in whispers, at least a couple of members of the Punjab Assembly, including one (Akhtar Rasool) who had played hockey at the international level for Pakistan, among the goons.

I had witnessed one of the most shameful incidents possible in a democracy.

Hundreds of Sharif supporters had climbed the main gate of the Supreme Court and stormed in. Nothing was done to stop them. The actions of Sharif's horde were akin to desecration. The highest court of Pakistan had been defiled.

In a letter to President Leghari on 28 November, the

Chief Justice said: 'I was informed by the members of my staff ... that ... arrangements had been made by the government party to bring people in buses from Lahore and other parts to stage a big demonstration in the Court.'

The custodian of Pakistan's judiciary was not exaggerating. As I finally got into my car to drive home, I saw the goons walking silently towards Punjab House in the vicinity of the Supreme Court.

Apparently, their buses were parked there and food arrangements had been made in Punjab House, a residence for persons of influence coming from the Punjab province.

'The police was informed and they promised to keep the crowd at [a] distance from the Court building ... but later on, during the proceedings in the Court room, a very big mob in a calculated manner forced entry and raided the Court room,' Shah's letter added.

Pointing out that the police did not lift a finger to restrain the mob, Shah requested the President under Article 190 of the Constitution to take necessary steps to provide army or paramilitary cover at the Supreme Court building and the residences of the Chief Justice and other judges hearing the contempt case, 'as hardly any trust can be reposed in the forces which are under the administrative control of the government'.

It was an unprecedented situation—the Chief Justice of Pakistan was asking the President of Pakistan to protect him from security forces reporting to the prime minister of Pakistan.

It was also a busy time for reporters in the Supreme Court. The press would often have to wait for long hours to get copies of Court orders. On occasion, the Court staff would jot down the names of news agencies and newspapers whose reporters wanted copies so that the correct number could be made available.

While handing out copies of a key order of Chief Justice Shah, a Court staffer began calling out the names of 'agencies' entitled to receive them: NNI (News Network International), PPI (Pakistan Press International), Associated Press of Pakistan (APP), and then, suddenly, he came to 'MI'.

The 'MI' representative leapt to his feet, grabbed the copy and ran—as reporters burst into laughter. 'MI' was not a news agency; it was an intelligence agency: Military Intelligence.

In order to get an authentic copy of the order, the MI representative had listed his 'agency' along with the rest. In my years in Pakistan, agencies, I came to realize, always meant intelligence agencies.

Meanwhile, Shah's brother judges were active. They were determined to tackle him in Court. Confounding the situation further, 'brother judge' Saiduzzaman Siddiqui took control of the administration of the Supreme Court, and two others, Irshad Hasan Khan and Khalil-ur-Rehman Khan, sitting in Quetta, passed an order holding 'in abeyance' the very appointment of Shah as Chief Justice. Meanwhile, judges loyal to Shah, sitting in Islamabad, sought to 'set at naught' the Quetta order.

It was all getting too confusing. Daily, one had to stretch the understanding of the law and the functioning of the Supreme Court further. A denouement, I felt, had to be at hand.

It came soon enough. On 29 November, Leghari wrote to Sharif endorsing the Chief Justice's demands that the Pakistan Army provide security to the Supreme Court building and the residences of all judges. 'There can be no greater evidence of the dismal failure of your government's administration than that provided by the unprecedentedly shameful events of the last two days,' the letter read.

The riposte came the same day. Expressing his regret at the 'intemperate language' used by Leghari, the prime minister attacked the President for accepting the assertions made by Chief Justice Shah. How could Leghari condemn the entire record of his ten-month-old government on the basis of a 'localized' incident in a courtroom?

'The high office of the Presidency ought not to be used in furtherance of an intra-judicial dispute ... I cannot accept that taking sides by the Presidency in delicate and sensitive matters is in the national interest,' Sharif wrote, rejecting the demand that the army provide security to the Supreme Court.

Army Chief Karamat, on his part, refused to intervene, merely marking the letter seeking army cover to the defence secretary for 'perusal and necessary instructions'. There would be no army cover for the Supreme Court or the Chief Justice; Sharif's continuance in office would be guaranteed by lack of action on the part of the COAS.

Karamat was different from the other army chiefs; he tried to reason with Sharif several times. But, as we were to see in the coming months, that was to no avail. Simply put, the powerful COAS chose not to act.

Time and again, in Pakistan's history, the army had chosen to intervene—taking power directly or ruling through proxies. Karamat, as army chief, perhaps felt that the cost of his actions would outweigh the benefits. My assessment was that Karamat, who had a carefully calibrated low profile, did not want to involve the military directly in the political affairs of Pakistan yet again.

Had the army been deployed at the Supreme Court and Sajjad Ali Shah allowed to function, the message to Sharif and Pakistan's democracy would have been clear— a regime change was in the works.

And then, on 2 December, history of sorts was again

made when rival factions led by the Chief Justice (described by the other factions as 'under restraint', or prohibited from passing orders) met at the Supreme Court.

The Chief Justice that day was a man in a hurry. Probably realizing that Sharif had come up trumps, Shah issued a most bizarre order—he suspended the thirteenth amendment to the Constitution—the one that had stripped the President of his powers to dismiss an elected government.

And what was Shah trying to do? In his overwhelming desire to get at Nawaz Sharif, the Chief Justice was providing President Leghari the opportunity to show the Sharif government the door.

Pointing out that persistent efforts were being made to get the President to sign official papers by threatening to impeach him, the order said the government had rejected the Supreme Court's request to have the army deployed at its premises. 'In such circumstances, there is no way out but to suspend the operation of the 13th Amendment ...' Shah and the judges supporting him held. The Court was adjourned promptly after the order was passed.

The other faction of nine judges, in a parallel sitting in the Court, declared that any order passed by a bench headed by the Chief Justice ('under restraint') was not to be implemented.

So, in effect, one bench of the Supreme Court was proposing and the other was disposing. What would the President do now? Which order would he follow? That of the 'minority' bench or of the 'majority'? Saiduzzaman Siddiqui and Co. being the 'majority' faction.

News began filtering in that a press conference had been scheduled by the President for 5 p.m. at the Aiwan-e-Sadar. The scene had shifted from the Supreme Court to the Presidency—would Leghari act, now that he was 'armed' with the powers of dismissal by a dubious Supreme Court order?

Leghari announced his decision to resign rather than sign a summary denotifying the appointment of Sajjad Ali Shah. The game was over. Leghari wasn't going home on some great point of principle. There was little he could do if the COAS was not inclined to back a possible dismissal of the government.

The crisis was 'over'. As envisaged in the Constitution, the Senate (Upper House) Chairman, Wasim Sajjad, took over as acting-President and proceeded to appoint Ajmal Mian as the Chief Justice. Sajjad Ali Shah's days were history.

Sharif's wordsmith, information minister Mushahid Hussain, said on 3 December that the end of the crisis was a 'sign of maturity and strength of democratic institutions'.

In a prepared statement, Hussain said the Pakistan Army had played a 'positive role' in stabilizing the situation by demonstrating a 'commendable commitment' to the Constitution, rule of law and the democratic political system.

The end of the crisis was a relief, but reflected the pernicious effects of continuing executive influence over the judiciary and demonstrated the lengths to which Nawaz Sharif would go to have his way.

The 'heavy mandate' of the prime minister could be deployed against anybody—including the Supreme Court. As events would show, this would not be his last effort in attempting to get institutions and individuals to do his bidding.

Finally, the battle became a personal one, with Shah determined to use his office to ensure that the prime minister showed some respect for the rule of law and the orders of the courts.

Sharif and Co. regarded the end of the crisis as a huge victory for themselves at the cost of subverting an institution that was finally showing some signs of independence.

Future events would show it was not to be an example of dealing with other institutions—especially the Pakistani army. But, for the time being, the prime minister was flying high.

4

Sharif, Karamat and Musharraf

❖

THE ARMY IS the most important political actor in Pakistan. Without being a formal political party, it can influence or manipulate most things in the country: from managing its nuclear weapons programme to conducting the census.

The fauj is everywhere; it's omnipotent; omnipresent. Wearing the khaki uniform allows you unprecedented status, and transforms you into being part of that tiny elite corps of Pakistanis whose writ runs everywhere.

In areas as disparate as running businesses to finding ghost schools, the army is the ubiquitous face of Pakistan's government. It builds roads and fights insurgencies; its membership is superior to any exclusive club.

From one phase of military rule to another, the military has always taken care of its own. And during direct military rule, the fauji, of course, is the protagonist. As I saw at first hand, both serving and retired officers come to occupy plum civilian jobs in Pakistan.

Given the weakness of other institutions, even civilian governments have taken recourse to using the military to get their jobs done. In the process, of course, they have succeeded in further undermining Pakistan's already weak civilian institutions.

Since the end of the 1980s, Pakistan has been running a low-cost war against India by backing militants in Jammu & Kashmir. At the same time, it saw no contradiction in running the massive Fauji Foundation, said to be the largest private sector employer in Pakistan.

In the military's scheme of things, a jehad in Kashmir and the Fauji Foundation can happily co-exist. Success—material or otherwise—was something that the army in Pakistan aimed for. And never mind the means.

In 1997, I got to see the annual report of the Foundation and it made me realize how far the fauj had gone in controlling the nation and the stakes it had in the economic stability of Pakistan. From cement factories to colleges—the Fauji Foundation ran them all. The Pakistani air force had its Shaheen Foundation and the navy also had the Baharia Foundation, but it was the former that commanded greater attention. (The Shaheen Foundation telecast some channels and you had to obtain a special antenna to watch those.)

A 12 November 2001 article in *Business Week* magazine had this to say about the Fauji Foundation:

> The Fauji Foundation is at the heart of the military's economic machine. With an annual turnover of more than $500 million and profits of $41 million, Fauji provides womb-to-tomb benefits for more than 8.5 million ex-military men and their dependents. Retired servicemen get preferential hiring for the 10,000 jobs at the foundation's wholly-owned companies. Thousands more find work at Fauji subsidiaries,

while top management jobs are reserved for retired generals...

The article continued:

> Just how big a slice of the economic pie the military controls remains a well-guarded secret, but it's safe to say it is by far the single biggest player. Fauji Fertilizer Co. was one of Pakistan's most profitable companies in 2000, earning $44 million on sales of $170 million. Outside of the Fauji network, Askari Commercial Bank, controlled by the Army Welfare Trust (AWT), is the country's largest private bank in terms of assets and profits. Military companies enjoy access to prime real estate, easy bank credit, and tax breaks, and routinely beat out civilian companies in bidding for contracts.
>
> Started in 1947 with a $3.6 million endowment from the departing British colonial administration to provide for the needs of World War II widows and their families, the Fauji Foundation remained a modest institution until the late 1970s, when it started expanding aggressively. Using money made by its 20 companies, the foundation spends $18 million a year running some of Pakistan's best hospitals and schools. For all that, Fauji Foundation Secretary, Brigadier (retired) Mumtaz Hussain denies that his group has any special privileges. 'The environment we deal with is ruthlessly competitive,' he says. 'If we offer better deals, we win. If we can't, we are nowhere. No crutches are available, never.'

Colonel E.A. Bokhari (retd), writing in the *Defence Journal* (January 1999), revealed that a very brief business profile of the Fauji Foundation would include the following:

Fully-Owned Projects include:

- Fauji Sugar Mills, Tando Mohammad Khan.
- Fauji Sugar Mills, Khoski.
- Fauji Sugar Mills, Sangla Hill.
- Fauji Sugarcane Experimental & Seed Multiplication Farm.
- Fauji Cereals.
- Fauji Corn Complex.
- Fauji Polypropylene Products Foundation Gas.

Shareholding Projects include:

- Fauji Fertilizer Company Limited.
- Fauji Oil Terminal and Distribution Company Limited.
- Fauji Cement Company Limited.
- Mari Gas Company Limited.

New Projects consist of:

- Fauji Kabirwala Power Company Limited.
- FFC-Jordan Fertilizer Company Limited.

Education:

- Colleges 2
- Schools 64
- Scholarships 1,30,942

Technical Training:

- Technical Training Centres 9
- Vocational Training Centres 66
- Fauji Institutes of Computer Sciences 2

Medical:

- Hospitals 12
- Day Health Centres 24
- Mobile Dispensaries 48
- Static Dispensaries 21

In his book, *Pakistan: Eye of the Storm*, Owen Bennett Jones puts the assets of the Pakistan Army at nearly $2 billion. Jones, a former BBC correspondent based in Pakistan, argues that the army's economic operations were profitable because the faujis could obtain both tax breaks and subsidies.

Institutionally, military personnel in Pakistan, as they rise up the ranks, are eligible for cheap plots according to their rank. So, a brigadier gets to buy an 'x' plot at a 'y' price.

I got an insight into the extent of the property the khakis owned when, in November 1999, the army chief, Pervez Musharraf, who had recently taken over after deposing Nawaz Sharif, declared his assets in an effort to encourage transparency.

A 2 November 1999 report filed by the official APP news agency gave these details:

I [General Musharraf] would like to declare all property owned by my whole family. My family consists of my parents, wife, my son and daughter. Both my son and daughter are married. The property owned by all of us is as under:

a. Property for which instalments are being paid:

    (1)   Under construction house in Army Housing Scheme Pt-II, Karachi.
    (2)   2000 sq. yards in DHA, Karachi.
    (3)   2 x Kanals[1] in Morgah Housing Scheme, Rawalpindi.
    (4)   1 and half Kanal in AWT Housing Scheme, Peshawar.
    (5)   8 x Marlas in LCCHS, Lahore.
    (6)   2 x Square agriculture land at Bahawalpur.

b. Parents' house in F7/3, Islamabad.
c. My daughter's house in DHA, Karachi.
d. 1 x Kanal plot in Eastridge Scheme (09).
e. 2 x Kanals in Sangar Housing Scheme, Gwadar.

I have paid all taxes (income, wealth and agriculture)
till the financial year ending 30th June, 1999.

At the time these details came out, I felt that the property
possessed by the general and members of his family was
excessive. But then, several friends informed me that this
was quite normal for senior army officers, as plots of land
were offered to them at preferential rates as they climbed
up the ranks. It was part and parcel of the perks that
came with the job.

The army is well networked and, over the years, has
perfected the job of protecting its institutional interests.
Even as it allowed a civilian façade of government since
1988, it retained the clout to influence decision-making
on key domestic issues or when it came to overseeing
Islamabad's India policy.

You can't anger the military and hope to survive as
prime minister in Pakistan. When, for the first time in
Pakistan's history, a civilian prime minister sacked his
chief of army staff, he violently disturbed the established
order in the country.

By sacking Jehangir Karamat as chief of army staff in
October 1998, Nawaz Sharif had felt that he had made
himself safe—the army could no longer dislodge him from
power. Uncharcteristically for an army chief in Pakistan,
Karamat went without a murmur, but Sharif had angered
the army sufficiently to ensure that powerful interests
within were waiting to get him.

It's not embedded in the country's 1973 Constitution,
but in Pakistan a civilian prime minister usually has limits

imposed on his power. Violating the *lakshman rekha* set by the army has always invited unhappy consequences.

Nawaz Sharif's growing incompetence, his inability to deliver on his promises and his ever-increasing desire to accumulate more and more personal power were evident as his rule continued. After the May 1998 nuclear tests, Pakistan's economy was in the doldrums and Sharif seemed to be living in his own world of make-believe.

In the name of the people, Sharif acted only to strengthen his personal power. Some critics believed that even the measures to Islamize Pakistan that he wanted to push through Parliament were to set himself up as 'Amir-ul-Momineen', leader of the faithful—quite like Mullah Omar who then held sway in neighbouring Afghanistan.

Also, Sharif was possibly the first prime minister since 1988 who, very publicly, tried to turn Ayesha Jalal's thesis on its head. In her book, *The State of Martial Rule*, Jalal had argued that an elected prime minister in Pakistan, in order that s/he succeed, had to act as the leader of the Opposition to tackle the established, army-led order.

But Sharif's actions were not intended to strengthen democracy or democratic institutions in Pakistan, but to strengthen his personal power. The coterie he had assembled around him was formidable. But as time would tell, the prime minister's attempts to become dictator were destined to fail.

Nawaz Sharif's ability to see off President Farooq Leghari and Chief Justice Sajjad Ali Shah in 1997, and the appointment of Rafiq Tarar as Leghari's replacement (he was said to be the choice of the late Abbaji—Sharif's father) had emboldened Sharif no end, and he came to believe, unwisely, that he could take on the army.

Well-known South Asia scholar Stephen P. Cohen, in the 1998 edition of his *The Pakistan Army*, predicted with uncanny accuracy what would happen if Sharif tried to do to the army what he had done to the country's Supreme Court.

Cohen wrote that the clash between Sharif and Chief Justice Sajjad Ali Shah in 1997 would not be the last of its kind. Because if the PM attempted to plant his own men in the army—as he had in the Supreme Court—there would be trouble afoot.

As I came to understand, COAS Jehangir Karamat was a careful man. The general rarely spoke in public, and when he did, the Inter-Services Public Relations (ISPR) Directorate, would relay his remarks. There were no off-the-cuff comments. But even though Karamat did not lift a finger to protect the Chief Justice in 1997, there had been indications from time to time that the chief of army staff was not happy with the state of affairs in the country.

And then, on 5 October 1998 Karamat dropped a bombshell. Without naming anyone, the COAS made clear his dissatisfaction with the state of affairs prevailing in the country. Speaking at the Pakistan Naval War College in Lahore, he said that in the present 'geo-strategic environment', the most important facet of national security was 'internal security'.

An ISPR release said:

> General Jehangir Karamat said that unlike countries with economic potential we could not afford the destabilizing effects of polarization, vendetta and insecurity-driven expedient policies. General Jehangir Karamat said that he maintained, as he had repeatedly stressed, that the need of the hour was total focus on the economy, the external linkages with China, Iran, Afghanistan, India, United States, the internal situation, especially Sindh, the sectarian aspect and finally the fears of the smaller provinces.

The Chairman Joint Chiefs of Staff Committee said that political mandate needed to be translated into institutional strength otherwise we would have a permanent election campaign environment in the country. This could be done, he said, by establishing a structurally-tiered system with responsibility at each level.

A National Security Council or Committee at the apex would institutionalize decision-making if it was backed by a team of credible advisors and a think-tank of experts. The other tiers would be at the Joint Staff, Ministry and Services levels. 'We also need neutral, competent and secure bureaucracy and administration at the federal and provincial levels,' he said.

In essence, Karamat was offering Sharif a bailout package and a power-sharing arrangement. The chief was trying to tell the prime minister politely that the army was beginning to lose patience with him.

The statement added:

In reply to another question, the Chief of Army Staff said that the political leaders he had been privileged to work with in the last three years and his own institution knew that he had never minced words on issues of national import. He added that he had been resisting pressures and had been providing unequivocal professional advice in what he considered to be the best interest of the country and the Service. He would continue to do this till his retirement in January '99. 'Inshallah,' he concluded.

In Pakistan, I met Karamat (he was known as General 'JK') just once and that, too, in a chance encounter. At a glittering reception hosted at the Aiwan-e-Sadar on 14

August 1997, Pakistan's Independence Day, I saw the army chief at a distance and went up and introduced myself as the correspondent of *The Hindu* newspaper. I shook hands with him, but it was scarcely more than a 'hello-and-goodbye' situation. Surrounded as he was by many others, there was no chance to talk to him.

My summation of Karamat was of a moderate, tough soldier, who had not wanted to intervene directly in the politics of Pakistan. Sharif's antics forced him to speak out, but he refrained from taking control of the reins of power.

All through the clash between Sharif, Leghari and Sajjad Ali Shah, Karamat had tried to counsel all sides, with no success. However, he didn't do anything to destabilize Sharif's elected government, possibly leading the prime minister to conclude that he was a weak man.

His October 1998 statement revealed that Karamat was getting increasingly impatient in the wake of the economic crisis following the nuclear tests and the looming default by Pakistan on its large debt repayments. Though he didn't name anyone, Karamat finally came out strongly against the destabilizing effects of polarization, vendetta and the so-called expediencies of 'insecurity-driven' policies. The chief also clearly stated that he had been providing professional advice in the best interests of the country to the politicians.

To me, what hit home was the very public statement that he had been 'resisting pressures', an indication that sections within the army were unhappy with Sharif and wanted him to go. By proposing a National Security Council, the army chief was suggesting a power-sharing arrangement between the faujis and the civilian government.

With Sharif failing to show any real leadership qualities,

Karamat had publicly suggested a new arrangement in which the prime minister, the army and 'technocrats' would jointly try to address the huge economic and political mess in which Pakistan had found itself.[2]

The country was rocked by Karamat's statement. It had, after all, indicated that the army was still willing to intervene when it felt the nation's interests, or its own interests, were threatened. But, under Karamat at least, it stopped short of direct, naked intervention in civilian affairs.

On 7 October, the Sharif government announced that Karamat had sought 'retirement on his own request'. The prime minister acceded to the request of the COAS and appointed Lt-General Pervez Musharraf as the new chief of army staff. 'He [Musharraf] has also been promoted to the rank of General,' Sharif announced.

'In his letter addressed to the prime minister, General Jehangir Karamat stated that given the context of his recent statement an unnecessary controversy had been generated as a result of which he thought it in the best interest of the country that he should like to step aside so that the right precedent is set for the future,' the Press Information Department said in a three-paragraph statement.

Evidently, Karamat didn't want to create a full-scale crisis. Simply put, after his statement and the response from Sharif, the army chief had just one choice—between going home, and asking his boys in Rawalpindi to move against the civilian government. It would take a year and five days before his successor, Pervez Musharraf, would show Nawaz Sharif his place.

Even as the issue of the military's support to democracy is taken with a whole bucket of salt, the fact is that, under the circumstances, Nawaz Sharif didn't quite realize that in Karamat he had a rare general who simply spoke up in October 1998; he did nothing to eject the prime minister from office.

The Musharraf experience would be different.

Not unusual in Pakistan, Sharif superseded two lieutenant-generals—the Pathan Ali Quli Khan (chief of general staff and brother-in-law of then power minister Gohar Ayub Khan) and the Punjabi Khalid Nawaz (quarter-master general)—when he appointed the Mohajir, Pervez Musharraf, as army chief on 7 October. Both the superseded officers chose premature retirement rather than serve under a junior.

Musharraf's appointment had a parallel in Zulfiqar Ali Bhutto's decision to anoint Mohammad Zia-ul-Haq, then fifty-two years of age, as chief of army staff in February 1976, as successor to Tikka Khan. In his masterly *Zulfi Bhutto of Pakistan*, Stanley Wolpert reveals that Tikka had recommended to the then prime minister that Muhammad Akbar Khan or Mohammad Shariff be appointed to replace him.

Wolpert writes that for the top job, Zulfikar Ali Bhutto superseded six senior lieutenant generals and picked the juniormost, Zia, for the job. Tikka Khan had not even mentioned Zia's name as his successor because he had only just been promoted to lieutenant-general. According to Wolpert, Bhutto's choice of Zia-ul-Haq was a mistake that would prove fatal.

Here, we must depart from the Bhutto–Zia and Sharif–Musharraf analogy. Unlike Zia, who pretended to be completely servile to Bhutto (Zulfi, Wolpert claims, used to call Zia-ul-Haq his monkey-general and was often put on show for foreign visitors), General Musharraf was a entirely different sort. Initially, Musharraf didn't say much in public, but it was soon clear that the man was in sharp contrast to Karamat—as Sharif would realize to his dismay.

At the time, a Pakistani friend told me that Musharraf was a clever man but had little vision. It would prove to be an accurate, far-seeing assessment.

Sharif selected Pervez Musharraf believing him to be the man who would pose the least threat to his personal power and be the most accommodating of his command and to his wishes. And by elevating the Mangla[3] corps commander to the top job, Sharif calculated that in a Punjabi–Pathan-dominated army, the Mohajir Musharraf would not prove a problem.

Musharraf, he failed to realize, may have been born in the lanes of Daryaganj in Delhi, but had little problem in building support for himself within the Pak army. As Musharraf has demonstrated since 1999, respect, within the army, for its chief, is not governed by ethnic background; it's institutional.

Nuggets of information available at the time also suggested that the army was seething with anger that its former chief, Karamat, had been sent home in disgrace by a civilian prime minister for the first time in Pakistan's history. Normally, it was the prime minister who had to go—Bhutto was even executed at Zia's instance.

I had written in *Frontline* (20 November 1998) that Sharif, apart from elevating Musharraf, had appointed Mohammad Ziauddin the new chief of the ISI Directorate. '*These appointments reflect the kind of control Sharif wants to exercise over the army,*' I had observed. '*The Karamat chapter may be closed, but it remains to be seen what sort of equation develops between Musharraf and Sharif.*'

Sharif had broken the power of the troika in Pakistan of the President, the prime minister and the COAS. Many enlightened Pakistanis felt that the 'balance of power' had been necessary and had been fundamentally altered, strengthening the hands of a whimsical prime minister.

Though Musharraf had a short honeymoon period with Sharif, there was nothing Karamat-like even in his initial statements after taking over. On 21 October 1998, during his first visit to the forward areas of Siachen after taking over as COAS, Musharraf delivered a blunt warning to India.

Pakistan, he stated, would not be cowed down by threats from across the border—the army was fully trained and adequately equipped to 'quash' the nefarious designs of the enemy. 'We are aware of the motives of the adversary and have the capability to effectively defend the territorial integrity of the country,' ISPR quoted Musharraf as saying.

'The Chief of Army Staff visited the entire Siachen front, mingled freely with the troops, spent the night with a deployed battalion and after having stayed two days in the sector returned to Rawalpindi in the afternoon,' the statement added.

Addressing troops in the Kharian and Mangla garrisons in the Punjab on 29 October in the Pakistani Punjab, Musharraf reminded them that the army was the most organized, disciplined and cohesive national institution. It was as strong as ever, he stressed. As an afterthought, Musharraf added that the army would remain 'apolitical'.

Such views were in sharp contrast to Karamat, who chose his words with care. On India, too, the former army chief was a measured speaker. Musharraf, however, had his own style and way of saying things.

However, initially at least, the prime minister felt that in Musharraf he had found a yes-man, who would follow his orders. It was evident that Sharif felt that he could deploy the new army chief and his massive institution to carry out whatever measure took his fancy.

At a press conference on 1 January 1999, Sharif's

information minister, Mushahid Hussian, now a close adviser to Musharraf, referred to the positive role played by the army in promoting economic development through construction of roads, revamping the Water and Power Development Authority (WAPDA), establishing the National Database Organization and exposing and eliminating 'ghost' (non-existent) schools.

By inviting the army to dispense justice, by asking it to conduct the census, by asking it to build roads, apart from performing a host of other functions, Sharif succeeded in further diminishing the admittedly weak civilian institutions of the Pakistani state.

His complete reliance on the army meant that civilian institutions were never allowed to develop—a situation the army was quite comfortable with. At all times, the army, despite its poor track record in governance and the defence of the country, wanted to shine as an institution which was indispensable.

The fauj had always wanted to maintain and perpetuate this larger-than-life image of itself in the country—even when not directly governing. Apart from its primary job of protecting the Pakistani nation, the army was more than happy with its extended role.

Nawaz Sharif himself was a creature of the Pakistani establishment, handpicked by Zia-ul-Haq's protégé, General Jilani, then governor of Punjab, to be first a provincial minister and then chief minister.

Soon after taking over from Karamat, Musharraf began making changes in the army command. Men loyal to him were to be given key appointments, decisions that would prove important in the future. Lt-General Muzaffar Hussain Usmani was appointed as corps commander, Karachi, and Lt-General Aziz Khan shifted to the key position of chief of general staff in Rawalpindi. The new chief was shoring up his position.

Aziz Khan and Usmani, along with the X corps commander in Rawalpindi, Mahmud Ahmed, would prove to be key players in the months to come—men who helped Musharraf survive as chief of army staff when Sharif tried to oust him in October 1999.

Though publicly supporting Sharif, General Musharraf was his own man. A larger role for the army in the country's affairs was far from antithetical to what General Musharraf wanted—a role that was being actively advocated by Nawaz Sharif—in the belief that the army had actually been brought to heel.

In November 1998, President Rafiq Tarar promulgated the Pakistan Armed Forces (Acting in Aid of the Civil Powers) Ordinance to assist the civilian government in maintaining law and order, and restoration of peace.

The Ordinance, promulgated about a month after the 17 October murder of the respected Hakim Said[4] in Karachi, was to apply to those areas of Sindh province where the army would be called in to act in the aid of civil power under Article 245 of the Pakistani Constitution.

It set up military courts to try offences listed under the Ordinance. Apart from heinous offences, Sharif created a new offence called 'civil commotion', which meant creation of internal disturbances in violation of law or intended to violate law, commencement or continuation of illegal strikes, go-slows, lock-outs, vehicle-snatching and lifting, damage or destruction to state or private property, random firing to create panic, distributing, publishing or pasting handbills, wall-chalking and writing graffiti intended to create unrest or fear, or a threat to law and order under Chapter VI of the Pakistan Penal Code.

The Ordinance made it plain that offences committed prior to its promulgation would also come under its purview. Pending cases in other courts of law could also be transferred to these military courts.

The military courts were yet another bid by Sharif to move ahead with his hare-brained scheme of dispensing quick justice. Rather than addressing the root causes of violence in Karachi and other parts of the country, and dealing with organized sectarian groups, the prime minister now involved the army in dispensing justice.

As expected, the legality of these military courts was challenged in the Supreme Court. Even before a seven-member bench of the Supreme Court began hearing the merits of the challenge, at least two persons convicted by the military courts in Karachi were hanged to death.

The first man, Ashraf Chakar (30) was executed on 31 December 1998 by the order of Military Court No. 3 on the charge of murdering a policeman. And, then, on 4 January 1999, Mohammed Rafi (22) was hanged in the Karachi Central Jail for kidnapping and raping a girl.

Soon after the two were hanged, the Supreme Court on 11 January stayed all hangings by the military court—but it was too late for Chakar and Rafi.

At around the same time, Nawaz Sharif escaped an attempt on his life near his private Raiwind residence in Punjab on 3 January. The massive blast, which killed four persons, including a policeman, seemed to energize Sharif further in his efforts to punish terrorists.

Subsequent information suggested that the attack was the work of Riaz Basra, the dreaded chief of the Sunni terrorist group, the Lashkar-e-Jhangvi. A day later, Attorney-General Chaudhry Mohammad Farooq read out a letter from Sharif in the Supreme Court in which he made the usual noises about the unprecedented threats that Pakistan faced from terrorism.

'If we are to progress we have to break the mould of lawless killings and eradicate the vortex of violence,' Sharif's letter read. 'Ever since I embarked on this campaign, I and my family have been receiving dire threats ... This is the first time in the history of our country that the person of the Prime Minister, and his family members, have been subjected to danger in this manner. These threats were translated into action on the road to Raiwind [Sharifs' family home near Lahore]. However, I have not been in the least deterred by these developments ... '

A major attack also took place on the Shia community in Karamdad Qureshi village in the Muzaffargarh district of southern Punjab. As many as seventeen persons were killed on 4 January 1999 as the ugly face of sectarian violence reared its head once again.

In the meantime, the Supreme Court dashed the prime minister's hopes that the military courts would continue as a means to deliver speedy justice. On 17 February 1999, the Pakistani Supreme Court declared that the military courts introduced by the Ordinance were unconstitutional.

'Ordinance No. XII of 1998 as amended up-to-date insofar as it allowed the establishment of military courts was unconstitutional, without lawful authority and of no legal effect,' the Court ruled. The Court clarified that its decision would not impact on the sentences and punishments handed down by the military courts (such as the executions of Chakar and Rafi) and those cases would be treated as past and closed transactions.

Clearly, the Supreme Court took the easy way out as any other finding would have had implications for those who handed down the verdicts and those who put in place the legal machinery for the military courts.

As Sharif blundered, Musharraf watched. After all, there was nothing the army could do if the military courts scheme was shot down by the Supreme Court. The army, under its new chief, had offered the fullest possible cooperation when it was required to.

The future would show how wrong Sharif's calculations about Musharraf had been. For better or for worse, the new army chief would take his own decisions and not confine himself to public suggestions such as the one made by his predecessor, Jehangir Karamat.

Musharraf, contrary to Sharif's impression of him, was able to keep the army with him despite the Punjabi–Pakhtun domination in the fauj. His Mohajir ethnicity, as Sharif would realize, did not interfere with his command of the army.

There is little doubt that the Pakistan Army is Punjabi–Pathan dominated, with a majority of officers and ranks coming from these two ethnic groups. Other than Mirza Aslam Beg, Musharraf is the only other Mohajir officer to have made it to the top job in the Pakistan Army. General Musharraf's ability to keep the flock together is dictated by the strong disciplinary roots of the Pakistan Army, including the need to safeguard its political and corporate interests.

Musharraf was more hawkish than his Punjabi predecessor, Jehangir Karamat. Given the fact that the Kargil incursion (see Chapter 7) was Musharraf's own brainchild, there was no question of the general going 'soft' on India.

Anti-Indianism put out strong roots in the Pakistan Army; India's ruination was almost the raison d'etre for the large military maintained by Pakistan. Musharraf exploited that ideology to the hilt to ensure his acceptance as the supreme leader.

Musharraf's hawkish views would have a fatal bearing on Sharif's attempts to build bridges with India as subsequent chapters on Prime Minister Vajpayee's visit to Lahore and the Kargil incursion will show.

5

Going Nuclear

*They even forgot how to talk to their neighbours,
and forgot their manners—their neighbourly manners.
They forgot the basic manners in culture, the
diplomatic culture ... Today, we have settled the
score with India. We have conducted five successful
nuclear explosions. I am thankful to God that He
made us do all this ...*

—Pakistani Prime Minister Nawaz Sharif
on 28 May 1998

IT WASN'T A good time to be an Indian in Pakistan.
Living through the Kargil conflict wasn't, personally for
me, as bad as the days between 11 May and 28 May
1998—the gap between the Indian and Pakistani nuclear
tests that inflamed bilateral relations and set the Indian
subcontinent up for international attention never seen
before.

Those seventeen days were, to my mind, the most harrowing of the years I spent in Islamabad. It was almost as if Indians in Pakistan had become persona non grata—while continuing our 'escorted' existence in the country.

If the hostility from the Pakistanis was direct and palpable, third-country diplomats were no less furious with us. Western diplomats, especially, felt they had been let down by India while neighbours were worried about the fallout from the tests. So charged with hostility became the environment that some spouses of Indian envoys stopped going for the diplomatic receptions—otherwise pretty much the routine during evenings in Islamabad.

I, too, personally experienced how bad it was. At every press conference or public function, I would be taken to task for what the Vajpayee government did on 11 and then again on 13 May.

Strangers, friends and acquaintances alike would seek me out to express their anger. I kept mostly silent (silence was a virtue that I came to acquire in Pakistan and, on the whole, it held me in good stead), but on some occasions I had to respond.

'Look,' I used to tell my Pakistani contacts, 'I don't represent the Government of India here. Far from it. I'm the representative of India's most respected newspaper. I have nothing to do with nuclear tests.'

But, like with other issues, this didn't cut much ice with the Pakistanis. For them, I was the face of India. To some of them I said, 'Why don't you write to the prime minister of India, expressing your feelings? Just leave me be.' I even offered to provide phone and fax numbers.

The small Pakistani activist community, too, was extremely upset by the Vajpayee government's actions and became acutely aware of the Pakistani response that was to follow.

A seminar was organized at Islamabad's Best Western Hotel by Pakistani NGOs in the middle of the seventeen days that shook the subcontinent. During the tea break, a Pakistani friend introduced me to a woman activist as an Indian journalist.

'What, they are still allowing you to remain here after what has happened? And you are in one piece?' she demanded to know. I was quite used to the mainstream anti-Indian responses in public, but this one from an activist flummoxed me. Clearly, she was furious at what India had done, and I was a convenient target for her disappointment, anger and frustration. It was only to be expected, given the impact of the 11 May nuclear tests conducted by India.

What the general feeling revealed was the extent of the anti-Indian anger amongst all sections of Pakistanis. At the time it disturbed me. Today, when I look back, I see that much of it was inevitable and natural.

As I have explained in Chapter 1, the principal lesson I learnt in Pakistan was to make a distinction between the people and the government. The difference stared you in the face. In the people who worked in our household, and in those friends I dealt with on a day-to-day basis, there was no trace of hostility. In fact, there was every evidence of affection.

It was this understanding from friends that permitted me to muddle through those seventeen stormy days before the Nawaz Sharif government 'settled the score' through its own nuclear tests.

To go back a bit, I have to say that the Pakistani government, to its credit, had been the first and only one to raise a hue-and-cry about the publicly declared intention of the National Democratic Alliance (NDA) government, soon after it took power in New Delhi in March 1998, to exercise the nuclear option.

India- and Pakistan-watching is almost like a fine art. One side watches the other closely; the parallel job has been going on for some fifty-eight years. So it was not entirely surprising that the one country able to read the BJP-led government's intentions in a flash was Pakistan.

Soon after the NDA government announced in its national agenda for governance on 18 March 1998, that it would 'exercise the option to induct nuclear weapons', Pakistan began expressing its concern.

Islamabad began to describe the NDA's intentions as an 'open threat', indicating that a 'fearsome situation' had been created. Also, implicit in the reaction was the threat to respond to Indian provocation.

In this situation, Pakistan would, if necessary, review its policy to safeguard its sovereignty, territorial integrity and national interest. Simultaneously, the Pakistani Foreign Office called upon the international community to take serious note of Indian intentions and exert pressure on New Delhi to show restraint.

If the Pakistanis were sensitive to Indian intentions, the US certainly didn't take the Pakistanis seriously. In April 1998, President Bill Clinton's special envoy, Bill Richardson, made a trip to South Asia that took him to Dhaka, New Delhi, Islamabad and Kabul. The cocky Richardson, who addressed a press conference at the US Information Centre in Islamabad after having met with the Taliban leadership in Kabul, was focussed on the one issue: getting Osama bin Laden.

A persistent Pakistani journalist tried to question Richardson on the intentions of the NDA government on the nuclear front, but Richardson, at the time US ambassador to the United Nations in New York, wanted to talk only about Afghanistan.

Having had meetings with the top Indian leadership,

including Prime Minister Atal Bihari Vajpayee, Richardson probably believed that India's nuclear intentions were a non-issue. He was to be proved wrong in just a couple of days.

A brilliant account of Richardson's meetings in New Delhi has been given by Jeffery Goldberg in *The New Yorker* (10 February 2003):

> [George] Fernandes [then India's Defence Minister], a self-described pacifist, told Richardson that India had no intention of exploding a nuclear device. Then he changed the subject to the situation in Burma. In other meetings, Richardson was given the same soothing message, and the mission to India was so relaxed that the assistant secretary of state, Karl Inderfurth, who was managing the trip, spent part of one day trying to set up a cricket demonstration for Richardson, a former minor-league baseball player. The demonstration was interrupted only once, so that Richardson could receive a six-minute intelligence briefing from a New Delhi-based CIA officer.

To give credit to the NDA government, it had fooled the Americans, but Goldberg, who had accompanied Richardson as a reporter, has revealed that it didn't have to try too hard. Richardson and Co. were supremely confident that the assurances they had been given were for real.

So, when the Indian nuclear tests happened on 11 May, there was surprise and anger in Washington. The US deputy secretary of state, Strobe Talbott, arrived in Islamabad on 15 May with a mission to induce, cajole or coerce Pakistan into not testing in response to the Indian tests.

'We made very, very clear to them the seriously negative consequences that would ensue from testing and the fact that they would be far, far better off if they chose the diplomatic road, the high road, the road of the rest of the world,' Talbott told reporters in Islamabad.

However, Talbott said nuclear tests by Pakistan were 'a live possibility', although another US official said that Pakistani leaders had apparently not made a final or irrevocable decision to go ahead.

'We are very aware of the political pressures that exist in Pakistan,' Talbott said to the press. 'But we hope that ... the government analyzes the situation and concludes that not going forward with the testing programme will rebound to the advantage of Pakistan.'

Clinton and his administration were, clearly, furious with India and the government of Prime Minister Vajpayee. This was reflected in Clinton promptly releasing to the press a 14 May letter written by Vajpayee in which he made the now-famous reference to China.

> We have an overt nuclear weapon state on our borders, a state which committed armed aggression against India in 1962. Although our relations with that country have improved in the last decade or so, an atmosphere of distress persists mainly due to the unresolved border problem. To add to the distress that country has materially helped another neighbour of ours to become a covert nuclear weapons state. At the hands of this bitter neighbour we have suffered three aggressions in the last fifty years.

The release of the letter was a major diplomatic embarrassment to the Vajpayee government and reflected the anger in Washington. Raising the China bogey didn't lead to India getting any sympathy from Washington.

On 11 May, Sharif was not in Pakistan but in Central Asia, when India conducted its nuclear tests. The not-in-favour foreign minister, Gohar Ayub Khan, had his moment of glory. From 11 May onwards, Khan gave a series of uninterrupted interviews and press conferences lambasting India.

Referring to the 6 April 1998 test of the *Ghauri* missile (widely believed to be a version of the North Korean *No Dong* missile, indicating the close nexus in ballistic missile deals between Pakistan and North Korea), Khan repeatedly warned that a nuclear attack by Pakistan would kill many more Indians, than if India were to launch one on Pakistan, since Indian cities were more densely populated.

Pakistan was obsessed with the Indian tests. There was nothing else in the newspapers but pressure on the Sharif government to respond. So smack in the middle of 11 May to 28 May tumult, Sharif addressed a press conference at his sprawling Prime Minister's Office.

Here, while the PM played his cards close to his chest, a woman Pakistani journalist was far from impressed by his speech. I remember her, after the press conference, running after the PM and imploring him: 'Mian Sahab, *aap* test *karen* (You must do the test, Prime Minister).'

The outpouring in the press had become so intense that I jokingly mentioned to a Pakistani friend that I had actually drawn up a list of Islamabad-based journalists who might 'explode themselves' if Pakistan did not conduct its tit-for-tat tests.

This friend, in a column for *The News*, wrote about the 'list' that an Islamabad-based Indian journalist had prepared. Since there were only two Indian journalists based in Islamabad, the list of possible suspects could not have been very long.

Mercifully, he had not mentioned any names of the Pakistanis on my list. So, when I called him to remonstrate against what he had done without telling me, he just laughed. 'I've been getting calls from my friends all morning,' he said complacently. 'They all want to know the names of the people on that list!'

Whatever noises Sharif may have made in the period between the Indian and Pakistani nuclear tests, it was evident to observers that the military establishment, and not the civilian government, had control over the Pakistani nuclear programme.

There was never any doubt in my mind on that score. A well-placed Pakistani source told me after the Pakistani nuclear tests that the army chief, Jehangir Karamat, used to get regular visits from senior generals pushing him to conduct the test.

As the diplomatic drama was enacted, with the Americans and Japanese in full cry, the military was doing its own thing. It had got the opportunity of a lifetime. The Pakistanis, on their own, could not have tested. The international community would have fallen upon them like a ton of bricks. But now it was India that had taken the first step. Pakistan merely had to follow the Indian lead. And, though the future was uncertain, the Pakistanis correctly calculated that whatever would happen to the Indians, would happen to them as well. The consequences for both would be equal.

The Pakistanis got their arithmetic right. Not all the inducements offered by the Americans and the rest of the international community was going to affect the Pakistani decision. Even if there was some evidence that Sharif may have thought differently, it wasn't articulated in public.

The situation was too serious for the airing of differences in public. Had that happened, the army would have sent the Sharif government packing a full seventeen months before October 1999. There could have been no compromise on the basics of the Pakistani response.

The billions on offer from the US could not have made up for the loss of Pakistani face. As in the case of the Sharif-versus-Sajjad Ali Shah battle, the 'mooch' factor played an important role here too.

India was openly boasting of its nuclear prowess. Live telecasts of Indian governmental gloating were being beamed into elite Pakistani homes hour after hour following 11 May. The Pakistani desire for a befitting response was certainly growing. And, the army, as the real custodian of Pakistani national interest, would have to come up with it.

Via a dish antenna installed on my terrace, I remember watching Indian channels (there was no ban on them at the time) relaying the pictures of a Sikh delegation presenting an emblematic sword to Prime Minister Vajpayee, which he promptly unsheathed and proceeded to wave around.

It was, without doubt, diplomacy at its worst. Gone were the days when it took days and weeks for the Pakistani public to get to know first-hand what the Indians were doing. This was instant provocation.

Mr Vajpayee and his government had gone overboard. As could be expected, the Indian mission in Islamabad constantly followed, assessed and analyzed the many statements emanating from the Pakistani establishment.

After ruining the relationship with China in the run-up to the tests (let's remember that Defence Minister George Fernandes was but a willing tool used by the prime minister and the Sangh parivar to this effect), the BJP-led government was ratcheting up tension with Pakistan through this very public display of emotion.

It left the Pakistanis with little strategic choice. It was clear to me from day one that it was only a matter of time before the Pakistanis would come up with a suitable nuclear reply. Having publicly declared their capability in the past, they had to put it to the test. And they had to prove to the Pakistani people that it actually existed.

There appeared to be some differences of opinion between the Indian mission in Islamabad and Delhi on the matter. While the high commission's assessment was clear that Islamabad would test, Delhi seemed less certain. That, perhaps, explained the statement made by Home Minister L.K. Advani on 18 May that dramatically raised the already boiling temperature in the subcontinent.

Warning Pakistan that it would face dire consequences if it continued to support a separatist insurgency in Kashmir, Advani claimed that 'Islamabad should realise the change in the geo-strategic situation in the region and the world'.[1]

While inviting Islamabad to 'join India in the common pursuit of peace', Advani at the same time warned Islamabad that 'any other course will be futile and costly for Pakistan'. At his hawkish best, the home minister said the Indian government did not rule out giving its troops the green light to engage in 'hot pursuit' of Kashmiri terrorists across the border. There was considerable speculation over the motives behind Advani's statement, but in the Pakistani establishment, at least, it was interpreted as a serious threat.

At 1 a.m. on 28 May, the Indian high commissioner to Pakistan, Satish Chandra, was summoned to the Pakistani Foreign Office and asked to convey an important message to his government: Pakistan had credible information in its possession that India was planning a pre-dawn strike against Pakistan's nuclear installations. Interestingly, the Pakistanis added, for telling propaganda effect, that Israelis were assisting the Indians in these 'strike plans'.

Later that day, I met Chandra in his office. What did I think of the post-midnight summons? 'The Pakistanis are going to test. They are building up their case for it,' I told the high commissioner.

An official statement issued that day said the Indian high commissioner had been asked to 'convey to New Delhi that we expected the Indian government to desist from any such irresponsible act'. Needless to add, the Pakistanis made it clear that any irresponsible act would warrant a 'swift and massive retaliation' with unforeseeable consequences.

The Israeli angle was just a twist in the tale. If the Pakistani 'bomb' was to be an Islamic one, adding the Israelis to this deadly Indian design would enhance the Islamist flavour of the bomb.

Pakistani columnist Rai Muhammad Saleh Azam has provided one of the best accounts of the run-up to the Pakistani government's decision to go nuclear. An article by him in *The Nation* was reproduced in the *Defence Journal* (June 2000):

> A meeting of the Defence Committee of the Cabinet (DCC) was convened on the morning of 15 May 1998 at the Prime Minister's Secretariat, Islamabad to discuss the situation arising out of the Indian nuclear tests. The meeting was chaired by the Prime Minister of Pakistan and attended by the Minister of Defence, the Minister of Foreign Affairs, Gohar Ayub Khan, the Minister of Finance & Economic Affairs, Sartaj Aziz, the Foreign Secretary, Shamshad Ahmed Khan and the three Chiefs of Staffs of the Army, Air Force and Navy, namely General Jehangir Karamat, Air Chief Marshal Pervaiz Mehdi Qureshi and Admiral Fasih Bokhari respectively.
>
> Since Dr Ishfaq Ahmed, Chairman of the PAEC

[Pakistan Atomic Energy Commission] was on a visit to the United States and Canada, the responsibility of giving a technical assessment of the Indian nuclear tests and Pakistan's preparedness to give a matching response to India fell on the shoulders of Dr Samar Mubarakmand, Member (Technical), PAEC. Dr Mubarakmand was in charge of the PAEC's Directorate of Technical Development (DTD), one of the most secretive organizations in the Pakistan nuclear programme, the location of which is one of Pakistan's best-kept secrets and unknown to the world. Dr Mubarakmand had supervised several cold tests since 1983 and was responsible for overseeing all of PAEC's classified projects. Also in attendance was Dr A.Q. Khan, Director of the Khan Research Laboratories (KRL), Kahuta.

There were two points on the DCC's agenda: Firstly, whether or not Pakistan should carry out nuclear tests in order to respond to India's nuclear tests. Secondly, if Pakistan does go ahead with the tests, then which of the two organizations, PAEC or KRL, should carry out the tests?

The discussions went on for a few hours and encompassed the financial, diplomatic, military, strategic and national security concerns. Finance Minister Sartaj Aziz was the only person who opposed the tests on financial grounds due to the economic recession, the low foreign exchange reserves of the country and the effect of inevitable economic sanctions which would be imposed on Pakistan if it carried out the tests. Prime Minister Nawaz Sharif neither opposed nor proposed the tests. The remainder spoke in favour of conducting the tests.

Azam said the order to conduct the tests was given on 18 May. Since the DCC meeting of 15 May had proved inconclusive, it is believed that a more exclusive DCC meeting was held on 16 or 17 May, attended only by the prime minister, the foreign minister, the finance minister and the three chiefs of staff of the Pakistani army, air force and navy. According to Azam, the fateful decision was taken at this meeting.

This account is rivetting:

On 19 May 1998, two teams of 140 PAEC scientists, engineers and technicians left for Chagai, Balochistan on two separate PIA Boeing 737 flights. Also on board were teams from the Wah Group, the Theoretical Group, the Directorate of Technical Development (DTD) and the Diagnostics Group. Some of the men and equipment were transported via road using NLC [National Logistics Centre] trucks escorted by the members of the Special Services Group (SSG), the elite commando force of the Pakistan Army.

The nuclear devices were themselves flown in completely knocked down (CKD) sub-assembly form on a Pakistan Air Force C-130 Hercules tactical transport aircraft from Rawalpindi to Chagai, escorted even within Pakistani airspace by four PAF F-16s armed with air-to-air missiles. The security of the devices was so strict that the PAF F-16 escort pilots had been secretly given standing orders that in the unlikely event of the C-130 being hijacked or flown outside of Pakistani airspace, they were to shoot down the aircraft before it left Pakistan's airspace. The F-16s were ordered to escort the C-130 to a designated airfield in Balochistan with their radio communications equipment turned off so that no orders, in the interim, could be conveyed to them to act otherwise. They were also ordered to ignore any orders to the contrary that got through to them during the duration of the flight even if such orders originated from Air Headquarters.

Once in Chagai, the parts of the nuclear devices were separately taken to the five 'zero rooms' in the kilometre-long tunnels at Ras Koh Hills in Chagai. Dr Samar Mubarakmand [from the PAEC] personally supervised the complete assembly of all five nuclear devices. Diagnostic cables were thereafter laid from the tunnel to the telemetry. The cables connected all five nuclear devices with a command observation post 10 km away. Afterwards, a complete simulated test was carried out by tele-command. This process of preparing the nuclear devices and laying of the cables and the establishment of the fully functional command and observation post took five days.

On 25 May 1998, soldiers of the Pakistan Army 5 Corps arrived to seal the tunnel. They were supervised by engineers and technicians from the Pakistan Army Engineering Corps, the Frontier Works Organisation (FWO) and the Special Development Works (SDW). Dr Samar Mubarakmand himself walked a total of five kilometres back and forth in the hot tunnels checking and re-checking the devices and the cables which would be forever buried under the concrete. Finally, the cables were plugged into nuclear devices. The process of sealing the tunnel thereafter began with the mixing of the cement and the sand. It took a total of 6,000 cement bags to seal the tunnel.

The tunnel was sealed by the afternoon of 26 May 1998 and by the afternoon of 27 May 1998, the cement had completely dried out due to the excessive heat of the desert. After the engineers certified that the concrete had hardened and the site was fit for the tests it was communicated to the Prime Minister via the GHQ that the site was ready. The date and time for Pakistan's rendezvous with destiny was set for 3:00 P.M. on the afternoon of 28 May 1998.

Expectedly, the Pakistani prime minister was deployed to make the announcement about the nuclear tests, a development that was being reported by international television channels having access to American satellite imagery. The developments in Chagai were, clearly, being tracked.

Nawaz Sharif said that Pakistan had settled its score with India—it was just the kind of language hawkish Pakistanis wanted to hear. The deed was done.

On his part, General Jehangir Karamat said in a public statement on 30 May that Pakistan's tests had corrected the strategic imbalance in the region and any 'further build-up' depended on India. Clearly, he had left the rhetoric in the hands of the civilian prime minister. 'This new balance in the military equation,' Karamat argued, 'could lead to restraint and rationality by learning from the painful process the US and former USSR had gone through in the Cold War era'. Events dictated by his successor, Pervez Musharraf, would show how wrong his assessment was.

At a press conference on the same day, Foreign Secretary Shamshad Ahmed, a clear favourite of the military establishment, clarified that only one nuclear test had been conducted on 30 May—bringing the total number of tests to six.

Ahmed left none in doubt about the intentions behind the Pakistani tests. 'After successfully conducting five nuclear tests on 28 May 1998, Pakistan completed the current series by another nuclear test today ... All the tests conducted were fully contained. There was no release of radioactivity. The results were as expected. The devices tested correspond to weapons configuration, compatible with delivery systems,' he said at a press conference carried live worldwide from the Pakistani Foreign Office.

He was declaring loudly and clearly—for India to hear and take note—that the Pakistani devices tested corresponded to weapons configuration and were compatible with delivery systems.

Ahmed argued that the 'high priests' of non-proliferation did not scratch below the surface. 'The symptom is their problem, the disease afflicts us,' he said, adding that the real causes of insecurity, conflict and tension were never addressed.

And, then he came to the real point: linking Kashmir to the nuclear issue. Soon Pakistani spokesmen would lay emphasis on saying that Kashmir had become a 'nuclear flashpoint'.

At the same time, Ahmed and his government, aware that Pakistan would now equally be in the international dock, stated that Islamabad was ready to resume a bilateral dialogue with India on all issues, including Kashmir, as well as discussing measures for mutual restraint.

Ahmed's press conference was of course carried live to all corners of the world from the Pakistan Foreign Office building. Yet again, Pakistan had proved that it retained the ability to provide a major international news story, whose implications would be known only in the future.

A day after his press conference, an Indian High Commission staffer, B.S. Rawat, was beaten up by a private Pakistani security guard outside his house in Islamabad. In the surcharged atmosphere between the two countries, this event added to the considerable tension that had built up over the past few weeks.

In New Delhi, the Pakistani high commissioner was

summoned by the Indian foreign secretary and, expectedly, a 'strong protest' was lodged with him by the Government of India. An official statement issued at the time said: '[The] foreign secretary told the high commissioner that India took very grave note of this incident which had very disturbing connotations and was entirely unacceptable. This abnormal incident reflects the inadequate security being provided to our mission officials despite repeated demarches made by us in the past.'

Though Pakistani intelligence wasn't found to be involved in the attack on Rawat (there appeared to have been some private animosity between the victim and the attacker), the incident sent nervous tremors through the small Indian community in Islamabad, coming as it did in the wake of the rival nuclear tests.

Retaliation against Pakistani officials in New Delhi was anticipated, and as a consequence, many Indian High Commission staffers in Islamabad, especially those marked for attention by Pakistani intelligence, were vulnerable. As had happened before, some of them chose to remain inside the High Commission premises—sleeping there at night—rather than come out and face more music from the Pakistanis.

Soon after the Indian nuclear tests of 11 May, an Indian diplomat advised me to take out all my money, kept in a savings dollar account (altogether legal in Pakistan). I wasn't convinced, telling myself they couldn't do anything to dollar accounts.

I would have time to repent my foolhardiness at leisure. On the midnight of 28 May, President Rafiq Tarar, personally picked to be the country's head of state by Nawaz Sharif's father, Abbaji, declared a state of Emergency, suspended all fundamental rights and froze all foreign currency accounts.

Foreign currency accounts, I came to realize, included mine. Diplomats and foreigners working for UN organizations were the only ones exempted from the Ordinance.

It was, to tell the truth, daylight robbery. Lakhs of Pakistanis, including those living overseas, lost their savings. As much as $11 billion was at stake. All of it was frozen by Tarar's action. Realizing there was going to be a run on the banks, Sharif's advisers had informed him that there was no way out but to freeze the accounts.

As a sop to account-holders, they allowed you to withdraw your dollars at the official exchange rate of Pakistani Rs 46 to the dollar at a time when the market exchange rate was over Rs 60. Pakistanis, clearly, did not have an option but to do what their government had dictated. The Government of Pakistan, in its wisdom, later made arrangements so that limited foreign exchange could be provided for emergency travel arrangements.

According to one assessment, three days after the Pakistani nuclear tests, the country's foreign exchange reserves fell to $1.27 billion—they had stood at $1.37 billion on 23 May 1998.

The foreign currency accounts were frozen because the government had no money to pay out. Prior to 28 May, successive Pakistani governments had been borrowing at higher rates to encash foreign currency demands.

Interestingly, all kinds of protection had been built into these foreign currency accounts in order to make investors, including overseas Pakistanis, feel safe. But, you see, the country had now become a nuclear power and ordinary people had to make sacrifices.

I was in a real soup. My salary and office expenses were remitted by *The Hindu* every month to a foreign currency account. How was this process to continue? If money could not be received in Pakistan, obviously a serious problem presented itself over the long term. A few months could have been managed, but permanently?

Along with this, my savings had been frozen. Withdrawing this money at the official rate would be quite useless. I decided to wait it out. I was not going to be subsidizing the Government of Pakistan even in a small way for its decision to become a nuclear weapons power. Shahid Khan, my PTI colleague, was in the same boat.

Almost every day, a trip to the bank became essential—simply because 'exemption' circulars were being issued thick and fast. And finally one day, weeks after the account was frozen, the bank informed me that since I was a foreigner, I could withdraw my money. Which I swiftly did, in spite of all the confusion that surrounded the circulars.

Ever since then, my savings in Pakistan were in 'cash dollars'—in the safe custody of a drawer in my house. They proved to be more secure there than anywhere else in Pakistan. Almost immediately, the government announced its decision to open a new series of foreign currency accounts, realizing inward remittances were falling drastically.

At the height of the crisis, I had spoken to Indian High Commission diplomats about the problem of the frozen accounts. They were frank: 'There's not much we can do with the government of Pakistan,' they said, 'but we can do one thing—we can get the accounts of the two Pakistani journalists in New Delhi frozen.'

Thanks, but no thanks, I said. Their logic dictated that if nothing could be done to address the issues that were plaguing you, the only option before you was to make life equally difficult for your counterparts across the border. How absurd is that?

That kind of bloody-minded thinking operated at the pettiest levels. Say, if the Pakistani political counsellor's telephone was out of order and wasn't being fixed in New Delhi, his/her counterpart's phone in Islamabad would also roll over and play dead.

So, till June 2000, when I left Islamabad for Singapore, my house was also my bank. My small savings didn't earn any interest in that period, but they were safe. Every month, I would take out my salary from the new foreign currency account as soon as it was deposited—once bitten, I was twice shy.

Later, I was to discover that I was among the lucky ones who didn't have to actually bankroll the disastrous economic policies pursued by the Government of Pakistan over the years.

Yang Shillong, representative of the Xinhua news agency, who had heard I'd gotten my money out, wasn't as lucky as I was. When he left for China at the end of his posting, Yang told me that he was leaving some $20,000 in his savings account as there was no point in exchanging it at the Rs 46-per-dollar rate that was on offer. I lost touch with Yang, and I don't know whether he ever saw his savings again.

Diplomats were luckier—at one level; and worse off at another. Their accounts were not frozen, but they couldn't change money at the market rate—they had to do it at the bank rate. There were, of course, ways to get around the problem and, I suspect, many took that route.

If Sharif's popularity among some soared for settling the score with India, his economic policies did not endear him to many. But one of his calculations paid off—having already used up people's dollar deposits—a large chunk of Pakistan's already brittle banking system would have certainly gone under had there been a run on the banks.

After the nuclear tests, Sharif's despotic nature began to show more and more of itself. In an address to the nation early in June, he asked the people of Pakistan to rein in their consumption of ghee and tea. An official account of his speech said that Pakistanis spent Rs 7 billion annually on drinking tea, so they should reduce that by half.

After dispossessing many of them of their dollar savings, the prime minister called on each overseas Pakistani to send US $1,000 back to their country in this, its time of need. He advised them to shun the 'hundi'[2] route and, instead, rely on Pakistani banks. Obviously, there wasn't much of a response to his appeal.

Some land reform measures—loans for the unemployed and a number of other schemes which never got implemented, of course—were also announced by the prime minister.

Most extraordinary of all was his decision to sell the Prime Minister's Secretariat—a sprawling, opulent building close to the Supreme Court and the Pakistani Foreign Office. In July 1998, the Privatization Commission tried to sell off the massive seven-storey structure—housing 400 office rooms and as many as twenty-nine kitchens—as part of the PM's 'austerity' drive after the country's nuclear tests.

Interestingly, the PM's Secretariat, possibly the most opulent building in Islamabad—it had cost some $20 million to build—found no takers. Sharif's bid to move to a humbler office came a cropper because the earlier one didn't sell.

Sharif was a 'gimmicky' PM, prone to making loud, boastful statements and being unable to implement most of what he promised to the people. So, very soon after taking office, he had begun to exhaust most of his goodwill. His interventions and pretentious statements made after the Pakistani nuclear tests were no different. Sharif had proven, too often, that his pet obsessions were more important to him than the Pakistani people.

A small incident, early in my stay in Pakistan, had underscored for me both his propensity for gimmickry and his profligacy. A friend of mine, Harinder 'Shammy' Baweja, then with *India Today*, came to Islamabad to interview Sharif. After a two-series interview spread over two days, conducted in Punjabi, the prime minister wanted to know how she saved her interviews.

He then proceeded to present her with a high-quality audiotape (bought from Harrods in London for £20), saying he recorded all his speeches on this brand of audiotape alone. Sharif, well known for his shopping sprees, suggested to Shammy that she, too, use those tapes. For the record, she presented the tape to me, and it remains with me—destined never to be opened.

Like in other parts of South Asia, political promise and practice in Pakistan rarely had anything to do with each other. Leaders wanted their people to be austere, but there was nothing to prevent the powers themselves from being profligate.

To return to the story. Sharif, like Vajpayee in Delhi, was under pressure from the rest of the world after the tests. Sanctions, imposed by key Western nations, threatened Pakistan more, but equally placed India's nuclear ambitions under the searchlight like never before.

Both India and Pakistan, after making belligerent noises at each other through most of May 1998, agreed that, notwithstanding the nuclear reality, they must continue the process of bilateral dialogue. This, I believed then, and do so now, was one way of dealing with the pressures being mounted on both countries by the United

States, Japan, the United Kingdom and other members of the international community.

On 12 June, the Indian Foreign Office spokesman, responding to concerns contained in a communiqué issued by G-8 foreign ministers in London, said that New Delhi remained committed to developing a framework of peaceful relations with Pakistan through a broadbased and sustained bilateral dialogue.

'This provides an effective means,' the spokesman said, 'of identifying the possibilities of mutually beneficial cooperation and [of] resolving outstanding issues through bilateral negotiations. It would also include consideration of CBMs [confidence-building measures] such as our proposal for a no-first-use agreement. In this process of dialogue, there is no place for third-party involvement of any kind whatsoever... It is a matter of regret that the G-8 Foreign Ministers' joint communique has not taken into account these proposals but has instead repeated unrealistic prescription, couched in the language of pressure.'

Symptomatic of the kind of pressures New Delhi had come to face was the spokesman's claim that India had been a responsible member of the international community and remained strongly committed to the objective of disarmament in general, and nuclear disarmament in particular.

'However,' he added in a long explanation, 'we would like to make it clear that India's security concerns cannot be viewed in a narrow South Asian construct. Indeed, the pursuit of non-proliferation in an arbitrary selective regional context remains the fundamental flaw in the global nuclear disarmament regime. The Government of India cannot consider any prescriptions which have the effect of undermining India's independent decision-making.

Like any sovereign nation, India will continue to take decisions in this regard on the basis of its own assessment and national security requirements.'

Following a visit by US President Bill Clinton to China, India reacted harshly to a US–China 'Joint Statement on South Asia'. India said on 27 June that it categorically rejected the notion of these two countries arrogating to themselves joint or individual responsibility for 'the maintenance of peace, stability and security in the region'.

'This approach reflects the hegemonic mentality of a bygone era in international relations and is completely unacceptable and out of place in the present-day world,' India said at the time, in a language that softened itself as New Delhi and Washington engaged in a dialogue, the details of which are still to be made public.

Ironically enough, the roots of the new engagement between India and the United States lay in the Indian nuclear tests of 11 and 13 May themselves. As India tried to get itself into the nuclear club, Washington began to realize that it could do business with the Vajpayee government.

The new American strategy was to talk to both India and Pakistan simultaneously through the person of Strobe Talbott, deputy secretary of state in the Clinton administration. Round upon round of talks with Indian External Affairs Minister Jaswant Singh and Pakistani Foreign Secretary Shamshad Ahmad commenced soon after India and Pakistan tested.

Soon the Americans would come to realize that the Indian nuclear programme could not be reversed despite all the harsh language that was used against New Delhi soon after the nuclear tests.

The Americans started telling both the Indians and Pakistanis, separately, of course, that delivery systems and warheads should be kept away from each other. They urged that the two countries not actually weaponize their new nuclear capabilities.

As pressure mounted on the two countries to do this and that, Prime Ministers Nawaz Sharif and Atal Bihari Vajpayee had their first meeting on 29 July 1998, on the sidelines of the SAARC summit in Colombo.

The Pakistanis had come prepared with a media strategy. Heavy doses of anti-India remarks appeared in interview form in select Sri Lankan newspapers even as Vajpayee arrived in Colombo.

The Vajpayee–Sharif cooperative body language that would become the subject of considerable discussion in future was yet not visible. In fact, in a 31 July statement, Pakistan blamed India for the failure of the talks in Colombo:

> At the heart of the problem lies the rigid and inflexible position which India continues to maintain in its refusal to address the issues of peace and security and the Jammu & Kashmir dispute. Pakistan considers it of the utmost importance that in accordance with the sequential order of the agreed agenda [the June 23, 1997 agreement] as well as the urgent necessity to address the issues of peace and security and Jammu & Kashmir, in keeping with the requirements of the security situation resulting from the nuclearization of South Asia, these two agenda items must be specifically and substantially dealt with on a priority basis.

The Pakistanis blamed Vajpayee for unilaterally stating after the talks that the dialogue process had been resumed. They, however, clarified that the two sides had agreed to remain in touch:

As announced by the Prime Minister of Pakistan in his inaugural address to the SAARC Summit, the Pakistan Foreign Secretary reiterated that Pakistan was willing to resume talks on the basis of the understandings arrived at Islamabad on 23rd June 1997. The Indian Foreign Secretary, however, did not agree to restore these understandings. Thus no basis exists for the resumption of the dialogue on account of India's refusal to honour the Islamabad Agreement.

However, in keeping with our positive approach, we hope that the two sides will remain in touch through diplomatic channels to overcome the difficulties for the resumption of the dialogue.

Whatever be the loud statements being made in the press, the rest of the world was bringing sufficient pressure on India and Pakistan to ensure that the bilateral process of dialogue could not be seen to be breaking down.

There would be more contacts between the two sides in the coming weeks and months—a path that would inexorably lead to the February 1999 meeting between Sharif and Vajpayee in Lahore.

This time period would also show American involvement as a de facto third party in the India–Pakistan equation; a position that suited India fine since it could always turn around and say that US–India dialogue had nothing to do with bilateral contacts with Pakistan.

I came to believe that the nuclear tests of May 1998 sent India–Pakistan relations on a dangerous downward spiral, emboldening Pakistan to believe that with a publicly proven nuclear response to India now available, they could engage in a conventional provocation.

6

Vajpayee in Lahore

❖

'INDIA AND PAKISTAN should not be seen raising the level of failure,' a top Pakistani diplomat told me in the lobby of Lahore's Pearl Continental Hotel soon after the meeting between Atal Bihari Vajpayee and Nawaz Sharif in February 1999.

The transition from a status-quo, jehad-oriented, hawkish foreign policy vis-à-vis India to a forward-looking, moderate, peace-oriented foreign policy which Mr Sharif appears to be advocating, is going to be very difficult. Such a transition cannot take place without Mr Sharif first cobbling a broad political consensus for it and then nudging the national security establishment to review its historic assumptions and accord its approval to a change of tack...but Mr Sharif has made no effort to take the security establishment or the Pakistani people into confidence. He has taken no steps to bring the political opposition

on board his non-ideological foreign policy agenda ...
Therefore, our fear is that, like his many other hastily
assembled initiatives in equally contentious areas of
economy and law, this (Lahore) initiative too is likely
to flounder on the rock of institutional confusion,
political indecision and jehadi counter-pressure.

—*The Friday Times,*
a few days after the Lahore summit.

From euphoria to disaster. That about sums up the
dramatic bus ride Indian Prime Minister Atal Bihari
Vajpayee undertook to Lahore in February 1999, nine
months after the two countries shattered South Asia's
calm by their nuclear tests.

The note of cheer accompanying the much-televised
bus ride ended with a whimper on the killing fields of
Kargil a few months later, but did enough to raise
expectations of a major breakthrough in India–Pakistan
relations. It looked like a dramatic improvement was at
hand.

Lahore symbolized the possibilities inherent in an
India–Pakistan détente. At the same time, it reflected the
dangers in trying to make peace without preparation and
having all actors on board.

Pakistani Prime Minister Nawaz Sharif, it would soon
become clear, couldn't command the loyalty of his army.
And, the Pakistani army, under Pervez Musharraf, was
not prepared to yield control over India policy, which was
almost synonymous with Pakistan's foreign policy, to the
civilian Prime Minister Nawaz Sharif.

Musharraf and the army and navy chiefs stayed away
from the reception organized for Vajpayee at the Wagah
border on 20 February—though the three of them did
salute the Indian prime minister in private at the Punjab

Governor's House later that day. However, there were no pictures in the press of the 'private' salute presented to Vajpayee by Musharraf.

The Indian inability to adopt a two-track approach to Pakistan—reaching out to the civilian and military leadership at the same time—was another factor that led to the eventual failure of the Lahore summit. There was no serious effort on the part of New Delhi to recognize the nuances within the Pakistani power structure.

If the civilian prime minister was one part of the structure, the army was another. And, it was clear that the army wanted no part in Sharif's decision to engage with India and that, too, in an orchestrated bus ride by the Indian prime minister into the heart of the Pakistani Punjab—Lahore.

Vajpayee's Lahore visit, I believe, in fact laid the foundation of a deeply embedded animosity between Sharif and Musharraf. It exaggerated the power struggle between the prime minister and the chief of army staff and led to disastrous results for Sharif.

I deal with this more extensively in separate chapters on Kargil and the October 1999 coup that ejected Sharif from office.

In retrospect, I have few doubts that the Musharraf strategy for the takeover of the Kargil heights had already been put in motion when Sharif hosted the *barakhana* in honour of Vajpayee at Lahore Fort on 20 February 1999.

Just as the Pakistani service chiefs skipped the Wagah reception, they were absent at the grand dinner hosted by Sharif for Vajpayee inside the Lahore Fort. Their presence was said to be required in Islamabad since the Chinese defence minister, Chi Haotian, was paying an unexpected visit to Pakistan's capital.

Foreign Minister Sartaj Aziz, too, was missing—he

was Chi's host in Islamabad where all three service chiefs had to be in attendance.

The barakhana and the use of the Lahore Fort were particularly 'Sharifian'—the prime minister liked to impress foreign visitors. The country's coffers may have been near empty, but Sharif was not a man known for restraint in these matters.

A previous guest of Sharif at the Lahore Fort had been the Saudi Crown Prince Abdullah. So, putting the Indian prime minister in the same category was, clearly, an 'honour'.[1]

If the Indian leadership displayed inadequate understanding of the Pakistani power structure, Nawaz Sharif was guilty of the same. After having removed Jehangir Karamat as the chief of the army staff, Sharif felt triumphant, perhaps believing that since Musharraf owed his appointment to him, the new army chief would remain loyal.

After initially engaging with him with enthusiasm on issues such as the setting-up of military courts to try civilians, Musharraf decided to express his displeasure at Sharif's bid to mend fences with India. Musharraf's posture was a clear signal to the prime minister that this army chief was no Jehangir Karamat. It was going to be a different ball game.

That the expectations from Lahore were pitched differently was evident in the differences of mood and reportage in the Indian and Pakistani press. As some visiting Indian reporters went overboard in their desire to see a breakthrough everywhere, Pakistani newspapers were distinctly downbeat—choosing to focus more on the protests against Vajpayee's trip than the gains of 'friendship' from the bus ride.

In the run-up to the Indian prime minister's visit, the

Jamaat-e-Islami had organized massive protests in Lahore and other parts of Pakistan. This led to clashes with the police at several places, involving the death of one protestor. Several police personnel were also injured.

As leading Indian newspapers came out with banner headlines such as 'New dawn over Lahore' and 'Vajpayee in Pakistan, steps into history', their Pakistani counterparts were surly in tone—pointing to the absence of the service chiefs in Wagah. The contrast could not have been more stark.

Sharif had failed to read the mood of the military. Whatever he knew or did not about the Kargil incursion, the fact is that the prime minister's writ didn't run when it came to Musharraf and the army.

The equation between the Pakistani prime minister and the chief of army staff that Sharif wanted to impose wasn't rooted in reality. Exhilarated as he was with the successful departures of President Leghari and Chief Justice Shah from office, the portly prime minister wrongly believed that Musharraf would behave as an underling.

I arrived in Lahore on 18 February to gauge the general mood and to report on the Jamaat's protests. It was clear that the last would be vigorous and organized—because the Jamaat is the Pakistani parallel to the Bharatiya Janata Party and allied Hindu chauvinist bodies.

On the night of 20 February, I saw an unusual lot of 'protesters' in the Pearl Continental Hotel's lobby—these were a harried and frightened group of high commissioners and ambassadors whose vehicles had been attacked by Jamaat goons.

While the Sri Lankan High Commissioner Alfred David had the windscreen of his vehicle smashed by the Jamaatis while entering Lahore from Islamabad, others could not make it for the banquet on time as the windscreens of their limousines had also been shattered en route to the Lahore Fort.[2]

These senior diplomats were thoroughly annoyed. Initially, they refused to go for the banquet being hosted in Vajpayee's honour, but later they relented after being assured that their security would be taken care of.

It was certainly embarrassing for Nawaz Sharif, especially since his brother, Shahbaz, was the chief minister of the Punjab. The Jamaatis had the full run of the place, though an agitated Lahore police would later deal most severely with this right-wing Islamist party.

A huge press corps had come from New Delhi in a special Airbus aircraft. As usual, it was made to stay away from the hotel housing the official delegation—in this case the impressive Pearl Continental Hotel. The press was put up at the nearby Avaari Hotel.

Vajpayee was received at the Wagah border by Nawaz Sharif. A 'half-hug' is the best way to describe the greeting that the Indian prime minister got from Sharif.

The man of the moment, however, proved to be Dev Anand, the Indian actor who stepped out from the bus along with Vajpayee. The evergreen film star was the cynosure of all attention.

It was a scene to be remembered. You couldn't blame many of the visiting Indians for believing that a major transformation in India–Pakistan relations was actually under way. After all, an Indian prime minister had actually crossed the international border in a bus after months of verbal abuse between the governments of the two countries.

I wrote in *Frontline* at the time:

The ice has been broken at last. When Atal Behari Vajpayee crossed the Wagah border checkpost on 20 February, he not only negotiated a formidable physical barrier but also broke through the mental barriers that prevented better relations between India and Pakistan. However, whether the initiative amounts to a genuine forward movement in terms of bilateral relations remains an open question.

In terms of atmospherics, it was an extraordinary occasion indeed—questions about substance notwithstanding. As the gold-coloured bus from Delhi, bound for Lahore, came to a carefully rehearsed stop, Prime Minister Nawaz Sharif opened the gate of Pakistan to receive the prime minister of India and his delegation of eminent persons, who had boarded the Delhi Transport Corporation (DTC) bus at Amritsar airport. Vajpayee's visit to Pakistan was the first by an Indian prime minister in a decade—the last one was by Rajiv Gandhi in July 1989.

On his arrival at Wagah, Vajpayee described the visit as a 'defining moment' in South Asian history. As one awaits the verdict of history, it can be safely said that the bus journey and its symbolism conveyed to the people of both countries that there is a desire at the highest level to overcome the bitterness and to improve relations.

It was a twenty-four-hour visit, but as Vajpayee claimed: 'It was brief, but substantive.' The two prime ministers were closeted for some twenty minutes at Wagah, no doubt setting the overall tone for the visit which was marked by warmth and friendliness from the Pakistani side. Sharif and Vajpayee had one-on-one interaction at least on two other occasions. Pokhran-II and the war of words and Pakistan's retaliatory nuclear tests that followed were forgotten for a moment as the two prime ministers attempted to address the nuclear issue in a post-Pokhran/Chagai environment.

Addressing a reception at the Punjab Governor's House in Lahore, Vajpayee resorted to poetry to build his image as a peacemaker. The Pakistani audience was suitably impressed by Vajpayee's oratorical skills, but not convinced when it came to justifying the 11 and 13 May 1998 nuclear tests and the belligerent posture adopted by New Delhi immediately afterwards.

The positive word-spin continued through the visit. In their banquet speeches at Lahore Fort, both Vajpayee and Sharif raised expectations of a major advance in the troubled relationship.

In his address, the Indian prime minister said:

> As we break bread together; a new century and a new millennium knocks on our doors. Fifty years of our Independence have gone by. On one side there is pride and on the other regret. Pride, because both the countries have been successful in retaining their independence; but regret because even after fifty years we have not liberated ourselves from the curse of poverty and unemployment.
>
> I am grateful to you, Mr Prime Minister, for hosting this banquet in such a historic location. It was in this magnificent fort that Shah Jahan was born; it is here that Akbar lived for over a decade.

He continued:

> We have also discussed those areas of relationship on which we do not see eye to eye. That is only inevitable. As we seek to resolve issues, we have to be conscious that there is nothing which cannot be solved through goodwill and direct dialogue. That is the only path.
>
> I am convinced that there is nothing in our bilateral relations that can ever be resolved through

violence. The solution of complex outstanding issues can only be sought in an atmosphere free from prejudice and by adopting the path of balance, moderation and realism. To those that preach, practise or foment violence, I have only one message: understand the simple truth of the path of peace and amity. That is why, as part of the composite dialogue process, we welcome sustained discussions on all outstanding issues, including Jammu & Kashmir. As we approach a new millennium, the future beckons us. It calls upon us, indeed demands of us, to think of the welfare of our children and their children, and of the generations that are yet to come.

I have brought but one message from India. There can be no greater legacy that we can leave behind than to do away with mistrust, to abjure and eliminate conflict, to erect an edifice of durable peace, amity, harmony and co-operation. I am confident that through our combined efforts we will succeed in doing so, no matter how hard we have to work in achieving it.

This was precisely the language the Pakistanis wanted to hear. Vajpayee was promising a sustained discussion on all issues—including Jammu & Kashmir. He wasn't ruling out anything—or placing any preconditions.

In turn, Sharif said in his prepared speech at the joint press conference with Vajpayee at Governor's House in Lahore on 21 February:

Neither Pakistan nor India has gained anything from the conflicts and tensions of the past fifty years. The peoples of the region risk losing out in the march of development if we remain caught in a vicious cycle of mistrust and suspicion.

If we look around us, confrontation is giving

way to cooperation. Complex disputes are being resolved. Nations are increasingly becoming engaged in mutually beneficial interaction.

There is no reason why these positive global trends should by-pass South Asia.

I would like a Pakistan-India relationship that is free of tensions and based on mutual trust and confidence. Should we achieve this, there is no limit to co-operation between our two countries.

I am convinced that the objectives of peace, progress and prosperity in South Asia can be achieved provided there is the will and commitment.

If the press could be held guilty of hyping up expectations from the tryst in Lahore, only Vajpayee and Sharif were to be blamed—for the flowery language that they used and for so blithely pointing to the 'tomorrow' that was to be ushered in.

However, Sharif did add in the same address that, 'We were able to undertake a comprehensive review of our bilateral relations. I have underscored to Prime Minister Vajpayee the immense potential of building a mutually beneficial co-operative relationship, once we achieve a final settlement of the Jammu & Kashmir issue.'

So, official Pakistan was saying that the 'immense potential' of good relations with Pakistan could be realized only after a final settlement of the Kashmir issue. But, whatever were the stated positions of the two countries, Sharif and Vajpayee had displayed a willingness to break from the past.

Behind the scenes, it was a different story. Vajpayee and Sharif had actually hit it off. Soon after his meetings with Sharif, the Indian prime minister told a senior Indian official that his discussions had gone off very well, but he wouldn't give the man any details!

Writing in *The Hindu* (3 April 1999), I reported:

> In a significant development, the Indian and Pakistani Prime Ministers agreed during their recent Lahore Summit that while Mr A.B. Vajpayee will not refer to Kashmir as an integral part of India in public, Mr Nawaz Sharif will reciprocate by not mentioning the UN resolutions on Kashmir.
>
> It has been reliably learnt by *The Hindu* that the Prime Minister, who had three meetings in Lahore on 20-21 February, had free-wheeling discussions on the Kashmir issue, not restricted to the official public positions of the two countries.

My report continued:

> In a radical proposal, Mr Vajpayee suggested to Mr Sharif that the two countries open the Line of Control (LoC) at Uri in Indian Kashmir to allow Kashmiris living close to it to meet each other.

Confirming my April 1999 report in *The Hindu*, A.G. Noorani (*Frontline*, March 2002) provided fresh details as revealed by Sartaj Aziz, former Pakistani foreign minister. When quizzed by Noorani about the nature of the understanding reached at Lahore, Aziz replied:

> The understanding at Lahore was the back-channel. While the dialogue would continue on different issues on the official level as far as Kashmir is concerned we must have people who can talk in private. The back-channel was established in New York in September 1998 in a one-to-one meeting. That was a preliminary. Lahore gave it a fillip.

Noorani then asked whether the prime ministers nominated their representatives for the backchannel. In response, Aziz said:

Absolutely. R.K. Mishra was nominated by the Indian side. Niaz A. Naik was nominated by Pakistan. Among others, Shahryar Khan's name was mentioned. The nominations were conveyed to each other after the New York meeting. They (the nominees) met in November-December 1998.

Soon after the Lahore visit of Vajpayee, I saw R.K Mishra in Islamabad on several occasions, including at dinners hosted by Indian High Commission officials.

At the time, I could not understand why he was being given so much importance. Later, everything would fall into place. R.K. Mishra's post-Kargil role would show that he was, indeed, Vajpayee's special emissary.

Sartaj Aziz revealed that the understanding at Lahore related to the creation of a backchannel, a channel that was used right through the Kargil crisis that was to engulf India and Pakistan in the months to follow.

As reported by me in *The Hindu*, the understandings reached by Vajpayee and Sharif were an effort to break the India–Pakistan logjam. There were two key implications here: that India and Pakistan would not dwell on their stated positions—if India did not refer to Kashmir as India's *atoot ang* (integral part)—and Pakistan would not speak of the UN Security Council resolutions on Kashmir.

It was a small, but important step forward that the two prime ministers had taken. There was an effort to move forward the relationship despite the deep differences that divided the two countries. Simultaneously, it was an effort to keep the rhetoric between India and Pakistan down.

The other aspect was the opening up of the Line of Control at Uri to allow Kashmiris living close to the LoC to meet each other. It was obvious that this was a radical proposal made by Vajpayee, one that Sharif was in a mood to consider.[3] Clearly, the trans-LoC bus service, proposed by India in October 2003, and which commenced in April 2005, is linked to this original suggestion by Vajpayee.

In the public domain, Lahore was a major success. Three major statements were issued, including the Lahore Declaration, but the most significant, undoubtedly, was a memorandum of understanding signed by the two foreign secretaries Shamshad Ahmad and Krishnan Raghunath.

It was the one agreement in which the United States, which had been playing a quiet, behind-the-scenes role in getting the two sides together, had a special interest.

The MoU said:

The two sides shall engage in bilateral consultations on security concepts, and nuclear doctrines, with a view to developing measures for confidence-building in the nuclear and conventional fields, aimed at avoidance of conflict.

The two sides undertake to provide each other with advance notification in respect of ballistic missile flight tests, and shall conclude a bilateral agreement in this regard.

The two sides are fully committed to undertaking national measures to reducing the risks of accidental or unauthorized use of nuclear weapons under their respective control. The two sides further undertake to notify each other immediately in the event of any accidental, unauthorized or unexplained incident that could create the risk of a fallout with adverse consequences for both sides, or an outbreak of a nuclear war between the two countries, as well as to adopt measures aimed at diminishing the possibility of such actions, or such incidents being misinterpreted by the other. The two sides shall identify/establish the appropriate communication mechanism for this purpose.

The two sides shall continue to abide by their respective unilateral moratorium on conducting further nuclear test explosions unless either side, in exercise of its national sovereignty, decides that extraordinary events have jeopardized its supreme interests.

It may not have been everything that the United States wanted, but the two countries directly concerned were on the right track. For these countries, which had been at each other's throats only a short while ago, this was, indeed, progress. For, the US and the rest of the Western world, the chief interest was in bringing India and Pakistan to heel and bind them to a new code of restrained conduct.

After all the separate efforts that Strobe Talbott had made with Indian External Affairs Minister Jaswant Singh and Pakistani Foreign Secretary Shamshad Ahmad, some positive results were beginning to show. These were, however, early days.

Here's what US State Department deputy spokesman, James Foley, had to say in Washington on 23 February 1999:

The Department of State warmly welcomes the successful summit meeting of the Indian and Pakistani Prime Ministers on Saturday and Sunday in Lahore, Pakistan. Prime Ministers Vajpayee of India and Sharif of Pakistan have committed their governments to intensify efforts to resolve the issues that have divided their countries for too long, including Kashmir.

We are pleased that they have discussed steps to address nuclear concerns, including confidence-building measures and methods to avoid accidental conflict. We also commend the attention paid in the

Lahore Declaration, issued at the end of the meeting, to improving the quality of life of the people of India and Pakistan. The two leaders clearly understand that economic growth and social progress are central to the futures of their countries, as they are to all countries around the world.

The success of the weekend's meeting demonstrates the ability of Pakistan and India to work together to resolve their differences and to look to the future, not to the past. While the United States and the international community have encouraged them to resolve their differences through face-to-face discussions at a senior level, the decisions to take this courageous step were made by the two Prime Ministers. They deserve the full credit for this successful meeting.

Some bits of the Lahore Declaration were a rehash of what was contained in the Shimla Agreement of 1972. Both the Shimla Agreement and the Lahore Declaration make a reference to the 'principles and purposes' of the United Nations Charter.

While the reference to the United Nations in the Lahore Declaration was aimed at appeasing the Pakistani interest, it also made a reference to the 'determination' of implementing the Shimla Agreement in letter and spirit. That must have pleased the Indian negotiators.

The third document, the joint statement, gave a fillip to the bilateral dialogue, stating categorically that the foreign ministers of the two countries would meet periodically to discuss all issues of mutual concern, including nuclear-related questions.

On the political side, Vajpayee's early morning visit to the Minar-e-Pakistan on 21 February was a major success. The Pakistan resolution was passed at the site of the

Minar back in 1940, and this is a much-revered monument for Pakistani nationalists.[4]

As a member of the RSS and the BJP, which believe in the concept of *akhand* Bharat (India's boundaries as they stood before 14 August 1947), Vajpayee made a telling point by visiting the Minar, making it clear that he recognized Pakistan as an independent nation. He pointed out that Pakistan's 'stamp' had been working in Pakistan for the past fifty-two years. It was sweet music to Pakistani ears, because many Pakistanis believe that many Indians have not—even after all these years—reconciled themselves to the creation of the 'land of the pure'.

Vajpayee certainly topped the charts in Pakistan with his remarks. He won many friends and, simultaneously, raised expectations in Pakistan that only the 'right wing' in India could do a deal with Pakistan, and that the Congress—which had been in power for forty-eight out of fifty-two years after independence—had not been able to settle with Pakistan.

But without the examination of the American role in what came to be known as the 'Lahore process', any analysis of the momentous events of February 1999 would be incomplete.

Just before the Lahore yatra of Vajpayee, US Deputy Secretary of State Strobe Talbott had paid a visit to both India and Pakistan for his separate, continuing dialogues with Jaswant Singh and Shamshad Ahmad. The policy approach adopted by the US, it seemed to me, was rather simple. Apart from publicly pressing India and Pakistan to sign the Comprehensive Nuclear Test Ban Treaty (CTBT) and the Nuclear Non-Proliferation Treaty (NPT), a number of suggestions were made separately to India and Pakistan in the nuclear field.

A Western diplomat informed me at the time that the

idea was to ensure both countries be prevented from deploying their nuclear weapons, and not marry their warheads and delivery systems, and discuss what the Americans and later, the Pakistanis, called a strategic restraint regime. Today, the American benchmarks for India and Pakistan are well known, but they were not so at the time.

In his *Engaging India* (Penguin, 2004), Strobe Talbott finally revealed the benchmarks that the US wanted India to meet: a signature on the CTBT, cooperation in negotiating a permanent ban on the production of fissile material, and a strategic restraint regime that would limit India's ballistic missile arsenal to the *Agni* and *Prithvi*.

Under this objective, Talbott says, the US wanted India to agree not to deploy missiles close to Pakistan and also not to mount warheads on rockets, nor store them nearby. Tough export controls on 'dangerous' technology were also on the US agenda.

The fifth benchmark, he said, employed language from the UN Security Council resolution 1172 passed in early June (1998) in calling on India and Pakistan to resume dialogue to address the root causes of terrorism in the two countries, including that flashpoint, Kashmir.

The idea was that after putting suggestions to India and Pakistan separately, the US would ensure that bilateral discussions would take place between New Delhi and Islamabad.

A joint statement after the eighth round of the Talbott–Jaswant dialogue was issued on 31 January 1999, and, soon after, Strobe Talbott was in Pakistan meeting Shamshad Ahmad and a host of other Pakistani leaders.

Though Talbott goes into great detail about the talks with India and Pakistan in his book, he's less forthcoming about the role played by the United States in the run-up to the Sharif–Vajpayee meeting in Lahore. Nevertheless, he does provide some new information.

According to Talbott, Foreign Secretaries Krishnan Raghunath and Shamshad Ahmad had moved ahead on procedural matters that could lead to institutionalized contacts. He also reveals that Prime Ministers Sharif and Vajpayee were having regular telephone conversations.

Talbott also speaks of the announcement by Vajpayee that he would travel by bus from Amritsar to Lahore, a gesture he compares favourably with US Secretary of State Richard Nixon's 1971 visit to China.

Actually, it was Sharif who invited Vajpayee to visit Pakistan in an interview with Shekhar Gupta published in the *Indian Express* (3 February 1999). This interview was the first sign that something new was happening on the India–Pakistan front:

> Pakistan Prime Minister Nawaz Sharif has offered to initiate direct, bilateral negotiations with India on the nuclear issue. He says this should begin soon, 'tomorrow, if possible', and should be at a high level. 'Let us now begin working at a level where things will work out,' he said, implying that it was time the negotiations were raised to higher political levels.
>
> In an interview at his Lahore residence on the eve of the visit of the US delegation led by Strobe Talbott, Sharif made his impatience with the current three-way nuclear talks quite clear. 'India doesn't want third-party intervention in Kashmir, so why a third-party role on the nuclear issue? Or else, let's have third party in Kashmir as well,' he said.
>
> But willy-nilly, he said, the third party (obviously Washington, though he did not name it) has already acquired a role. 'They ask you things and they ask us the same things. Why must it go on like this?' he

asked. 'Why can't we talk directly? Why do we have to go on approaching each other via Bhatinda?' he said, using a common Punjabi metaphor to describe a circuitous, muddled approach to an issue.

If Vajpayee responded positively on this, Sharif said he will be more than willing 'to take the initiative'. He also said he will be happy to raise the level of the discussions in consultations with Vajpayee. 'It is time the political leadership moved in and set a road map on all this. Then the officials can follow up in a time-bound manner.'

The interview, which Talbott doesn't refer to at all in his otherwise meticulously researched book, continued:

'I would say, let us discuss the nuclear issue, the missile issue, also the issue of conventional weapons. We can finalize treaties and agreements that will reduce threats and fears. Let's talk about an approach to CTBT and FMCT,' he said. 'The [nuclear] threat,' he said, 'is all here. So why not resolve the issue between ourselves?'

'I interact with the officials a lot. I understand their point,' he said, but complained that he gets 'impatient' when he sees no movement. The problem with officials, he says, is that they get deadlocked 'even over a comma or a full stop or over which word should come before the other'. This, he says, slows things down. '*Ajeeb maamla hai* (It is a strange state of affairs).'

Sharif says while it is good that a few things, like the cricket tour and the Delhi-Lahore bus have come through, the pace of this process is far too slow. 'We should do in five months what we can do in five years. We should aim to settle at least 50 per cent of our problems by year 2000.'

'There has to be a departure from status quo. What fifty years of status quo has given us, we can all see with our eyes,' he said, delicately answering a question on whether it was possible for either side to move from frozen positions on Kashmir. 'Let's approach this with an open mind. Why can't a solution then be found?' he asked. He did, however, state repeatedly that Kashmir is a key issue. 'It is a major issue and if there is no progress on it, it will not serve the ends of normalization.'

Sharif underlined his evolving equation with Vajpayee whom he repeatedly described as 'a good man, *ek behad sharif insaan* (an extremely decent man)', and said that the two of them conversed often on the phone. 'I firmly believe that Mr Vajpayee has the same views on our relationship as I do. That is why people on both sides now expect progress,' he said.

That there had been previous contacts between the two governments was evident from the prompt response from New Delhi. On the same day that the interview appeared, a ministry of external affairs spokesman said in New Delhi:

In the context of reports indicating that Pakistan Prime Minister Nawaz Sharif would welcome a visit by Prime Minister Vajpayee to Pakistan on board the inaugural Delhi-Lahore bus service, [it was] said that it is the intention of the Prime Minister to travel to Lahore on the inaugural run of the Delhi-Lahore bus service. He looks forward to meeting Sharif and other Pakistani leaders as well as the people of Pakistan. His visit will be one more manifestation of India's abiding desire to build peaceful, friendly and cooperative relations with Pakistan, the spokesman added.

Talbott, obviously, has not been keen to focus on the American role in bringing the two sides together. In *Engaging India*, the former deputy secretary of state shows acute frustration with both India and Pakistan (more with Pakistan) over the lack of progress on the 'big biryani' (the strategic restraint regime between India and Pakistan) in his January–February talks with Jaswant Singh and Shamshad Ahmad, but then points out the 'very good' news that 'suddenly' India and Pakistan were talking to each other.

In his book, Talbott stressed that India and Pakistan had embarked on this new journey of dialogue on their own. The American role was there for all to see—including this reporter—but the Americans, obviously, wanted to play it down.

In October 2004, US Secretary of State Colin Powell revealed in an interview to *USA Today* the part that Washington played in setting up a telephone call in April 2003 between Prime Ministers Vajpayee and Mir Zafarullah Khan Jamali.

It's clear that on any occasion of a major engagement between India and Pakistan, the leaderships of the two countries would like to stress the 'independence' of their actions and aver that it was better to engage directly rather than go through a third party.

In the chapter on Kargil, I deal with the key role played by the United States in ending the conflict. This role was one that favoured India, but it showed, yet again, the kind of clout the US could exercise in the post-Pokhran II era.

So, when Vajpayee boarded the bus to Lahore, there was no doubt in my mind that both he and Nawaz Sharif were under pressure to relieve the tension that had been built up by the West over the nuclear status of the two countries.

In the rest of the world (whatever India and Pakistan thought of themselves), the view was that South Asia had become a dangerous place after the May 1998 nuclear tests. Anything that reduced this image of danger emanating from India and Pakistan would be welcome.

Look at how quickly the bus ferrying Vajpayee moved to Lahore. On 3 February itself, the BJP leader accepted Sharif's invitation to commence talks 'tomorrow' and a mere seventeen days later, the Indian prime minister was dining with his Pakistani counterpart at Lahore Fort.

The speed displayed by the Indians in accepting the Pakistani offer for a visit by Vajpayee must, surely, be a record in itself. Neither of the two establishments are known for their innovation, or speed in accepting a proposal made by the other. The trip to Lahore, clearly, was different.

Lahore left a mixed legacy. At one level, it displayed what was possible if there was a willingness to move ahead. At another, it revealed that the crucial power centre in Pakistan—the army—was not convinced by the civilian prime minister's desire to make friends with the Indians.

Looking back, I believe that the Jamaatis were quietly encouraged by the army to engage in their street protests; what Musharraf could not say in public, could be articulated by Qazi Hussain Ahmed and other leaders of the Jamaat. These called on Vajpayee to rebuild the Babri Masjid demolished on 6 December 1992, and asked India to agree to a plebiscite on Kashmir.

Lahore also displayed the growing clout of the United States in the affairs of the subcontinent. It was becoming clear that the American hand in manipulating Pakistani policy had now been extended to India as well.

I have referred to the fact that both Nawaz Sharif and

the Government of India failed to engage the Pakistan Army and take its leadership along the path of rapprochement with New Delhi.

The Clinton administration and its whiz-kids who spent so much time in first dissecting Indian and Pakistani intentions after May 1998, too, failed to comprehend the ground realities in Pakistan as far as the military was concerned.

The Clinton administration, which would successfully use General Anthony Zinni, head of the US Central Command from 1997 to 2000, to end the Pakistani intrusion into Kargil, could do precious little else, as it became evident that Musharraf had his own agenda— both in regard to India and to Nawaz Sharif.

Unlike Indian assessors of the Pakistani military, who came to their conclusions from studying the 'ethnic' origins of senior officers or the length of their beards, the US had considerable access to the top echelons of the faujis in Pakistan.

Whether it used or failed to use this access in preparation for and during the Lahore summit is a question only key players in the Clinton administration can answer.

7

From Lahore to Kargil

❖

- ... to take such action as will defreeze [the] Kashmir problem, weaken India's resolve and bring her to a conference table without provoking a general war. However the eleme.it of escalation is always present in such struggles. So, whilst confining our action to the Kashmir area we must not be unmindful that India may in desperation involve us in a general war or violate Pakistani territory where we are weak. We must therefore be prepared for such [a] contingency.

- To expect quick results in this struggle, when India has much larger forces than us, would be unrealistic. Therefore our action should be such that can be sustained over a long period.

- As a general rule Hindu morale would not stand more than a couple of hard blows delivered at the right time and place. Such opportunities should therefore be sought and exploited.

—*'Political Aim for Struggle in Kashmir'—Annexure G to GHQ Letter No. 4050/5/MO-1 dated 29 August 1965. Directive from President Ayub Khan to General Mohammed Musa, Commander-in-Chief Pakistan Army.*

—Quoted in *A History of the Pakistan Army,* Brian Cloughley, Oxford University Press, 1999

ON 20 FEBRUARY 1999, I had stood, along with hundreds of other reporters, watching Atal Bihari Vajpayee's gleaming bus roll past the Wagah border. Less than four months later, on 3 June 1999, I stood, lonely, inside the Indian mission in Islamabad, watching an International Committee of the Red Cross official hand over a captured Indian prisoner-of-war, Flight Lieutenant Nachiketa of the Indian Air Force, to high commission officials.

Could all this have happened in the space of less than four months? What kind of countries were India and Pakistan? Who was to blame for the war in Kargil? Was there hope for the subcontinent when India and Pakistan, after dramatic gestures of friendship, descended to conflict mode so easily?

I knew some of the answers. But Kargil brought home to me the contradictions of the Pakistani power structure. What unfurled was a tragic story, where there were no winners on the battlefield, only losers.

For Pakistan, it was always about Kashmir. Whether it was in Operation Gibraltar in 1965 or in Kargil in 1999, the broad contours of Pakistan's military and foreign policy have not shifted much. The larger strategic objective has always been to prise Kashmir away from India.

The Pakistani establishment never really forgot the ignominy of 1971 when half the country was lost due to the power-hungry nature of the West Pakistani elite. Simultaneously, West Pakistani hegemony roused Bangladeshi nationalism, a process aided by the Government of India.

Islamabad's support to Khalistani terrorists in the Indian Punjab and later, to Kashmiri separatists, was an obvious 'response' from the Pakistani establishment to the rout suffered in 1971 with India's abetment.

Through the 1990s, Pakistan supported a host of militant–terrorist groups like the Hizbul Mujahideen, the Harkat-ul-Ansar (later Harkat-ul-Mujahideen) and the Lashkar-e-Taiba in its desire to bleed India. Foreign terrorist elements, from Pakistan, Afghanistan and Central Asia, were sent to Kashmir for purposes of the larger internationalist jehad. The Pakistan Army, without having to sacrifice its own men, had the Inter-Services Intelligence (ISI) Directorate send thousands of young men to fight the jehad in Kashmir. Also, the Pakistani establishment took some care that the terrorist movement was not armed with weapons that could trigger a full-scale confrontation with India.

For instance, the use of a Stinger missile to, say, bring down an Indian Airlines aircraft (something that the jehadis would be more than willing to do) in Jammu & Kashmir would have brought India and Pakistan to the brink of confrontation.

However, the May 1998 nuclear tests by India and Pakistan and, importantly, a change in the leadership of the Pakistan Army made Islamabad abandon such a 'low-risk' policy and, instead, the seeds of the Kargil conflict were laid. With a nuclear shield in place, Pakistan felt confident in waging what it thought would be a limited battle with India.

Many Pakistani commentators have written about the fact that plans for a Kargil-type operation had been discussed among the army brass on many occasions. But the man who operationalized this limited war game was the army chief, Pervez Musharraf.

A Special Services Group (SSG) commando, Musharraf, and some of his close associates like chief of staff Muhammad Aziz Khan, and 10 Corps Commander Mahmud Ahamed, were the key men in charge of the Kargil operation. Other corps commanders, as well as the navy and air force chiefs, were probably not even aware of General Musharraf's plans.

I returned to New Delhi after the heady days of the Lahore summit for a short break in March 1999. The Lahore Declaration and the rest of the Vajpayee visit to Pakistan were still being digested by analysts and strategic thinkers in the capital. For many in India, a new dawn in relations with Pakistan appeared to have broken.

The first suggestions that all was not well came soon enough. But these, though just signs, were confusing all the same. What was one to make of these conflicting signals? Initially, one simply reported the events without comprehending their full import, but later I wrote in *Frontline* (18 June 1999):

> The first signs of trouble came soon after the Lahore summit between [Nawaz] Sharif and Atal Behari Vajpayee. The appointment of Javed Nasir, a former chief of the Inter-Services Intelligence (ISI), as the head of the Pakistani Gurdwara Prabanadhak Committee, and Sharif's action in granting an audience

to Ganga Singh Dhillon, a symbol of the discredited
Khalistan movement, were pointers that trust between
the two countries remained at a premium.

While Pakistan was planting or had already planted its
men in the shape of the Northern Light Infantry (NLI)
personnel and a sprinkling of Mujahideen fighters on the
heights of Kargil, the Government of India was announcing
unilateral visa relaxations for select categories of Pakistanis.

Of course, Pakistan took considerable pains to hide
the fact that the 'fighters' along the LoC were 'mujahideen'
and not regular army personnel. As time wore on in the
conflict, this patent falsehood used by Musharraf and Co.
was exposed for what it was.

In the mean time, what was India doing after Lahore?
On 27 March 1999, the Government of India opened a
'camp visa office' at the Gaddafi Stadium in Lahore to
issue 1,000 visas for the India–Pakistan one-day cricket
game in Mohali in the Indian Punjab.

The winds of change were blowing, but they were
blowing from India to Pakistan and not back. A few days
earlier, on 19 March, the foreign ministers of India and
Pakistan met in Nuwara Eliya, Sri Lanka, and worked out
a schedule for further meetings between the two sides.

Kargil, from the Indian point of view, was a colossal
intelligence–military failure and had it not been for some
alert Gujjars the discovery of Pakistani personnel on the
heights of Indian territory would have taken some more
time.

But that is another story.

Pictures taken by Western photographers showed that
concrete bunkers had been constructed in Kargil to protect
heavy guns. In some places, only the barrels of the heavy
guns protruded from the Pakistani defences—all indications
that even as Vajpayee's bus was rolling into Lahore, NLI

men and a few assorted mujahideen were already sitting in Kargil.

As the Indian Army began military action to evict the intruders in the second half of May, it became clear that the heady days of the Lahore summit had transformed themselves into a limited war in the Kargil battlefields.

The sense of disappointment and let-down, so palpable in India, was reflected in Prime Minister Vajpayee's address to the Indian nation on 7 June 1999:

> You know very well that our relations with Pakistan, as with all our neighbours, were improving rapidly: The Prime Ministers and other ministers of the two countries were in regular contact; dialogue among officials of the two countries was proceeding constructively, and satisfactorily; areas of cooperation had been identified...most important, people-to-people contacts and exchanges had opened up as never before in fifty years—there had been an outpouring of goodwill on both sides.
>
> In the midst of all this, regulars of the Pakistan Army and infiltrators have been sent across. Fomenting insurgency here was heinous enough. But this time army regulars have been sent. They have been sent to occupy our territory. And, having occupied it, to choke off our links with other parts of our country—in particular with Siachen and Ladakh. This step has been taken after a great deal of preparation. It was a preplanned operation. It is also a repudiation of the letter and spirit of the Lahore Declaration. It is a violation not just one Article of the Shimla Agreement, but an eightfold violation of that solemn Agreement.

On 17 May 1999, Pakistani papers reported that India had launched a major military offensive in Kargil. Earlier, a Srinagar-datelined Associated Press report summed up the confusion that existed in the early days of the Kargil war:

> Amidst unconfirmed reports of capturing two or three Indian strategic border posts by Kashmiri freedom fighters, fierce fighting between Indian troops and freedom fighters in the mountains of Kashmir have left at least seventeen combatants dead, officials said on Friday.
>
> Military officials said ten militants and seven Indian soldiers were killed Thursday night in the fighting in the Kargil region...the area is 80 miles north-east of Srinagar. Unconfirmed reports Thursday said the militants captured two or three Indian border posts. An [Indian] Army spokesman refused to comment.
>
> However, [Indian] defence minister George Fernandes, who was visiting the area of Leh on the eastern side of Kashmir, was quoted as saying Thursday that 'no post had fallen'. 'Pakistan troops capture strategic posts,' said a headline in the *Kashmir Monitor*, a local English-language weekly. Similar reports appeared in some Urdu-language papers in Srinagar. Pakistan had no immediate comment on the fighting.[1]

Earlier, on 15 May, Pakistani newspaper *The Nation* reported that Pakistan had captured 'five strategic posts' in the Kargil sector. Again, on 18 May, it said that Pakistan continued to occupy the 'twenty posts' it had wrested from the Indian Army.

This report was denied several days later by the Inter-Services Public Relations (ISPR) Directorate, but, in retrospect, one can see that these reports—whatever the number of Indian posts captured was reported to be—were largely correct.

Pakistan also built up the theory that whatever was happening was a 'reaction' to Indian aggressive designs—going back to the time of the occupation of Siachen by India.

That Pakistan was in denial and unable to come to terms with the foolishness of its actions would soon become clear. Musharraf's army, of course, had no intentions of changing course. And Pakistan would have to pay a heavy international diplomatic price for what some of its generals had plotted.

Time and again, parrot-like, the Pakistani establishment said that its troops were not involved in Kargil, and it was the brave mujahideen who were able to take on the Indian Army.

In a press statement on 21 June 1999, Pakistan blamed India for violating the LoC[2] in Chorbat la in 1972 and in Qamar in 1988, for its blockade of the Neelum Valley from 1996 to 1998 by artillery shelling and its 'current ground attacks' against Pakistani posts along the LoC.

As India launched air strikes and heavy barrages of artillery at Pakistani-occupied positions in Kargil and Drass, it would have become evident to the Pakistanis that New Delhi had no intention of accepting the new positions occupied by the NLI, at that time a paramilitary force under the direct command of the Pakistan army, during winter.

That the 'mujahideen' had official blessings from the army became clear as their bodies began to come home. On 25 June, the coffin of Sikandar Gul, a Hizbul Mujahideen militant killed in Kargil, had the honour of being draped with the Pakistani national flag, with a floral wreath coming from none other than Chief of Army Staff Pervez Musharraf (reported in *Frontline*, 16 July 1999).

The best account of what Musharraf and Co. had done was provided by a Pakistani reporter, Ghulam Hasnain, who had to leave the country temporarily after his story appeared in *Time* magazine.

It included a first person account by an unnamed thirty-year-old Pakistani soldier of his seventy-seven days on Indian territory, fighting and suffering at elevations of up to 5,400 metres:

In February (1999), I was ordered to cross the Line of Control and climb some mountains that the Indians controlled. My commanding officers would not allow me to take my AK-47 rifle. I was against going to an Indian hill without a weapon, but I saw that everybody who was being sent across the LOC was going there empty-handed. We were told it was for the sake of secrecy.

It took us three days of walking and climbing to reach the Indian posts near Kargil. We found they were empty, and our job was to prepare some makeshift bunkers. All we had were tents.

The first five days were hell. The M-17 military helicopter did not come with our food supplies. We just had Energile [a protein-enriched food pack used in high-altitude warfare] and ice. Sometimes we ate ice with sugar. There was jubilation when the helicopter came with real food.

The skirmishes with the Indians started in May. In the early days we mowed down many of them. Those Indians were crazy. They came like ants. First you see four, and you kill them. Then there are ten, then fifty, then 100 and then 400. Our fingers got tired of shooting at them. We felt sorry for them. Sometimes they came in such large numbers we were afraid of using up all our ammunition. There is no instant resupply, so you have to be very careful. We were always worried that we would use up all our ammunition on one attacking Indian party and would have none left when a new group came. But God was always with us. You could see lots of bodies strewn down below or in the gorges. They were just rotting there. We also suffered a lot of casualties, many more than officials in Pakistan are claiming. During my stay up there, seventeen of my friends died while fighting the Indians.

There is so much exchange of fire that you cannot eat the ice now or drink the water, which is laced with cordite. Even the streams down below the mountains are contaminated. Lots of soldiers are facing stomach problems because of this. We had no proper bunkers, so we dug a 5-m tunnel into the snow. When the Indian shells started landing on us, we would crawl into this tunnel for safety. You don't get enough space to spread your legs in the tents. You always sleep sitting up. Sometimes there is so much firing, you cannot relieve yourself even if you want to.

On the ridges now we have disposable rocket-launchers, surface-to-air missiles and machine-guns, including anti-aircraft guns. On one occasion I was positioned on a mountain facing the Drass-Kargil highway. It's fun to target the Indian convoys.

Our officers are very strict. A young soldier from Punjab died in front of me because of altitude sickness. The soldier came from the plains. He fell sick soon after coming up. He offered our commanding officer 200,000 rupees [about $4,000] to let him go down, but the offer was refused. He died four days later. We didn't know his name. I tried to find out, but they refused to tell me. If you die up in the mountains, there is no way to lift your body and take it down. Most of the time we slide the bodies downward. All the men who are fighting on those ridges know that they are in a hole from which they cannot come out alive. You can only return dead. There are a rare few like me, who somehow by fate got the chance to leave the mountains.[3]

In the same issue of *Time*, Hasnain also provides further information about what the Pakistanis were up to in Kargil:

As far back as last November, the first batch of Pakistani troops from the Northern Light Infantry

Regiment—a unit experienced in mountain warfare—
crept over the 3,500-m-high passes along the LoC to
occupy the high ridges that the Indian Army held in
the summer. To avoid raising suspicion, even among
local Pakistanis, they went without weapons. Their
task was to build new bunkers on the ridges—but as
far as possible from the empty Indian positions that
would be unsafe because they are marked on Indian
Army maps. Pakistan was 'stretching' the LoC to its
advantage, to be able to block at will India's strategic
road from the Kashmir Valley to distant Ladakh—
the military base for that other source of conflict
between India and Pakistan, the 6,600-m-high Siachen
Glacier.

Near the town of Kargil in Indian-held Kashmir,
Pakistani soldiers have assembled a Chinese-made
57-mm anti-aircraft gun inside a man-made cave
protected by steel girders and concrete. It sits on top
of a 3,000-m-high ridge that overlooks a 500-m
stretch of the Kargil road. When a lookout spots a
vehicle, he shouts 'Allahu Akbar (God is great)', and
the gunner pulls the trigger. The soldiers cheer each
hit. The weapon has scattered convoys and made
Indian troop deployments hazardous. Bombs and
artillery shells fired by the Indians have failed to
penetrate the cave.

Islamabad insists that the soldiers on the Indian
ridges are Islamic mujahedin, or holy warriors, fighting
for the freedom of Kashmir. That was the alibi
Pakistan used for its military advance. Men from the
Northern Light Infantry Regiment and later the
Khyber Rifles were used because of their high-altitude
experience and because they are from the region.
They were encouraged to look like mujahedin, and
they discarded their uniforms for traditional shalwar

kameez, or tracksuits, grew beards and wore traditional white religious skullcaps. The soldiers say that when they reached the heights in February, some genuine mujahedin were at the abandoned Indian positions. But these men left after a few days because they could not survive in the high altitudes. They are now used for reconnaissance and as porters.

It was the first, solid piece of writing that exposed the Pakistani establishment. Not written by an Indian, it carried great credibility. I promptly filed details in the *Time* stories for *The Hindu*.

Hasnain also put in context the heavy odds that the Indian soldiers faced. Also, these articles thoroughly exposed the Pakistani establishment's deception that only mujahideen were fighting in Kargil.

As I will show, Kargil was a diplomatic disaster of epic proportions for Pakistan. It exposed the state as a liar. In these days of satellite imagery, it's not easy for governments and states to move men and material without being spotted by the spy satellites deployed by countries like the United States and Russia.

And, having taken the first step, Pakistan had to continue lying to cover up for the rest of whatever was happening. In the days and weeks that marked the Kargil war, the Pakistani establishment was exposed daily before the international press, but it made little difference to the overall trajectory of propaganda coming from General Headquarters (GHQ) in Rawalpindi. Kargil was like waving a red rag at a bull. Musharraf and Co. had concluded that with Pakistan now a publicly declared nuclear power, it could withstand military pressure from India.

No longer was Pakistan subservient to India in military terms; it was not a question of the 'father of the bomb'

Abdul Qadeer Khan boasting that Pakistan had the bomb; it had been tested and demonstrated.

Pakistan was a nuclear power, at par with India. So, in the mindset of the few generals who planned and plotted Kargil, Pakistan could now change the strategic equation in Kashmir. A conventional incursion was possible under Islamabad's very public nuclear deterrent.

This adventurist line of thinking in Pakistan should continue to disturb the Indian establishment at the highest levels. Kargil showed that a nuclear power is not automatically 'sensible' about its decision to use or not to use this most horrific weapon created by humankind.

If Kargil was about Siachen, as claimed, why did the Pakistan Army wait all those years before responding? The new Pakistani strategic belief that nuclear weapons could be used and the installation of an irresponsible military leadership led the establishment to believe that this was the right time to move against India.

Additionally, Musharraf was perturbed about his prime minister's unilateralist desire to befriend India and invite the arch enemy's prime minister to dinner at the Lahore Fort. India policy simply could not be left to the civilians. It was too important an area for the Pakistan Army to give up its leadership role in it.

The idea was to cut off India's communication links to Siachen and force it to negoatiate on Kashmir from a position of weakness. The planners and plotters of Kargil felt that India would accept the fait accompli and then discuss Kashmir in a realistic manner with the Pakistanis. That, however, remained in the imagination of the generals who authored the incursion. Nothing of the sort would happen.

I remain convinced that a thinking, mild-mannered COAS like Jehangir Karamat would not, perhaps, have taken the fateful decision to do a Kargil. Nawaz Sharif's decision to appoint Pervez Musharraf as the army chief after removing Karamat had much to do with Kargil happening at all.

Undoubtedly, Musharraf was the man in charge and he took the decision to go ahead with the Kargil operation. One of the questions that has troubled analysts is: how much did Nawaz Sharif know about Kargil? Was he an accomplice? Or was he taken for a ride by Musharraf? Or did he know a little, but not everything? Or was he simply incapable of understanding what the faujis were trying to tell him? Or did the khakis tell him just a little, knowing full well that he would not ask any more questions?

Having discussed this issue with a variety of people, including senior third-country diplomats based in Islamabad during and after Kargil, I believe that Sharif was informed in general terms about some 'action' to be taken, but not about its specifics. The army had decided how much to tell Sharif and how much to withhold from him.

In any case, Sharif, comfortable with the fact that he had installed his own man as army chief, didn't think at the time that Musharraf would do anything as audacious as undermine an India-friendly policy set in motion by Pakistan's most powerful civilian prime minister, who had even sent an army chief home without triggering a coup.

At the best of times, Sharif did not have much of an attention span. Surindar Nihal Singh, one of India's best-known newspaper editors, then with a Gulf newspaper, came to interview Nawaz Sharif.

The prime minister had a good conversation with Nihal Singh in Punjabi, but informed him that he could take 'answers' to the questions posed from the PM's information minister, Mushahid Hussain!

On the Kargil front, meanwhile, diplomatic manoeuvres were becoming as important as military ones. A verbatim record of the 29 May 1999 conversation between Musharraf in China and his chief of staff, Muhammad Aziz Khan, in Pakistan, shows that the Indian establishment was told categorically by Sharif that he was not responsible for what was happening in Kargil.

'Have you listened to yesterday's news regarding Mian Sahab [Nawaz Sharif] speaking to his counterpart [Atal Bihari Vajpayee],' Aziz said to Musharraf. 'He [Sharif] told him [Vajpayee] that the spirit of Lahore Declaration and *escalation has been done by your* [Musharraf's] *people.* Specially wanted to speak to me thereafter. He told [the] Indian PM that they should have waited instead of upping the ante by using Air Force and all other means. He [Sharif] told him [Vajpayee] that he suggested [foreign minister] Sartaj Aziz could go to New Delhi to explore the possibility of defusing the tension.'

This telephone conversation between Musharraf and Aziz Khan, reportedly taped by the Research & Analysis Wing, India's external intelligence agency, was released by New Delhi as part of its diplomatic war against Pakistan. A deliberate effort was being made by the Vajpayee government to drive a wedge between Musharraf and Sharif.

The manner in which Aziz Khan put it across to his boss suggested that the information was on PTV's main news bulletin. It was not. If Indian intelligence was listening in on the Musharraf–Aziz conversation, Pakistani intelligence was obviously listening to what Nawaz Sharif was telling Vajpayee. Needless to say, Musharraf and his generals didn't like Sharif's 'independent' policy on India.

On the war front, the Indian Air Force began air strikes as heavy-duty artillery guns began pounding

Pakistani positions on 26 May. In Islamabad, the war seemed far away; the front line was distant.

All that was going to change. For the first time, the war was coming close to Islamabad. On the afternoon of 27 May, Islamabad's press circles were abuzz with reports that an Indian aircraft had been shot down.

Late in the afternoon, foreign wire agencies put out the first stories that two Indian aircraft had been downed. Soon, I would get a call that an 'important' press conference was to be held at the Press Information Department's headquarters at Zero Point in Islamabad.

It was the first time during my stay in Pakistan that I was actually getting a glimpse of an operational army officer speaking to the press. All of us reporters could anticipate what he was going to say.

Major General Anis Bajwa, vice chief of general staff, told us that two Indian aircraft—a MiG 21 and a MiG 27—had been shot down. While Flight Lieutenant Nachiketa, piloting the MiG 21, had been taken prisoner, Squadron Leader Ajay Ahuja, flying the Mig 27, had been 'unfortunately killed'. Information Minister Mushahid Hussain was also present at the press conference.

As I wrote in *Frontline* (18 June 1999) about the incident, 'Ahuja's body was handed over to the Indian side on 28 May, and the Indian Army stated that the body bore bullet wounds...reports also suggest that Ahuja had ejected safely and had used his parachute. Foreign journalists, who were taken by Pakistani authorities to see both the crashed aircraft, saw Ahuja's personal effects, including his personal weapon, which had his name engraved on it.'

One Western reporter told me after visiting the crash site that Ahuja had, perhaps, put up some resistance, and had been shot dead by Pakistani soldiers after being captured, but this could not be verified.[4]

The very next day, 28 May, an Indian MI 17 helicopter was brought down. 'The downing of the Indian helicopter gunship is the result of the collective operation of the Mujahideen in the Council,' Syed Salahuddin, chief of the United Jehad Council and head of the Hizbul Mujahideen, said in a statement.

It was a patently false claim. The Pakistani military was responsible for bringing down the MI 17, not the mujahideen. But the propaganda was obvious.

The whole situation was turning surreal for the Indians living in Islamabad: the couple of people outside the high commission and those within. Here was a situation where a limited war was being fought—and we continued to live in and report from Islamabad.

The Indian High Commission prepared evacuation plans for its staff, and they included me and my family. Indian diplomats also chose to destroy all papers in case an evacuation of the mission was to take place. They didn't want any documents to fall into Pakistani hands.

Returning home from the Bajwa press conference, I had informed Minu about the shooting down of the MiGs. She looked stricken. 'Let's go. Let's leave,' she told me. 'I don't want to stay here any more.' Her response was understandable since I had told her that we might have to leave at half-an-hour's notice should war break out.

But since Kargil was a 'war' that Pakistani soldiers were not officially fighting, it gave us some breathing space. Though colleagues in the Pakistani press would pose questions at me about the 'war', by and large our lives didn't change much. We were able to live through the crisis and I was able to report without any new restrictions.

I attended all the press conferences and briefings

organized by the Foreign Office and the information ministry. Analyzing the daily briefings, and positing them on what had previously been said, provided huge insight into what the Pakistanis were doing or not doing.

I believe that the turning point of the Kargil war came on 27 May after the shooting down of the two MiG aircraft, which, as Chief of General Staff Aziz Khan told Musharraf by telephone in Beijing, had been ascribed to the prowess of the mujahideen.

From what I could glean later, there was tremendous pressure on the Government of India to launch retaliatory air strikes against Pakistan; strikes which would not have necessarily been restricted to the Kargil sector. It could have taken the form of, say, a predawn attack on Pakistani aircraft sitting at one of their bases.

Given the mood in New Delhi, such an eventuality could not have been ruled out on the evening of 27 May. But New Delhi resisted these pressures. There were no retaliatory strikes; nor was there going to be the opening of another front like the Indian side had made in 1965.

This, in my view, won India considerable respect abroad; it displayed that New Delhi was acting with restraint in the face of extreme provocation from Pakistan. Launching air strikes or opening another front would have generalized the war and could have led to events taking on a momentum of their own.

If India had escalated the war, Pakistan, too, would have followed suit. As it was, threats about the use of nuclear weapons were a feature of Pakistan's response during the entire period of the Kargil war.

Pakistan's chief diplomat and foreign secretary, Shamshad Ahmad, said on 30 May 1999, right at the beginning of the conflict, that Islamabad would not hesitate to use 'any weapon' in its self-defence.[5]

'We will not hesitate to use any weapon in our arsenal to defend our territorial integrity,' Ahmad stated categorically. No great analysis is required to conclude that by 'any' weapon, the foreign secretary meant even one of a nuclear kind.

If the foreign secretary of the country was hurling such threats, others could not be far behind. On 24 June, the official Associated Press of Pakistan news agency quoted Prime Minister Sharif as saying in Gultiari in Pakistan's Shakma sector that if the present confrontation continued along the borders, 'the damage...will never be repaired'.

Sharif blamed India for creating a warlike situation along the LoC, adding that 'defence-wise', Pakistan was one of the strongest countries in the world. The *Ghauri* and *Shaheen* missiles, Sharif told Pakistani troops, were symbols of Pakistani might.

Here, the prime minister was mouthing the army line. Whatever may have been his private views, in public Sharif was echoing what the rest of the establishment was saying. The contradictions in the prime minister's persona became obvious.

Other Pakistani officials were more direct in making their nuclear threats. Raja Muhammad Zafar-ul-Haq, Leader of the House in the Pakistani Senate and one of Sharif's factotums, said in the Pakistani Upper House on 30 June that Islamabad would use nuclear weapons if its security was threatened.

'We made it (nuclear weapons) for what—it's not something sacrosanct to be kept in your arsenal even if your throat is cut down by someone,' Haq was quoted as saying.[6] 'It's our duty and right to defend ourselves with all the military might at our disposal.'

In the midst of all this, Pakistan was finding that

international pressure was building up and calls for respecting the LoC were growing. In a statement on 20 June 1999, the G-8 group of nations expressed their concern at the continuing military confrontation in Kashmir.

Blaming the conflict on the infiltration of armed intruders that had violated the LoC, the G-8 said, 'We regard any military action to change the status quo as irresponsible.'

'We therefore call for the immediate end of these actions, restoration of the Line of Control, and for the parties to work towards...the resumption of a dialogue between India and Pakistan,' the statement added.

The battle for Kargil was not being fought on the icy heights of the subcontinent alone, but on the diplomatic trenches in Europe and America.

On 21 June, India said, 'We welcome the statement issued by the G-8 countries calling on Pakistan to undo its armed intrusion and fully respect the Line of Control. We expect that Pakistan will heed this call and act to immediately put an end to its irresponsible conduct and fully restore the status quo ante on the Line of Control. Until that happens the action of our armed forces will continue.'

Pakistan's interpretation of the G-8 statement was, of course, altogether different. 'India has suffered a serious diplomatic setback as its efforts for endorsement of her stand by the G-8 have been rebuffed.'

Islamabad's 21 June statement continued:

> The G-8 have said that 'any military action to change the status quo is irresponsible'. Pakistan is not trying to change the Line of Control. We consider this reference to be a clear recognition that India's military actions have violated the Line of Control, e.g., in

Chorbat La in 1972, Siachen in 1984, Qamara in 1988, its blockade of the Neelum Valley from 1996 to 1998 by artillery shelling, and its current ground attacks against Pakistan posts along the Line of Control and its aerial incursions. All of these are denounced by the G-8 as 'irresponsible'. The G-8 have called for an end to 'these actions'.

Most importantly, the G-8 communique on Kashmir is an affirmation that the international community has become engaged on the Kashmir issue whether India likes it or not. Kashmir has been 'internationalized'. This is due to the valiant efforts of the Kashmiri Mujahideen...

It couldn't have gotten worse for Pakistan. The world was focussed on the fighting that was going on between Pakistan and India; it was calling for an end to conflict— restoration of the LoC—and Pakistan insisted that these were references to events beginning in the 1970s.

The G-8 statement was the sum total of what influential developed nations, including Russia, were telling Pakistan. But Islamabad was in denial. In an incredible formulation, Pakistan even saw the G-8 statement as evidence of 'internationalization' of the Kashmir issue.

Essentially, Pakistan's adventurist behaviour had been placed in the international spotlight as never before. As events in the next few weeks would show, Pakistan had suffered a debilitating credibility crisis by engineering the Kargil crisis by sending in regular troops and then falsely claiming that mujahideen were involved.

The international tide was turning against Pakistan. On 15 June, US President Bill Clinton telephoned Nawaz Sharif and urged him to withdraw troops from the Indian zone of the LoC in order to reduce tensions with India.

Reuters reported that the telephone conversation lasted

twenty minutes. The report quoted White House spokesman P.J. Crawley as saying that Pakistani forces 'have crossed over the Line of Control in Kashmir and the President indicated that he did not see how progress can be made on this issue until those forces are withdrawn'.

Clinton also encouraged Sharif to continue direct dialogue with India. The same report said that the US President had spoken to Vajpayee, urging him to show restraint. It had become clear that Pakistan's bluff on Kargil had been called.

The last thing that the world wanted was an escalation in the fighting. If Pakistan did not restore the status quo on the LoC, the danger of India escalating the war, as election time approached, was a very real one.

It was in this crucial period that the United States firmly planted itself as a third party in the affair. Clinton and assisting key advisers like Strobe Talbott and Anthony Zinni took it upon themselves to intervene diplomatically in a bid to end the crisis.

On the bilateral front, Sharif had made contact with Vajpayee by telephone on 28 May and offered to send his foreign minster, Sartaj Aziz, for discussions to New Delhi. Aziz went to Delhi on 12 June, armed with a brief from the Pakistan Army that at the first meeting he must give no understanding or commitment on the ground situation.

That was exactly what happened. Sartaj Aziz journeyed to New Delhi for a day and, on return, he told journalists at the Chaklala air base in Rawalpindi that the problem across the LoC was nothing new.

My 13 June report in *The Hindu* quoted Aziz as saying, 'The fact that we started the Lahore process did not mean that anything in Kashmir became normal and the problems along the Line of Control were finished. It has its own dynamic and has been going on all the time.'

The report continued:

> Mr Aziz said the atmosphere in New Delhi was 'fairly gloomy' as India had suffered a number of casualties. He conceded that India had sent across its message clearly—that the Kargil area should be cleared of infiltrators...
>
> In reply to another question, Mr Aziz said there was no agreement between India and Pakistan on who were the intruders, where they had intruded and how far they had gone. 'So we need some kind of expert discussion where we are, how far the Line of Control is, what is happening. To do that, we need a better atmosphere. Once we do that, then we will see whether their [Indian] assessment is correct or our assessment is correct,' he said, adding that the situation needed an enabling environment to be created by India.

Sartaj Aziz is one of those old-school Pakistanis who mean well. It was, however, clear that he didn't have much autonomy in negotiating with the Indians and had the task of balancing the demands of the army and a prime minister who didn't want further escalation of the fierce fighting that was going on in Kargil.

In any case, the situation was such that Sartaj Aziz didn't have much to negotiate with. His government had a weak hand. And, as alarm mounted in the West that these two South Asian nations could actually use their nuclear weapons, the pressure on Pakistan to withdraw the infiltrators and on India to exercise restraint would only grow.

The Clinton administration came to realize that it needed a military man to talk to General Musharraf.

As the fighting continued, Anthony Zinni, who headed the US central command, arrived to put pressure on

Musharraf. The Americans felt that a uniform-to-uniform conversation, which took place on 24 June, could make Musharraf see reason.

The US Deputy Assistant Secretary of State, Gibson Lampher, was also in Pakistan, and proceeded to New Delhi on 25 June to brief the Indian side on what had transpired in Pakistan. In the book *Battle Ready* that Zinni co-authored with Tom Clancy, he writes that in the American assessment Pakistan and India stood at the brink of a larger war. According to Zinni, he was asked to head a presidential mission to persuade both Musharraf and Sharif to pull back their troops.

The general's account said that during his meeting with Pakistani leaders he told them bluntly that if Islamabad did not bring back its troops, a nuclear catastrophe loomed large.

Zinni correctly assessed the situation as one of imminent loss of face for the Pakistani leaders. In order for this not to happen, the Americans offered a meeting with President Clinton which would be announced only after a withdrawal of troops.

Strobe Talbott and Bruce Reidel of the American National Security Council have also written accounts of the Kargil diplomacy conducted with Pakistan and India. Talbott writes in his book *Engaging India* that soon after the Zinni meetings, the Clinton administration let it be known in Washington that if Sharif did not order a pull-out, the US would hold up a $100-million loan from the International Monetary Fund to Pakistan.[7]

It's no coincidence that Niaz Naik, a trusted aide of Nawaz Sharif, left for New Delhi on 26 June for backchannel contacts in New Delhi. Sharif was trying everything: winning over the Americans, a bilateral settlement with India and, as a last-ditch effort, roping in the Chinese as well. The Americans had got him worried.

Sharif took off for China though his plan was to be able to sign some kind of bilateral agreement for a pullback of forces during the course of the visit through the good offices of Niaz Naik in India and his Indian counterpart, R.K. Mishra, then editor of the Ambani-owned newspaper, *The Observer of Business and Politics*. That plan did not materialize.

While Pakistan claimed on 3 July that Sharif had paid a 'successful visit' to China, the message emerging from the Chinese was quite different. A Chinese spokesman said in Beijing on 1 July that the priority 'at present' was to avert further deterioration of the situation and to prevent further escalation of the conflict.

'We sincerely hope that both India and Pakistan can earnestly respect the Line of Control in Kashmir, resume negotiatons as soon as possible and seek a fair and reasonable settlement of all their differences,' the Chinese foreign ministry spokesman emphasized.

There was nothing 'extra' in this for the Pakistanis. Their time-tested allies were saying what the rest of the world was virtually saying: that the Line of Control should be respected and that the conflict should not escalate further. If the prime minister was expecting unqualified backing for what the Pakistanis had done in Kargil, then Sharif's visit to Beijing was a failure.

On 26 June, my PTI colleague in Islamabad, Shahid Khan, reported that the former foreign secretary, Naik, had left for New Delhi by a special aircraft. The report was on the ball.

In my own despatch on that day, I added that R.K. Mishra had travelled to Islamabad on 1 June, along with a senior external affairs ministry official, Vivek Katju.[8]

That was the first time that the backchannel became public knowledge. It indicated that the BJP-led government, all through the Kargil conflict, was engaged in backchannel contacts with the Pakistanis, holding discussions with the 'enemy' as Indian soldiers engaged in fierce battles to capture key heights from the Pakistanis.

In a bid to drive a wedge between Musharraf and Sharif, New Delhi decided that the Pakistani prime minister, Vajpayee's new friend, should be given a chance to listen to the Musharraf–Aziz Khan tape about Kargil.

Days after the key 29 May conversation between Musharraf and his Chief of Staff Aziz Khan, R.K. Mishra and Vivek Katju arrived in Islamabad with the tape to be played for Sharif's benefit.

I knew at the time that the two were staying at the Mariott Hotel in Islamabad, but it would take a little more time to learn the details of what the Mishra–Katju mission was about.[9]

By playing the tape to Sharif, the Indian side wanted to show the prime minister that he had been stabbed in the back by General Musharraf. Also that, since he was not really a party to the Kargil intrusion, he should make efforts to rein in the army chief and order a pull-out of troops.

On 29 June, Niaz Naik laid bare the framework of the deal that Pakistan wanted with India on the Kargil pull-out. In retrospect, it was clear that this was Nawaz Sharif's initiative, not one that had the support of Pervez Musharraf.

After his discussions in New Delhi, Naik told the BBC that a meeting between the directors general of military operation of the two countries had been talked about. They could prepare a schedule of the 'so-called withdrawal, the timing and the methodology, etc.'

'And, once that's done, if the two Prime Ministers can agree with the time-frame, then the whole thing can be wrapped up as soon as possible...if you ask my personal opinion, I think the situation will be resolved. I can't say that a deal is in the offing, but efforts are being made in that direction...so that the Lahore process...can be resumed and accelerated,' Naik was quoted as saying.[10]

Sharif failed in his efforts to set up a bilateral meeting with Vajpayee to reach a settlement on the pull-out of troops. New Delhi, perhaps, had understood by the time that the Pakistani leader was getting desperate and had little option but to withdraw forces.

Much has been written about how the Kargil conflict came to an end. Bruce Reidel, a key aide to President Bill Clinton, provided the first account. Strobe Talbott, who was virtually a special envoy for India–Pakistan affairs, has devoted a whole chapter on how the Kargil war came to an end in *Engaging India*. I shall not go into the details of how the conflict was ended by the US, but many methods, including threats of withholding monetary aid, were used by the Americans.

There's little doubt that US intervention proved beneficial for India in the short term. It helped to end the Kargil conflict. When Sharif travelled to the United States on 3 July, the prime minister of Pakistan knew he was going to sign on the US's dotted line. There was little else he could do.

On 4 July, Pakistan signed the climb-down-from-Kargil agreement with the US. The text of the agreement read:

> President Clinton and Prime Minister Sharif share the view that the current fighting in the Kargil region of Kashmir is dangerous and contains the seeds of a wider conflict. They also agreed that it was vital for the peace of South Asia that the Line of Control in Kashmir be respected by both parties, in accordance with the 1972 Shimla Accord.

It was agreed between the President and the Prime Minister that *concrete steps will be taken for the restoration of the Line of Control in accordance with the Shimla Agreement* [emphasis mine]. The President urged an immediate cessation of the hostilities once these steps are taken.

The Prime Minister and the President agreed that the bilateral dialogue begun in February provides the best forum for resolving all issues dividing India and Pakistan, including Kashmir. The President said he would take a personal interest in expeditious resumption and intensification of those bilateral efforts, *once the sanctity of the Line of Control has been fully restored* [my emphasis again]. The President reaffirmed his intent to pay an early visit to South Asia.

The repercussions of and the actual modus operandi for the Kargil withdrawal are detailed in the next chapter. In sum, Kargil exposed the Pakistani establishment as never before. It was a massive diplomatic setback for Pakistan, because Islamabad's standing as a credible international interlocutor was badly shaken.

The Pakistani state repeatedly lied to its own people: that it was the mujahideen and not regular troops that were fighting across the LoC. Indian Army personnel did launch a major fightback, but an end to the Kargil conflict was brokered by the United States, which kept India informed of its discussions with Pakistan.

Tiger Hill was retaken by the Indian Army on 4 July—the same day on which Sharif signed the pullback agreement with Clinton. Kargil was a diplomatic defeat for Pakistan—all key international players wanted the conflict to end and the sanctity of the Line of Control restored.

To me, the story about Kargil was not about bravery on the battlefield. It was about the sheer futility of it all. And, sitting in the press gallery of the Pakistani Senate, the articulate Aitazaz Ahsan of the Pakistan People's Party (PPP), brought this home to me very clearly. The Indian press had been full of stories about how well the Pakistani soldiers were equipped with rations and gear. But Aitazaz Ahsan dispelled all those notions.

He told the Senate that post mortems conducted on the bodies of Pakistani soldiers who died in the Kargil war, had shown that 'grass' had been found in their stomachs.[11] So much for their rations.

So, with heavy Indian artillery barrages and air strikes, the supply lines to the Pakistani soldiers had been cut and some of them were killed not by Indian bombs or bullets, but by the lack of food: they were forced to eat grass.

Putting Pakistani casualties in perspective, journalist M.A. Niazi revealed that 267 Pakistani soldiers were killed during the Kargil war and 228 wounded.[12] Not a small number for an army that claimed the mujahideen and not its men had been fighting on the heights of Kargil.

Kargil was a mindless war. It backfired badly on the Pakistan Army and directly led to the seizure of power by the military under Pervez Musharraf in October 1999.

8

The Fallout from Kargil

❖

*Everyone has been on board. This is the kind of
disinformation going on all around and
disinformation, which is trying to create dissension
between military and the government. Everyone has
been on board.*

—Pervez Musharraf to the BBC in Skardu on
16 July 1999, when asked if Nawaz Sharif had
been kept informed about the Kargil intrusion

PERVEZ MUSHARRAF AND his key generals were
humiliated by the terms of the withdrawal agreed to
between Prime Minister Sharif and President Clinton on 4
July. Days before this, on 26 June, Musharraf said on
record in Karachi that withdrawal of Pakistani forces
would be the prime minister's decision, adding that there
would be no unilateral pullback from Kargil.[1]

However, since the die had been cast, Musharraf had no choice at the time but to go along with Sharif. The army chief was keeping his powder dry. The COAS knew that the big boys in Washington were watching every move. Musharraf had no choice but to deliver on the withdrawal.

After returning home from Washington via London on 8 July, Sharif chaired a meeting of the Defence Committee of the Cabinet (DCC), where it was decided to 'appeal' to the mujahideen to withdraw from Kargil.

An official statement said after the DCC meeting on 9 July:

> The DCC also expressed satisfaction that the joint statement issued in Washington had included the main elements of Pakistan's position, i.e., respect for the Line of Control by both India and Pakistan, de-escalation of the volatile situation in Kargil and, subsequently, the resumption of the dialogue for a final settlement of the Kashmir dispute as part of the Lahore process.
>
> The DCC, therefore, decided that Pakistan should appeal to the Mujahideen to help resolve the current Kargil situation and to provide an opportunity to the international community to play an active role for the realization of the legitimate aspirations of the Kashmiri people and to promote peace and development in South Asia.

After concluding an agreement with Bill Clinton, the prime minister had got down to the job of selling the idea of the climbdown from Kargil to the Pakistani people. The DCC meeting had set this process in motion.

A face-saving device had been found in that President Clinton had decided to take a personal interest in resolving the Kashmir situation. That was the selling point. So, an appeal was made to the jehadis to help resolve the situation.

The United Jehad Council, headed by Hizbul Mujahideen's Syed Salahuddin, initially said that they were shocked at the 'baseless news' appearing in some newspapers. A statement issued in the name of 'Abu Shahbaz' on 10 July 'strongly refuted reports' that the mujahideen had agreed to withdraw from the heights of Kargil.

The next day the full Pakistani Cabinet met and noted that the mujahideen 'had responded positively' to the appeal made by the government to 'help resolve' the Kargil situation.

There was, however, no ambiguity on what had been agreed to with President Clinton. Sharif has proclaimed several times that he wasn't aware of Kargil, but he was second to none in upholding the sacrifices that were made by the 'martyrs'.

A statement issued after the Cabinet meeting on 10 July said:

> Recent developments in Kargil have vindicated Pakistan's position that the international community must pay attention to the Kashmir issue so that the core issue retarding peace in South Asia is resolved amicably. The Cabinet acclaimed the heroic contribution of the Kashmiri freedom fighters, particularly the martyrs of Kargil, who laid down their lives for a just and legitimate cause. While stating that their sacrifices would not be in vain, the Cabinet underlined Pakistan's policy of providing moral, diplomatic and political support to the freedom struggle of the people of Jammu & Kashmir.

The Cabinet also took note of the public commitment of the President of the United States to take a personal interest in resolving the Kashmir issue through negotiations. The Cabinet was of the considered view that the Prime Minister's peace initiative had helped to internalize [sic] the Kashmir issue in a manner that had never been done before, while *peace in the region had been preserved* (emphasis added).

So, what was the civilian government saying here? It was claiming success that it had 'preserved' peace in the region after so many lives—Pakistani and Indian—had been lost in a mindless conflict.

Yes, it had 'internationalized' the India–Pakistan conflict like never before, but this, in effect, worked to Pakistan's disadvantage. Kargil demonstrated to the world that Pakistan spoke with a forked tongue; Kargil brought no benefits to Pakistan, the issue simply worsened Pakistan's reputation as an untrustworthy state. President Clinton's promise of taking a personal interest was a sop to Nawaz Sharif—nothing more, nothing less.

But, the prime minister and his civilian associates had got something to tell the Pakistani people. Sharif's diplomacy had pulled the chestnuts out of the fire. The withdrawal from Kargil was being given the gloss of success; not the paint of failure.

In a front-page report, *The News* reported on 9 July that the Pakistani government would start 'taking concrete steps within seventy-two hours' to implement the 4 July Washington agreement for the withdrawal of the 'mujahideen'.

On 10 July, Pakistan's withdrawal from the Kaksar sector began. The next day began the pull-out from

Mushkoh. Also, on 11 July, the Indian and Pakistani directors general of military operations met in Attari. Moves for a negotiated disengagement from Kargil were well under way.

In a press briefing on 11 July, the foreign minister, Sartaj Aziz, said that following the mujahideen's 'positive response' to 'our appeal', the Indian and Pakistani governments had been 'in contact' on the question of restoring the Line of Control.

'The DGMOs of the two countries met today and agreed on the modalities for de-escalation including sector-wise cessation of ground and air operations to facilitate the mujahideen's disengagement.

'We have been informed that disengagement from Kaksar sector which began yesterday has been proceeding satisfactorily. The disengagement from Mushkoh sector will commence tonight. Gradually the disengagement will be completed in the entire area,' Aziz added.

In keeping with the official line of 'bravado' in the face of capitulation, the foreign minister stated, 'The mujahideen's success has made it amply clear that Kashmir is a volcano. Like Kargil, it can erupt again if the legitimate aspirations of the Kashmiris are not realized soon.'

On 12 July, the Government of India took 'military credit' for what was clearly a negotiated disengagement between the two sides though substantial ground pressure was mounted on the Pakistanis by Indian troops.

Given the fact that India was in election mode, the entire Kargil crisis was used by the BJP-led government to try and cling on to power in New Delhi.

An official Indian statement claimed that Operation Vijay had been a 'resounding success'. With Pakistani forces having been 'defeated on the ground...status quo ante' on the Line of Control in the Kargil sector 'is being restored'. It said:

Almost the entire sub-sector Batalik and the sub-sector Dras have been cleared of Pakistani aggression in the last forty-eight hours...the pressure of our decisive military action in the other two sub-sectors of Mushkoh Valley and Kaksar was also proving unbearable for the Pakistani Army.

Pakistan being faced with the inevitable, their DGMO called his Indian counterpart on the evening of 9th July. He sought an early meeting. Our DGMO suggested that the meeting be held at the Border Security Force reception hall, on our side of the Joint Check Post, at Attari on Amritsar-Lahore Road on the 11th afternoon. Our DGMO also informed him that we expected Pakistan would begin withdrawing its troops from the Kaksar sub-sector even before this meeting, and that this withdrawal will be completed by 12th morning.

During the 11 July meeting, India claimed that its DGMO informed his Pakistani counterpart that Pakistani forces 'must withdraw well north of the Line of Control by the morning of the 16th of July. The Pakistani DGMO said that Pakistan would comply with this schedule.'

In line with the policy of taking credit, the 12 July statement added:

The withdrawal of Pakistani forces has been brought about by the skill, determination and valour of our armed forces, who rolled back Pakistan's aggression from Kargil ... Our forces have not de-escalated their action, nor has any disengagement taken place. The Indian Army is not impeding by fire the retreat of Pakistani forces. After this withdrawal has been completed, we expect that Pakistan will reaffirm the inviolability and sanctity of the Line of Control.

In fact, the disengagement process followed the script suggested by Pakistani interlocutor Niaz Naik, who was acting at Sharif's behest. On 30 June, Naik said that Indian and Pakistani DGMOs could meet soon to prepare a schedule of withdrawal from Kargil.

He told the BBC after talks with Prime Minister Vajpayee on 27 June: 'We just discussed that yes, why not, the D[G]MOs should get together, they have to prepare a schedule of so-called withdrawal, the timing and the methodology etc.

'And once that's done, if the two Prime Ministers can agree with the time-frame, then the whole thing can be wrapped up as early as possible,' Naik added.

Barring that India did not finally agree to a meeting between Sharif and Vajpayee, the rest of the process went according to script. Instead of meeting Vajpayee, the Pakistani prime minister, who had by now become alarmed at the prospect of the conflict continuing and escalating, rushed to Washington and signed the agreement with Clinton.

The Indians, who were kept in the picture, did not want to have a bilateral agreement to end the Kargil intrusion. They were quite content to have the Americans end the conflict by exerting enormous pressure on Sharif.

As can be believed, the Pakistani military and General Musharraf kept up the façade that their troops were not directly involved in the Kargil operation despite the fact that no one was buying this line.

On 13 July, the mujahideen officially conceded that they were 'changing their positions' along the Kargil front. 'For the time being, the mujahideen have formulated a new strategy to carry out their operations by changing their positions on the present Kargil front,' the UJC said in a statement

When asked 'where' the 'mujahideen' were withdrawing to at a press briefing, the ISPR chief, Rashid Qureshi, responded:

> They [mujahideen] are not coming to Pakistan as they belong to Indian-occupied Kashmir and it is up to them where they go...the disengagement between the two sides is meant for de-escalation...mujahideen are people from the occupied Kashmir and they resorted to all this in sheer frustration...[2]

General Musharraf stayed with the story that regular troops were not involved in the Kargil intrusion—that his boys had merely been restricted to 'aggressive patrolling' on the Line of Control.

Musharraf, of course, when asked if he would look back at Kargil as a failure, told the BBC in Skardu on 16 July:

> Definitely not. Not at all, it is a great military success. It is a great success by the mujahideen and our actions on the Line of Control have been extremely successful and all their [Indian] actions to come across the Line of Control have been foiled. And, therefore, I would say that as far as the army is concerned, it is a great success because we do not have any ingress by the Indians across the Line of Control. It has been a great success by the mujahideen who caused a lot of damage and who operated across the Line of Control.

So, if India was claiming that simple military pressure was responsible for the pull-out, official Pakistan felt that the Kargil operation had been a great success.

Many in the Pakistani press did not share Musharraf's assessment.

Others too. A former ISI chief, Asad Durrani, popular on the cocktails and dinner circuit during the time I was in Pakistan, wrote:

> We had chinks in our armour, but as the events unfolded it was the Indian external pincer that forced us to agree to restore the LoC... Pakistan was pressured to restore the *status quo ante*, not only because the West desired to prevent turmoil in the region, but also due to our comparative vulnerability to coercion... It (Kargil) has not only brought home the realities of international politics... it has also taught us to regard events in their correct perspective, rather than getting carried away by self-serving hopes and hypes.[3]

Another senior analyst, Rifaat Hussain, considered close to the permanent establishment, wrote:

> The main problem with the Pakistan-backed Kargil operation by Kashmiri mujahideen was that it did not have a well-thought-out diplomatic exit strategy. Islamabad erroneously believed that New Delhi and the world at large will accept the mujahideen occupation of the Kargil hills as a fait accompli...[4]

Hussain's criticism was not that Kargil was 'done' with Pakistan's 'backing', but the fact that there was no exit strategy that had been worked out by the establishment.

But the best comment that I read on Kargil came from Fakir Aijazuddin in the *Dawn*:

> Whoever conceived the Kargil expedition had the instinct of the ill-fated mountaineer George Mallory who climbed up Mount Everest—because it was there. Like Mallory, he saw the way up clearly enough...[but] reaching the peak is not what matters. Climbing down without losing one's life [Mallory lost his] is more important.

The Indians came to Lahore with an olive branch. We responded with Kargil. Today, the Indian nation is on a war footing, demanding vengeance and we are advocating ahimsa. Never in the fifty years of Independence have we seemed less like a State and more like a stringless Pinocchio capering to a dance choreographed at Blair House (where Mr Sharif met Mr Clinton in Washington on 4 July).

Mercifully for India and Pakistan, the withdrawal from Kargil proceeded without a hitch. Tensions abated with India, but soon it was becoming evident that tensions within the Pakistani establishment—between Prime Minister Sharif and his army chief—were growing.

Musharraf did accept that he had to withdraw, but he did so with extreme reluctance and because the American pressure was on. In the face of international pressure, Musharraf had no choice but to go along with Prime Minister Sharif.

In the days and weeks that followed the withdrawal, the mujahideen and their backers became active in the major cities of Pakistan. From Lahore to Peshawar to Islamabad, rallies were organized, I believe, with the support and consent of the Pakistan Army, to provide a forum to bash Nawaz Sharif for his decision to withdraw from Kargil.

Musharraf and his key generals were seething with anger that Sharif had flown to Washington and signed a unilateral, climbdown agreement. Given that the mujahideen had always been supported by the Pakistani state, the signal was given to organize protests against the Kargil 'sell-out' and pin the blame for the capitulation on the civilian prime minister.

In Lahore, the Jamaat-e-Islami held a huge rally, at which posters of Clinton holding a 'pocket-sized' Sharif on his lap were freely distributed. The prime minister was attacked for his actions repeatedly.

Jamaat chief Qazi Hussein Ahmed, the financier and backer of the Hizbul Mujahideen, thundered at the Lahore rally that Pakistan and Nawaz Sharif could no longer 'co-exist'.

The qazi said that Sharif was a coward who had fallen at the feet of President Clinton. He claimed that it was Indian Prime Minister Vajpayee who had first okayed the withdrawal plan from Kargil and only then had Clinton presented it to Sharif.

'Kashmir and Pakistan cannot be separated from each other. Pakistan is Kashmir and Kashmir is Pakistan. Indian control over Kashmir is Indian control over Pakistan,' the Jamaat chief thundered.[5]

The Jamiat Ulema-I-Islam-Fazal (JUI-F) of Maulana Fazlur Rehman didn't take long in getting in on the act along with the Lashkar-e-Taiba of Hafiz Muhammad Saeed. In addition to Indians and 'Hindus', the JUI-F began to threaten Americans. In a rally at Islamabad's Aabpara Chowk on 30 July, the JUI-F warned American nationals living in Pakistan that they would be targets for attack.

Addressing a rally in Peshawar on 24 July, Rehman brought the focus on the situation in Afghanistan. 'We will be justified in killing the Americans if Afghanistan is attacked....If the US attacks in Afghanistan, we will consider it a war between Americans and the Muslims....Osama [bin Laden] is a guest in Afghanistan and we Pakhtuns are duty-bound to protect our guests.'

At Aapbara Chowk in the heart of Islamabad, I saw Hafiz Saeed up close, addressing the faithful and using colourful language against India. When the rally was winding up, I saw that Saeed and his colleagues got into several 'gleaming double cabs', or pick-up trucks, with official, green 'AJK' (Azad Jammu & Kashmir) number plates.

If sanction for proof of Pakistani establishment support was required for the cause of groups like the Lashkar, it was there for me to see as an Indian reporter. No more proof than the use of vehicles bearing official number plates was needed to show official approval.

In Pakistan, only government vehicles bear green number plates. So, one could only conclude that the government was aware that Mr Saeed had the status of one of its officials. I hadn't heard it second-hand, I had seen it on the streets of Islamabad.

All around the rally venue, volunteers were collecting money for the Kashmir jehad. For an Indian reporter, it was unreal. Here was the reality: jehad had official sanction and creatures like Saeed were involved in its implementation.

The Lashkar broadly drew its 'recruits' from the Pakistani Punjab and had its training camps too in the province. Its connection with Afghanistan was the least in terms of logistics and training, leading to speculation that in the event of anything happening in Afghanistan, the 'jehad' against India could be continued from the Pakistani Punjab without interruption.

It was evident that the Pakistani military intelligence establishment was furious at the decision of the civilian government to pull back from the heights of Kargil. As I wrote in *Frontline*, the withdrawal did not signal any change of approach:

Pakistan has begun calling back its men from Kargil, but it is clear that there is no change in its policy of sending *'jehadi* elements' into Kashmir. If anything, an army that is smarting from the experience of having to listen to political dictates may step up the infiltration into Kashmir from other areas on the LoC—or try some desperate actions elsewhere. The acknowledgement of 'valiant actions' by the mujahideen is not mere talk; the Pakistani establishment genuinely believes it.[6]

The 3 November 1999 high-profile attack on the Badami Bagh Cantonment in Srinagar showed the mujahideen's resolve. It was the first such strike by the Lahskar-e-Taiba on a major military installation in Kashmir: the 15 Corps headquarters.

In the August 1999 issue of the Lashkar mouthpiece, *Voice of Islam*, Hafiz Saeed had stated that 'jehadi' groups had conveyed to the Sharif government their 'rejection' of the government withdrawal of Kargil.

This, too, was backing an elaborate lie, for all the 'infiltrating' had been done by soldiers of the Northern Light Infantry and other regular troops of the Pakistan Army. At best, some mujahideen were 'present'—as suppliers or porters.

Saeed claimed that 'jihadic activities' in all parts of Kashmir had been stepped up. 'The increasing number of mujahideen attacks in Kashmir sent a wave of mourning all over India. Their celebrations ended abruptly. Indian Army officers became the biggest target of the mujahideen in this war...' he wrote with glee.

He argued that Kargil had presented a 'golden opportunity' for Pakistan to fight a decisive war to liberate Kashmir and to avenge the 'defeat of 1971'. The truth was out: the 'jehadis' too shared the view that 1971 still had to be avenged.

In another piece in the same issue of the *Voice of Islam*, Faroq Ahmed wrote:

First of all, as a result of withdrawal [from Kargil] Pakistan's stand on Kashmir that it supports mujahideen only morally stands negated. In fact Pakistan is so embarrassed and confounded after the retreat that it does not know as to what stand it should take. On the other hand, India's stand that the resistance movement in the [Kashmir] Valley is not indigenous stands vindicated.

In the meantime, the Pakistan Army was having to come to terms with its own role in Kargil, especially dealing with the dead, the wounded and their families.

Brigadier Rashid Qureshi, the military spokesman during the Kargil conflict, later promoted to the rank of major-general for his 'stellar performance', said in Islamabad on 28 July that as many as 267 Pakistani troops were killed during the Kargil war.

Earlier, on 12 July, when the process of disengagement between India and Pakistan was underway, the same brigadier had said that 187 Pakistani soldiers had been killed and twenty-four were missing.

Confirming the figures of the dead at 267, M.A. Niazi wrote in *The Nation* that another 228 soldiers were wounded in the conflict.

On 1 August, *The News* reported that families living in the Northern Areas, from where the bulk of the Northern Light Infantry's recruits come, were bitter that the contributions made by NLI men in battle were 'being credited to the Kashmiri mujahideen'.

The report said:

Though Prime Minister Nawaz Sharif subsequently paid a visit to Skardu and met the aggrieved families, and efforts were belatedly being made to acknowledge the sacrifices of NLI jawans through the official media and other means, it would take some time to heal the wounds and console the embittered families.

The funeral of Sepoy Ibadullah of Chitral Scouts in Chitral was also a big event. Besides the officers and jawans of the Chitral Scouts, the deputy commissioner and the elite of the district joined the funeral. The mourners at the funeral recalled how jawans of the Chitral Scouts had tried to outdo each other while volunteering to be sent to the Kashmir side of the LoC. However, none of these emotive scenes were reported in the newspapers or filmed by our television cameras because the official policy was to play down battles for Dras, Kargil and Batalik.

Musharraf and Sharif were finally forced to abandon the position that regular troops had not been involved in the Kargil intrusion. Both in July and early August, the army chief visited homes of military personnel killed during Kargil to address family grievances.

This policy change came to fruition when a special investiture ceremony was held in the presidential palace, Aiwan-e-Sadar, with President Rafiq Tarar, Prime Minister Sharif and Musharraf in attendance, on 14 August 1999.

The actions credited to the 'Kashmiri mujahideen' were now being accounted to the army. That was the result of the impact of the disaffection among the families, officers and jawans. The NLI was also given the status of a regular regiment in the Pakistan Army.

I wrote in *The Hindu* of this investiture ceremony that an overwhelming number of the sixty-four personnel honoured for their role in Kargil were from the NLI:

> Havildar Major Nasir Ali Shah and Gunner Mohammad Kamal (both from Army Air Defence) were given the Tamgha-e-Jurrat [a rough equivalent

of the Indian Vir Chakra] for shooting down with a missile an Indian Air Force helicopter on 28 May in the Kargil area.[7]

In the 29 May taped conversation between Chief of General Staff Aziz Khan (in Rawalpindi) and Pervez Musharraf (in Beijing) released by then Indian Defence Minister George Fernandes in New Delhi, this action of downing the MI-17 helicopter was ascribed to the mujahideen. 'This [the chopper] has fallen in their [Indian] area. We have not claimed it. We have got it claimed through the mujahideen,' Aziz is heard telling Musharraf.

A month-and-a-half down the line, Musharraf and Co. had to change their minds about the rightful claimants to the shooting: Nasir Ali Shah and Mohammad Kamal—both of the Pakistan Army—had to be given medals by President Tarar.

The wheel had come full circle. Pakistan was now officially claiming what had been tagged to the mujahideen for purposes of propaganda. The veneer had worn off.

The language used in the citations was crude. My report in *The Hindu* noted:

> For instance, Captain Sardar Izhar Haider (posthumous) got the Sitara-e-Jurrat (the Indian equivalent of the Mahavir Chakra) for sending fifty 'enemy' soldiers to 'jahannum' (hell). The phrase 'sent to hell' figured in at least half-a-dozen other citations.
>
> Naik Talib Hussein and Gunner Shafqat Ali (Air Defence) were presented with the Tamgha-e-Jurrat...for shooting down the MiG-27 aircraft piloted by Flt. Lt. Nachiketa on 27 May.

Days before the investiture ceremony, tensions between India and Pakistan again rose after the Indian Air Force shot down a Pakistan Navy Berguet Atlantique maritime patrol aircraft in the Rann of Kutch on 10 August.

Sixteen Pakistan Navy personnel, including five officers, were killed in the IAF action. While India claimed that the aircraft had intruded into its territory, Islamabad stated that wreckage of the Berguet was found two kilometres inside Pakistani territory.

The fact is that the IAF was looking to hit a Pakistani aircraft ever since Flight Lieutenant Nachiketa's MiG-27 was shot down on 27 May and Squadron Leader Ajay Ahuja's MiG-21 came down in Pakistan territory due to an engine problem. Whatever be the truth of the rival claims, the fact is that shooting down the Atlantique was an effort by the IAF to 'settle the score' for the loss of its MiGs.

The Pakistani side claimed that the Indian director-general of military operations telephoned his Pakistani counterpart and took responsibility for shooting the plane by 'alleging intrusion for two minutes'.

'It was a cowardly act,' Prime Minister Sharif said at the Mehran naval base in Karachi during a ceremony to honour the sixteen persons killed in the Indian attack. Sharif reiterated the Pakistani claim that the aircraft was shot in Pakistani territory and was an act of 'military aggression' by India.

A day after the Atlantique was shot down, Pakistan confirmed firing a missile at an IAF aircraft in the Rann of Kutch area. Information Minister Mushahid Hussain claimed at a press conference that each time India had acted, Pakistan had responded in a very strong manner. It was an attempt to settle scores.

On 17 August, India announced its draft 'nuclear doctrine', which spoke of a 'triad of aircraft, mobile land-based missiles and sea-based assets' meant to ensure survivability. The draft did not define the concept of a minimum deterrent, stressing, 'This is a dynamic concept related to the strategic environment, technological imperatives and the needs of national security. The actual size, components, deployment and employment of nuclear forces will be decided in the light of these factors.'

As expected, the Pakistani response was 'strong'. Foreign Secretary Shamshad Ahmad, whose hawkish postures I have referred to before, was the one chosen by the permanent establishment of Pakistan to respond to the draft Indian doctrine.

Arguing that the 'doctrine' pointed to strengthening of India's conventional forces as well, Ahmad warned during a press briefing on 19 August, 'The growing imbalance in conventional military capabilities will intensify Pakistan's reliance on its nuclear capabilities to deter the use of threat of aggression by India.'

The message was clear. A conventionally weak Pakistan, without resources to buy new weapons, was saying that it would increasingly depend on the nuclear option in the wake of any threat of aggression by India.

In effect, Ahmad was threatening the use of nuclear weapons if Pakistan was faced by even a conventional threat. The strategic logic was evident.

Internally, the investiture ceremony had done nothing to dilute the differences between Sharif and Musharraf. Gone was the trust that had led to Musharraf's appointment after Jehangir Karamat was eased out in 1998.

Musharraf, in the immediate aftermath of the Kargil war, had told the BBC that everyone was on board as far as taking a decision on Kargil was concerned. At the time, in the middle of July, it was not clear why the army chief had taken such pains to drive this point home. That would, however, soon become clear.

Just as the Kargil tide was beginning to ebb, the former foreign secretary, Niaz Naik, got in on the act once again. It's now clear to me that Naik was acting at the instance of Nawaz Sharif, who was beginning to show increasing signs of panic that Musharraf had no intention of restricting his role to that of an army chief.

The suave Naik, speaking to a *Jang* reporter after a function of the Pakistan–China Friendship Society on 13 September in Karachi, said:

> Lack of coordination in the Kargil planning was a major factor for undermining the emerging Pak-India agreement on Kashmir [to have been clinched] in September or October this year. A main factor which prevented a Kashmir accord between the two countries was Kargil where a military exercise was begun, but the lack of coordination between the planners subverted a deal on Kashmir...if the Prime Minister had known about it, Kargil may not have erupted at all.

Naik was essentially making the point that the army was the one that had subverted a deal and that Sharif did not receive 'proper feedback' from the planners of Kargil. His remarks came at a time when Sharif was beginning to feel the heat from Musharraf.

A denial that came from Naik later (one Pakistani press report said at the time that the army chief had telephoned the former foreign secretary before it was issued) had little or no meaning.

Naik's remarks in Karachi would also serve to set the stage for a meeting between the prime minister's younger brother and Punjab chief minister, Shahbaz Sharif, along with the ISI Directorate chief, Lt-General Khwaja Ziauddin, with senior US State Department officials in Washington in the middle of September.

The remarks projected Sharif as a 'man of peace' who had been misled by Musharraf. An agreement on Kashmir with the Indians, favoured by the prime minister, had been thrown off the rails by the general. The 'political pitch', which was not so clear then, would be evident in the days that followed.

Ayaz Amir, my favourite Pakistani columnist, was the one who alerted Pakistanis (and me, of course) to the mood in Rawalpindi. In his weekly column tellingly entitled 'Testing ponies and waiting stallions', Amir, a retired army captain and batch-mate of several serving generals at the time, wrote in *Dawn* on 17 September that Sharif's relationship with Rawalpindi was fraught and tense because of the Kargil fiasco:

> ...Kargil has dealt a blow to the unity of the governing class, driving a wedge between the heavy mandate [of Nawaz Sharif] and Rawalpindi. While both have had their fingers burnt, both are trying to put the blame for this fiasco on the shoulders of the other. In the shades of Islamabad this is the real cat-and-mouse game being played...
>
> In the giant stables in Rawalpindi where Pakistan's champion stallions are kept, the mood is dark; some would go so far as to say even dangerous. One indication of this is the almost permanent scowl that has come to sit on the army chief's face. A carefree man before Kargil, he now looks visibly unhappy. Niaz Naik has only made matters worse. Whatever he may have meant to convey, his remarks in Karachi will be taken by the army high command as another attempt at putting the entire blame for Kargil on its shoulders while absolving the civilian leadership of all responsibility...will the sullen mood that can be felt in Rawalpindi pass or will it gel into something

harder? To know the answer to this question is to understand how Pakistani politics will unfold in the critical months that lie ahead.

If Amir was subtle, the American State Department was not. On 20 September, the Americans waded into the skirmishes going on between Sharif and Musharraf. If the tension between the army and the civilian government was known only to some people, the Americans made it public knowledge.

In a report datelined New York, the Reuters news agency quoted a senior US official, widely believed to have been then Assistant Secretary of State for South Asia, Karl Inderfurth, as saying:

> We hope there will be no return to the days of interrupted democracy in Pakistan...we would strongly oppose any attempt to change the government through extra-constitutional means.

The American statement flowed from the meetings that Shahbaz Sharif and Ziauddin had with senior Clinton administration officials. The Sharifs were trying to 'cash in' on what they felt was a private 'IoU' signed by President Bill Clinton as part of the 4 July Kargil joint statement.

What the Americans did was to place the ongoing power struggle between the army and the Sharifs in the public domain. While Sharif may have himself triggered the 12 October coup, the fact is that it had been in the making for quite some time—ever since differences over Kargil became apparent. The question was only one of timing.

On 20 September, General Musharraf replaced Mangla Corps Commander Lt-General Salim Haider with Tauqir

Zia. Haider was reported to have some leanings towards Nawaz Sharif. The Mangla Corps is supposed to be one of Pakistan's 'strike corps'.

Officially, the ISPR Directorate expressed surprise at the comments coming out of Washington. Brigadier Rashid Qureshi said the army did not know what had prompted the comments. 'There is nothing that the army is doing. Ask the [Sharif] government what we are doing,' Qureshi remarked.

Musharraf himself sent a clear message to Sharif. Speaking to reporters at the Mariott Hotel on 23 September, the general said he would finish his tenure as chief of the army staff—he wasn't going to be sacked or sent home like his predecessor.

Owen Bennett Jones, former BBC correspondent in Pakistan, has provided a fascinating account of the fear that had gripped Sharif. Referring to the joint visit to Skardu by Sharif and Musharraf on 8 and 9 September, Jones pointed out that the trip got off on a bad start due to the absence of 10 Corps Commander Mahmud Ahmed. Skardu fell under the direct charge of 10 Corps.

Jones writes in his book *Pakistan: In the Eye of the Storm* (Viking, 2002), that Musharraf was showing off his new Italian-made pistol to Information Minister Mushahid Hussain in the lobby of Hotel Shangri La outside Skardu on 8 September.

When the prime minister walked into the lobby, Mushahid called Sharif over to take a peek at the new pistol. According to Jones, the prime minister didn't want to know how the pistol worked, he only wanted to know whom it was being aimed at.

My own sources revealed later that the brigadier responsible for Sharif's security had been replaced by a Musharraf loyalist. This, according to the sources, sent the prime minister into a tizzy. He was now convinced that Musharraf was going to act against him.

A meeting between the general and some of Sharif's emissaries, including Shahbaz Sharif, indicated that a 'compromise solution' had been worked out between the two sides.

The contours of this understanding were spelt out on 30 September when it was announced that the army chief's tenure would be co-terminus with that of the chairman, Joint Chiefs of Staff Committee (JCSC). Musharraf was now to hold both the posts of COAS and chairman, JCSC, till his tenure was to 'end' on 6 October 2001.

A spokesman for the prime minister, while making this announcement, hoped that 'this step will once and for all set at rest the uncalled-for rumours and speculation about the change of command in the army, that some vested interest[s] were fanning in pursuance of their political agenda'.

To many, including the majority of analysts in the Indian High Commission, it appeared that the shadows stretching over the Sharif government had lifted. That was, however, not to be the case.

Fasih Bokhari, who quit as naval chief on 2 October following Musharraf's permanent appointment as JCSC chief, is quoted by Owen Bennett Jones as saying that Musharraf and Sharif—the two points of power in Pakistan—were on a collision course.

On 7 October, Sharif held what was to be his last formal press conference as prime minister. Though it was ostensibly focussed on new projects, the PM took just one question, and that was, significantly, on Afghanistan.

The prime minister revealed that persons who had received training in Afghanistan camps had been found to be involved in a string of sectarian attacks in Pakistan. A delegation led by his loyalist ISI chief had visited Afghanistan and asked the Taliban to close down the camps.

Just after the press conference concluded, I managed to ask the prime minister if he considered Kargil to be a closed chapter. 'Your question has now become old,' he told me. 'New issues have now come up.'

That was the last time I saw Nawaz Sharif as prime minister in public.

On 9 October, it became clear once again that the temporary and precarious truce brokered by Shahbaz Sharif with General Musharraf had collapsed. The general relieved Quetta Corps Commander Lt-General Tariq Pervez of his command following an unauthorized meeting Tariq Pervez had with Nawaz Sharif.

Tariq Pervez, a cousin of the then communications minister Nadir Pervez, instead of reporting to the Rawalpindi headquarters, chose to retire prematurely— even though he was supposed to be in office till February 2000.

The very next day a senior Intelligence Bureau official, Col. Pervez Jamal, was given his marching orders by the military. During Nawaz Sharif's tenure, the 'civilian' Intelligence Bureau was reporting to his factotum, Senator Saifur Rehman.

Making sense of all these goings-on for an Indian correspondent was maddeningly difficult. First-hand access to information on what was going on between Musharraf and Sharif was impossible. But, at the same time, if you were following the press carefully, and talking to diplomats and others, the contours of the bigger picture did present themselves.

As an example, here is what I wrote in *The Hindu* on

10 October, two days before General Musharraf staged his coup:

> Clearly, the speculation [that Sharif was planning to replace Musharraf as Army Chief] was intense enough for the government to come out with such a statement [that no such move was afoot]. However, this step does not preclude the appointment of a new COAS if the Prime Minister so desires.

Two days later, on 12 October 1999, the prime minister did exactly that: he tried to appoint a new chief of army staff. But Sharif could not ensure that his nominee would take office.

9

The March of the 111 Brigade

❖

What is the Constitution? It is a booklet with ten or twelve pages. I can tear them up and say that from tomorrow we shall live under a different system. Is there anybody to stop me? Today, the people will follow wherever I lead. All the politicians, including the once mighty Mr Bhutto, will follow me with their tails wagging.

—Zia-ul-Haq speaking in Teheran,
18 September 1977

TWENTY-TWO YEARS LATER, when one of Zia-ul-Haq's successors, Pervez Musharraf, ousted the elected Prime Minister Nawaz Sharif on 12 October 1999, the chief of army staff was not at liberty to make such a politically incorrect statement. The world had changed a little.

But domestic politics had not changed much in Pakistan, as the actions of General Musharraf showed, and the world, too, seems willing to accept a limited form of uniformed government, when it comes to Pakistan.

On their part, the people of Pakistan had little choice. Governments have always been removed for them—by the President or by the army—they have never actually exercised their right to vote out a government.

Going by the norms of constitutional propriety, Musharraf's actions in taking power on 12 October were out of line. But, in Pakistan, politics is not that simple. The army has always been the power hanging over the civilian prime minister: manipulating events from its perch.

A conflict between political rectitude and what took place on 12 October was evident, but army intervention in civilian politics hardly comes as a surprise to the people of Pakistan. It's part and parcel of the order of things.

Besides, Sharif was an unpopular and autocratic ruler. You just have to look at his treatment of *Friday Times* editor Najam Sethi and columnist Hussain Haqqani— both were imprisoned and beaten by his goons for not toeing his line—to comprehend the depths to which his 'democratic' rule had sunk.

The economy was in the doldrums. Foreign loan repayments had mounted while Sharif rolled out more and more populist schemes, which had no impact on the country since they were never implemented. Every once in a while he would appear before the press and announce a new scheme.

So when Sharif went, few tears were shed for him. There were no street protests against the sacking; even his own partymen in the Pakistan Muslim League had precious little to say. The 'heavy mandate' simply collapsed.

In a country like Pakistan, intervention by the army is

never far away in the public reckoning. Musharraf's coup, while it could not be called popular, certainly brought a sense of relief to the common people that an unpopular leader had been removed.

I could see that Musharraf and Sharif were on a collision course after Kargil. The prime minister's Mohajir general had bared his teeth; there was no patron–client relationship here.

Musharraf, it may be recalled, had the support of the vast majority of corps commanders and had even tried to elicit the support of the other service chiefs in his desire to square-off with Sharif when the time came. The general sense among the corps commanders was that they would not allow a repeat of what Sharif had done to Musharraf's predecessor, Jehangir Karamat.

For me, 12 October was just another day. The usual checks for stories—and the usual conversations with my Pakistani journalist friends—carried on through the day.

Just after five in the evening, I received a telephone call from a friend in the Pakistani press. 'Musharraf has been sacked!' he screamed into the phone. 'Ziauddin is the new army chief. PTV just announced it.'

'What?' I responded.

'He's been removed! Let's see what happens. Switch on your television,' my friend said, ending the conversation abruptly.

I had been aware that the differences between Musharraf and Sharif were growing, notwithstanding some efforts at patching up. But I, too, was surprised that matters had come so suddenly to a head.

After the announcement on the 5 p.m. PTV bulletin of the new appointment, I waited with bated breath for the next bulletin at 6 p.m. As the bulletin began, PTV World, which is a satellite channel, went off the air. Something was clearly wrong.

I switched to the main PTV terrestrial channel. The news continued as usual—the situation in Chechnya and the daily dose of propaganda on Kashmir took centre stage. The wait continued. The weather report commenced. Still no announcement.

Newsreader Shaista Zaid, whose image would soon be telecast round the world in the hours to come, read that crucial piece of information only after the weather report—repeating the 5 p.m. bulletin that Musharraf had been sacked and ISI chief Khwaja Ziauddin was to be his successor.

Inside the PTV headquarters opposite the stately Margala Hills, a bizarre drama had ensued, as we learnt later. A posse of armymen, led by a Major Nisar, had been asked to rush to the PTV headquarters to ensure that the news item was not telecast again. The major's presence had ensured that the story of Musharraf's sacking was withheld during the main bulletin.

Naturally, Nawaz Sharif had been watching the bulletin in his Prime Minister's House. When he saw that Ziauddin's appointment had not been covered, he had sent his military secretary, Javed Iqbal, to the PTV headquarters.

After a brief confrontation between Brigadier Iqbal and Major Nisar, Shaista Zaid finally came on after the weather report and announced to the people of Pakistan that Sharif had appointed a new army chief.

As the bulletin ended, I jumped into my car and drove to the PTV station—in time to see what the march of the 111 Brigade was all about.

Ever so often, my Pakistani friends had told me that coups in Pakistan were a simple affair: a jeep from the 111 Brigade drove in from Rawalpindi and the country passed from civilian to military hands. I used to think that it was a big joke they were playing on me. It clearly wasn't.

Standing along with other reporters outside the PTV gate, one could soon see army reinforcements coming in. Since the gate was locked, the soldiers had to clamber over. That picture made the coup for the media—it was the only active sign of a military takeover in Pakistan.

Apart from the Shaista Zaid announcement that Musharraf had been sacked and the picture of troops scaling the PTV gate, the press had little else to show to the rest of the world that the army had seized power. Such is the nature of coups in Pakistan.

Soon, word spread that the troops were acting at the behest of the Rawalpindi-based X Corps Commander Mahmud Ahmed. After satisfying ourselves that the drama was, indeed, over, most of the reporters drove towards the Prime Minister's House, barely a kilometre away from the PTV office.

Here, no entry was permitted. I could see that troops had taken position and there was no way we could get any closer to our objective. No one was being allowed to go in or out of the Prime Minister's House, which commands an imperial view of Islamabad. Army trucks were parked across the roads.

An army officer in civilian clothes, who said he was a captain, began shouting insults aimed against the Sharif government. 'I'm thrilled that Nawaz has gone,' was one of them. The prime minister was in army custody.

Driving around the city, one saw it was unreasonably calm. A few soldiers could be seen lounging around outside the Parliament building and the offices of Radio Pakistan. The 111 Brigade had marched in and quietly taken over control of Islamabad.

There was no resistance. Once more, Pakistan passed peacefully from civilian to military rule.

It was all very reminiscent of General Zia-ul-Haq's coup, more than two decades ago, which had been just as clinical. On 5 July 1977, General Zia-ul-Haq executed his Operation Fair Play. Faiz Ali Chishti, X Corps Commander at the time, had ordered his troops into action at 2 a.m. on 5 July.

By 2.15 a.m., K.M. Arif writes in his book *Working with Zia*, Prime Minister Zulfiqar Ali Bhutto and senior Pakistan People's Party leaders Abdul Hafeez Peerzada, Maluana Kausar Niazi, Mumtaz Ali Bhutto, Hamid Raza Gilani, Sheikh Rashid, Ghulam Mustafa Khar and General Tikka Khan were in custody.

Arif, who was Zia's vice-chief of army staff and key aide, made the point that there was little or no resistance to General Zia's action given the deliberate planning and execution that went into it. In the end, the result was the same in both 1977 and 1999—the military took complete control of Pakistan without a shot being fired.

Here, I am not drawing any mechanical linkages between the events of 1977 and 1999. Every military intervention had its specific circumstances; it took place when the chief of army staff felt threatened or simply believed it was time to take power.

Evidently, Nawaz Sharif's decision to make Pervez Musharraf's tenure as COAS co-terminus with chief, Joint Chiefs of Staff Committee, had been just a ploy to lull the general into thinking that all was now well and the peace pipe was ready for smoking.

The prime minister's paranoia, however, had been growing. On 10 October, he had set off for Dubai to meet Sheikh Zayed Bin Sultan Nahyan in a special aircraft, taking with him ISI boss Ziauddin, son Hussain Nawaz and speech-writer Nazir Naji. The plot for 12 October was hatched on board the flight because the prime minister suspected that Musharraf and Co. had bugged both his house and telephones.

Owen Bennett Jones says in his book *Pakistan: In the Eye of the Storm*, by 4.30 p.m. on 12 October, Sharif had signed the orders for Musharraf's removal and Ziauddin's appointment as the new COAS. Soon after, Ziauddin began making calls to different corps commanders, seeking their support.

Jones writes that the man who called X Corps Commander Mahmud Ahmad and the chief of general staff Aziz Khan with the news, while they were playing tennis, was Saeed-uz-Zafar, the Peshawar-based corps commander, who was acting-chief during Musharraf's trip to Colombo. The Mahmud Ahmad–Aziz Khan duo acted quickly and took charge of matters till their chief was able to return to Pakistan.

As the news of Musharraf's sacking was announced on state media, the prime minister wanted to ensure there was no way that the general, who was on a scheduled visit to Sri Lanka, could return to Pakistan. He issued patently illegal orders that PIA flight PK 805 carrying Musharraf from Colombo (the plane had 198 other passengers and crew on board) was not to be allowed to land in Karachi.

The FIR filed in the case on 10 November 1999 by Lieutenant-Colonel Atiq uz Zaman Kiyani, protocol officer in the Karachi corps headquarters stated:

> At about 1840 hours Corps Commander 5 Corps Lieutenant-General Muzaffar H. Usmani, along with Major Zaffar Ullah Khan Wazir, arrived at the [Karachi] airport. I, along with Brigadier Tariq Ali Khan, Commander Logistic Area and Brigadier Naveed Nasar, Commander ASF, received the corps commander. I came to know at the airport that flight PK 805 has been refused permission to land at its

destination, i.e. Karachi Airport, by ATC (Air Traffic Control). The Karachi airfield was closed, runway lights were switched off and [the] runway was physically blocked by parking crash tender vehicles at three different places. While other flights scheduled to land at Karachi were diverted to Sukkur and Nawabshah, flight PK-805 was refused landing even at Nawabshah, which was the planned alternate airfield of flight PK-805. I also came to know that flight PK-805 was ordered not to land anywhere in Pakistan.

Despite critical low fuel-endurance, the pilot had been ordered to proceed to a foreign country at his own risk. Later on, after the landing of flight PK-805 at about 1948 hours, I came to know that only approximately ten minutes' fuel was left, which showed an intent and criminal conspiracy to cause the plane to crash [and] thus physically eliminate and murder COAS General Pervez Musharraf and passengers by an act of terrorism of hijacking with an intent to cause crash of plane by lack of fuel for the reason as no airfield was allowed to be open for its landing. In this manner the conspiracy was to physically eliminate and murder COAS General Pervez Musharraf and 198 passengers on board flight PK-805 with deliberate criminal intent which is apparent from the act, conduct and orders/conversation of persons, including the then Prime Minister Mohammed Nawaz Sharif...

At about 1845 hours, army troops ex-5 Corps Reserve arrived at Jinnah Terminal to take over the ATC, and it was army troops ex-5 Corps Reserve who got the runway cleared, runway lights switched on and blockade removed on [the] army's order to facilitate landing of Flight PK-805. The ATC was

instructed by the army to allow Flight PK-805 to
land at Karachi Airport. Approximately at 1948
hours flight PK-805 thus landed safely at Karachi
Airport.

It was clear that Sharif felt that Musharraf would be a
threat to him if he was allowed to land in Pakistan. And,
as the pilot of the aircraft, Sarwat Hussain, revealed, he
did not have sufficient fuel to take him outside Pakistan.
Previously, Musharraf, when told that the aircraft could
land at Ahmedabad in India, had been quoted as saying,
'Over my dead body.'

In his statement of 9 March 2000, before the anti-
terrorism court in Karachi, the ousted prime minister
addressed some of these issues himself:

> I was constrained to do so [order Musharraf's sacking]
> as I had received credible information that General
> (Retd) Pervez Musharraf was planning to overthrow
> my legally established government by unconstitutional
> means and to achieve that end he had been taking
> certain measures by keeping my movements under
> surveillance, by abruptly changing [the] commander
> of triple one [111] Brigade and replacing him by a
> person of his own confidence...he also got bugged
> various rooms of the Prime Minister's House and
> Prime Minister's Office. I could not hold a meeting in
> the PM House or discuss any important or sensitive
> matter without raising the volume of the TV in order
> to avoid eavesdropping.

Sharif's condition, I must add, was no different from that
of an Indian diplomat living in Islamabad. Diplomats
were under instructions that if 'sensitive matters' were to
be discussed, the volume levels of their televisions/music
systems should be raised at all times. It would appear that

the general had reduced the prime minister to the status of a frightened Indian living under constant surveillance in Pakistan.

The prime minister, in his account, denied that he had a meeting with the now-retired Quetta corps commander Tariq Pervez. 'Despite instructions issued by the defence secretary to the ISPR, no contradiction was issued,' Sharif said in his 9 March statement.

The account added a vivid picture of Sharif's experience:

> I also noticed all of a sudden the army contingent posted at PM House was equipped with modern gadgetry such as headphones and latest sensitive devices....The circumstances giving rise to these unfortunate developments date back to the Kargil issue.

Mian Sahib, as the prime minister was known, said he was innocent of the charges of high treason (which carried the death penalty), hijacking, and attempting to murder General Musharraf. In his defence, Sharif stated that he had been falsely implicated in the case. The ousted prime minister explained why he acted as he did:

> I had reliable secret information that...Musharraf had planned taking over of the lawfully established government. It was suspected that his plan could be carried through on his arrival from Colombo...the news of the change of the then COAS was flashed on the PTV at 5.00 pm and within minutes, i.e. 5.20 pm, the army took control of the Islamabad PTV Centre. The PM House was taken over by the army before 6.30 pm. The Corps Commander 5 Corps Lt. General Muzaffar Usmani...had also reached the Karachi Airport by 6.00 o'clock on the pretext of

receiving...Musharraf...thus the order for retirement
of...Musharraf and appointment of General Ziauddin
was frustrated, defied and made inoperative under a
pre-conceived plan hatched by some senior
commanders of the army, who owed personal loyalty
and allegiance not to the institution, but to the
retired General Pervez Musharraf.

Clearly, Sharif's take was different. The sacked prime
minister's defence was that the plot to remove him from
office was to go into effect immediately after Musharraf
returned from Colombo.

Whatever be the truth, the fact is that Sharif came out
badly in the whole case. He had given the army action
some justification when he ordered that the plane be
allowed to land neither in Karachi nor in Nawabshah.

Post-12 October, the interest shifted to what Musharraf
would or would not do. The Pakistan Muslim League was
strangely silent. To me, the most pointed and yet nuanced
response to the events of 12 October came from that
stellar voice of civil society, the Human Rights Commission
of Pakistan (HRCP).

Expressing deep anguish and concern, the HRCP felt
that the army takeover would do little to serve the long-
term political prospects of the people, of democracy or
even of the armed forces themselves. 'The armed forces,'
the HRCP warned, 'should recognize that the order they
impose may be orderly...but it will nevertheless lack
legitimacy and...popular consent'.

The HRCP critique said: 'It [the previous government]
has interpreted popular mandate as a sanction for major
decisions not even by the consensus of the majority party
but by the undebated whims and wishes of the leader of
the party and his near ones...some of the worst
consequences of this were blatant violation of human

rights, rise in fundamentalism and creation of new tensions in federal bonds.'

With Sharif in army custody, Musharraf, after a belated but dramatic arrival in Karachi, prepared to address the Pakistani people on television. At 11 p.m. on the same day, PTV, whose transmission had been interrupted, came back on air with the announcement that the Nawaz Sharif government had been dismissed and that the COAS would address the nation.

The general began his brief address to a nation glued to their TV sets at 2.50 a.m. on 13 October. He said the army had moved in as a 'last resort' to prevent any further destabilization of the country. The ousted prime minister was accused of attempting to politicize and destabilize the army and create dissension within its ranks.

Late on the night of 15 October, Musharraf issued an emergency proclamation in the name of the three chiefs of staff and the army's corps commanders. He placed the Constitution in abeyance, the elected assemblies were suspended, the prime minister, federal and provincial ministers ceased to hold office and the whole of Pakistan came under the control of the armed forces.

A Provisional Constitutional Order No. 1 of 1999 was also issued—laying the path to legitimacy in the future. It allowed courts to function, but these could not issue orders against the Chief Executive (as Musharraf chose to anoint himself), and fundamental rights not in conflict with the emergency proclamation, or with orders from the Chief Executive, would remain in force.

The 'Chief Executive' phrase was key to the altered equation. Recognizing the changes that had taken place in the rest of the world, General Musharraf realized that he could not proclaim himself to be the Chief Martial Law Administrator (CMLA), as his predecessors Ayub Khan,

Yahya Khan and Zia-ul-Haq had been free to do. Even the civilian Zulfiqar Ali Bhutto had inherited the title of CMLA from Yahya Khan.

Internally, too, this new title of Chief Executive would soften the blow for the people and the press. It was part of a strategy that, in the case of Pervez Musharraf, actually worked to his advantage.

After an initial period of attempted isolation, both by the United States and India, Musharraf, especially after the 11 September attacks in the US in 2001, has had few issues as far as attaining international legitimacy goes.

The Chief Executive, who formed a new National Security Council, a Cabinet of ministers to work under the guidance of the NSC, a think-tank entitled the National Reconstruction Bureau, and the National Accountability Bureau to nab the corrupt, sounded genuine and sincere in his professed concern for the Pakistani people in his first statements to them.

And then, on 17 October, Musharraf laid down six objectives for himself: rebuilding national confidence and morale; strengthening the Pakistani federation; removing inter-provincial disharmony and restoring national cohesion; reviving the economy and restoring investor confidence; ensuring law and order and dispensing speedy justice; de-politicizing state institutions; devolving power to the grass-roots level and ensuring swift and across-the-board accountability.

The general's description of the state of Pakistan had obvious elements of what a failed state might look like:

There is despondency and hopelessness surrounding us...the slide has been gradual but has rapidly accelerated in the last many years. Today, we have reached a stage where our economy has crumbled, our credibility is lost, state institutions lie demolished, provincial disharmony has caused cracks in the Federation and people who were once brothers are now at each other's throats.

... In sum, we have lost our honour, our dignity or respect in the comity of nations. Is this the democracy our Quaid-e-Azam envisaged? Is this the way to enter the new millennium?...Quite clearly, what Pakistan has experienced has been merely a label of democracy, not the essence of it...I shall not allow the people to be taken back to the era of sham democracy but to a true one. And I promise you I will, Inshallah.'

Among the key appointments he made was that of the 'legal wizard' Sharifuddin Pirzada as member of the National Security Council and senior adviser to the Chief Executive. Pirzada has been described by *Dawn* columnist Ardeshir Cowasjee as the '*jadoogar* of Jeddah' on account of his association with the Organization of Islamic Conference (OIC) as its Secretary General.

Pirzada has been key to lending legitimacy to successive illegal military regimes in Pakistan by manipulating the country's Constitution. So, when he received his new designations on 25 October, most Pakistanis were not surprised.

In 1961, during Ayub's military regime, Pirzada had been appointed adviser to the Constitution Commission of Pakistan. He had later served as Pakistan's foreign minister from 1966 to 1968.

Pirzada had returned to government with Zia-ul-Haq—in the period between 1979 and 1984 he had been the country's Attorney-General and law minister—and had then worked as OIC Secretary-General during 1985–88 in Jeddah.

The 'jadoogar' would prove useful in the years ahead

when Musharraf had to protect himself from, possibly, ill consequences of some his actions through the vehicle of a Legal Framework Order (LFO) in August 2002. Through such dexterous political management, has Musharraf contrived to stay in power. He has managed to create and manipulate with ease a new faction of the Pakistan Muslim League—staffed even by several leading lights who served Nawaz Sharif.

The general has entered into alliances with the right-wing Muttahida Majlis-e-Amal (MMA), an alliance of the Jamaat-e-Islami and the Jamiat Ulema-e-Islam (Fazal). At the same time, he has tried to appease the United States by adopting a tough political posture against extremist and terrorist elements.

Using the Zia-ul-Haq route, Musharraf, who appointed himself President in June 2001, a decision linked to his visit to Agra for talks with India in July 2001, held a referendum on 30 April 2002, which extended his 'term' as President for another five years.

In May 2000, a twelve-judge bench of the Pakistan Supreme Court validated the Musharraf coup on the basis of the dubious 'doctrine of State necessity', which the Court claimed was recognized in Islam, and also accepted by some eminent international jurists.

It also held:

- All past and closed transactions, as well as such executive actions as were required for the orderly running of the state and all acts, which tended to advance or promote the good of the people, are also validated.

- General Musharraf having validly assumed power by means of an extra-constitutional step, in the interest of the state and for the welfare of the people, is entitled to perform and promulgate measures that, among other things, would establish or lead to the establishment of the declared objectives of the Chief Executive.

- A three-year period from the date of military takeover, which was to end on 12 October 2002, was given to the Chief Executive to fulfil his objectives.

- Elections to the National Assembly, Senate and Provincial Assemblies were to be held by 12 October 2002.

The Supreme Court also said there would probably have been no need for Musharraf's takeover had Article 58(2)(b) of the Constitution not been deleted from the 1973 Constitution (by Parliament in 1997 at Sharif's instance). This key provision had 'provided checks and balances between the powers of the President and the Prime Minister to let the system run without any let or hindrance to forestall the situation in which martial law can be imposed'.

It said there was an 'implied consent' of the people of Pakistan to the army takeover 'in that no protests worth the name, or agitations, have been launched against the army take-over and/or its continuance'.

This was not the first time that 'implied consent' had been invoked in the defence of a military ruler. Pakistani courts have shown little or no spine in bending before the superiority of the military, and Supreme Court judges—barring a few honourable exceptions—have submitted to fresh oath-taking ceremonies after an army takeover.

For individuals to 'imply consent' is one thing, for the Supreme Court to do so is quite another. In Pakistan, the courts have still to demonstrate their independence when it comes to dealing with the military. Quiet acquiescence is the easier way out—an adverse judgment can attract adverse consequences for the judges in question.

As per the Supreme Court judgment of May 2000, Musharraf allowed elections to be held in October 2002—three years after his coup. The Pakistan Muslim Leaque (Q), backed by the permanent establishment, took power with Mir Zafarullah Khan Jamali as prime minister.

By coming to an arrangement with the MMA, Musharraf managed to get himself elected President of Pakistan on 1 January 2004 by the legislature. A seventeenth amendment to the Pakistani Constitution was also passed, which legalized the 1999 coup.

As part of the 'deal' with the MMA, the President was to give up his job as army chief at the end of December 2004, a commitment, clearly, he never had any intention of adhering to. Subsequent events were to prove that Musharraf did this only in order to 'legalize' his rule.

The fact is that the President, like his predecessors, draws his authority solely from the uniform that he wears. If he sheds that costume, he is denuded of power, subject to the authority of any successor that comes in.

After taking power in October 1999, the President made many grandiose promises. One of his main focus areas was *ehtesab* or 'accountability'. To that end, Lt-General Syed Amjad was given charge of dealing with the corrupt, and recovering loans from defaulters.

Amjad did a fair job of trying to net in the top defaulters, many of whom were part of previous governments. As time went on, Musharraf seemed to lose interest in accountability and many previous actors in the Sharif regime returned to favour, making a mockery of the process of 'ehtesab'.

In October 1999, State Bank Governor Mohammad Yaqub told the press that Rs 356 billion was owed to banks in Pakistan. Of this loan defaults stood at Rs 211 billion and non-performing loans at Rs 145 billion.

Of the defaults of Rs 211 billion, as much as Rs 100 billion was owed by 322 families/groups, Yaqub said. And, a mere number of twenty-five families/groups owed as much as Rs 30 billion to Pakistani banks.

A tiny coterie of parliamentarians, retired military personnel and feudals dabbling in business have drained Pakistan of its resources. It is this broad class of people that has called the shots in government too.

Remember that key members of the Nawaz Sharif government made the transition to the 'king's party', or the ruling faction of the Muslim League, with relative ease. This group has never had any problems in Pakistan— all doors of power are always open to it. Musharraf, Nawaz Sharif and Benazir Bhutto all belong to this group.

The new Chief Executive held his first press conference at Chaghai Auditorium (Pakistan's Pokhran) on 1 November in the PTV headquarters in Islamabad. Journalists were asked to arrive three hours before time so that men of the SSG could frisk them and check any item being taken inside the venue.

It was a far cry from Sharif's press conferences where PID officials just waved you in. This time it was, after all, the chief of the permanent establishment of Pakistan who was going to be addressing us.

Musharraf spoke clearly and directly. He sat alone on the stage—there were no aides with him. It was clear that he was in command. As I realized quickly, here was a man who loved to talk. He's probably the most interviewed leader in the world these days—just check out his official website for evidence of this.

To me, the high point of the long press conference was a question from a bearded, shalwar-kameez–clad Pakistani reporter. In chaste Urdu, this correspondent asked the general: '*Ayub Khan ne ham ko Gohar Ayub Khan diya, Zia-ul-Haq ne ham ko Ijaz-ul-Haq diya, kya aap ham ko Bilal Musharraf denge* (Field Marshal Ayub Khan gave Pakistan and Pakistanis [his son] Gohar Ayub Khan [who was Sharif's foreign minister], Zia-ul-Haq gave [his son] Ijaz-ul-Haq [leading luminary of the Muslim League] and now will Musharraf's 'gift' be [his son] Bilal Musharraf?)'?

For a moment, the easy-talking general was stumped, and the assembled press corps burst into laughter. And, then came the response: 'Thank you, you know my son's name.'

It could have been dismissed as a joke. But, in a country where rulers have been more interested in perpetuating themselves than in governance, the exchange was significant.

It was also a sign that the press would not behave like a poodle; Musharraf would have to account for his actions to this vigilant wing of Pakistani civil society.

10

Musharraf, India and Kandahar

❖

THERE WAS A lot of bluster in General Pervez
Musharraf's approach to India after he took over as Chief
Executive. His commando image, the picture of the man
responsible for plotting and planning Kargil, and the face
of the saviour of the Kashmir mujahideen, was clearly in
focus.

The general is a man who gives as good as he gets. If
you ask him a question politely, he'll give you a polite
answer. If you get tough with him, he'll return the
compliment in like mode. And, importantly, one needs to
remember that he's not really accountable to anybody.

The only persons that can—gently—question him are
his corps commanders; nobody else. Musharraf has never
had to answer a question in Parliament—he has been
outside the pale of Pakistan's democratic system in his
seven years in the saddle. Shooting from the hip comes
easily to those who don't have to account for their
actions.

The military and the jehadis have been the best of friends; the jehadis have been supported and nurtured by the ISI Directorate as part of a low-cost, bleed-India policy for the longest time. And with the general taking over, it appeared that the jehadis had been given the green signal to go hammer-and-tongs at India in a bid to erase the ignominy of Kargil.

At all the rallies organized by the Jamaat-e-Islami, the Harkat-ul-Mujahideen and the Lashkar-e-Taiba, the anger against the Nawaz Sharif government for ending the Kargil intrusion had been evident. These groups now had a point to prove: their 'jehad' for the 'liberation' of Kashmir would continue. On 3 November 1999, the Lashkar struck at the 15 Corps headquarters in Srinagar—its most audacious attack ever. Even before the strike, the Lashkar had stated they would be carrying out sensational attacks in Kashmir.

(It's important to remember here, that the 'activist' policy towards the jehad in both Kashmir and Afghanistan was a pre-11 September 2001 phenomenon, when the world's view of Pakistan, and its ability to sponsor militancy and terrorism, changed dramatically.)

Addressing his first press conference on 1 November, the general said that Indian hostility would be met with hostility, peace with peace and threats with threats. 'I will ensure the honour and dignity of this country. Nobody threatens us without getting a threatening response,' he announced.

Musharraf delineated the contours of a more Kashmir-centric approach in the composite dialogue process with India. 'We would like to resolve all our differences [with India], and when I say all our differences, I mean the core issue of Kashmir first of all—or simultaneously at least.

'But if there is any design to address issues other than

Kashmir and sideline the Kashmir issue then I am not part of it. The Kashmir issue has to be addressed and with that all other issues can be addressed. If this is the attitude we see from across the border, I can assure that I will be going far ahead of them [the Indians] in this area.'

The reaction in India to Musharraf's takeover was one of confusion. On that fateful day, External Affairs Minister Jaswant Singh said, 'We are concerned over the developments in Pakistan. But there is no cause for alarm or anxiety.'[1]

On 14 October, Pakistani Foreign Secretary Shamshad Ahmad met Indian High Commissioner G. Parthasarathy in Islamabad and told him that the military regime wanted tension-free and good relations with India.

The very next day Defence Minister George Fernandes said that developments in Pakistan were an 'internal matter'.[2] In a more formal reaction, the external affairs ministry spokesman said that Pakistan was effectively under martial law and expressed concern at the 'direction in which the country was moving'.

In response to the remarks made by Musharraf at his 1 November press conference, the Foreign Office stated:

> ... India harbours no enmity towards the people of Pakistan. India has always taken the initiative towards improving relations, as it did again last year by putting in place the composite dialogue process to build confidence and trust, establish a stable structure of cooperation and address all outstanding issues. The Prime Minister had sought to reinforce this approach through his historic visit to Lahore in February 1999.
>
> Pakistan's armed intrusion and aggression in Kargil was, of course, a violation of the Line of Control, but more than that it was betrayal of trust.

Pakistan must, therefore, facilitate a restoration of trust through actions, abandon its state-sponsored cross-border terrorism against India in Jammu & Kashmir and elsewhere, and it must also cease hostile anti-India propaganda.

The language coming out of New Delhi as well as Islamabad was easily translated on both sides. No strangers to a war of words, the two countries had commenced upon a fresh round, with a military leadership now in place in Pakistan.

In what appeared to be a pre-emptive move to isolate Musharraf and Pakistan, India announced on 4 November that due to the 'military coup d'état in Pakistan and the consequent concern and disquiet expressed in the region and beyond, the Government of India has informed the SAARC chairperson and Nepal, as the host country of a productive meeting, it would be appropriate to defer the Summit for the time being.'

It was an absolute snub. There had been little change in the security situation in the region and, in fact, Musharraf had announced his decision to pull back troops from the international border. Objective analysis could only lead to one conclusion—the Indian side was hitting at Musharraf personally.

But Musharraf's body language was equally tough— something apparent to anyone watching him on television. In an interview to the BBC's Zafar Abbas on 5 November, Musharraf made apparent his distaste for the Lahore process agreed to between Prime Ministers Vajpayee and Sharif in February 1999.

When asked about the 'Lahore process', Musharraf said in Urdu: '*Lahore process ho, ya phalana process ho, ya dhimkana process ho...*' (Whether it is the Lahore process or this or that process...)'. The Chief Executive also boasted that if the Indian side was willing to talk Kashmir, he was willing to take ten steps for each one taken by New Delhi.

If Musharraf had used 'phalana' and 'dhimkana' for the Lahore process, his newly-appointed foreign minister, Abdul Sattar, a former foreign secretary and high commissioner to India, was more precise in his choice of words. At his press conference, Sattar was asked whether the Lahore documents would form the basis for negotiations with India or would a fresh framework have to be negotiated? His response: 'There are scores of agreements between India and Pakistan. The Lahore agreement between Pakistan and India was one of them. We will scour that agreement for positive aspects and we'll be prepared to implement them.'

This distancing of Pakistan from Lahore was important for the military regime. None too happy with Nawaz Sharif for having gone over the heads of the army to invite Vajpayee to Lahore in the first place, Musharraf and Sattar were making a point to their domestic audience as well: We're not following the lead given by the ousted Prime Minister.

For those Indians living in Pakistan, it was clear that relations were in a steep nosedive. With the jehadis stepping up their actions and the verbal abuse mounting between the two sides, the bilateral front looked bad.

Meanwhile, what of the Americans, who were smack in the middle of the India–Pakistan 'peace process'—with the Clinton administration having invested a great deal of time and energy in the form of the Strobe Talbott parallel dialogue with both India and Pakistan?

It was clear that the Americans were going to deal with Pakistan—albeit in a limited and restricted way. But deal they would. Assistant Secretary of State for South Asia Karl Inderfurth said in Washington:

Despite our deep disappointment with this latest
setback to democracy in Pakistan, we have no choice
but to stay engaged. We cannot walk away because
Pakistan is important. It is important because stability
or the lack thereof in Pakistan will have an impact on
Pakistan's neighbours, the region and beyond.

We will be pursuing in the days ahead far more
commitments from General Musharraf...including
[on] cross-border terrorism. The Indians have said
that they cannot resume the Lahore process until
cross-border terrorism ceases. We believe steps like
that should and must be taken. We will press very
hard for that.[3]

On 18 October, American ambassador to Pakistan, William
B. Milam, had gone out of his way to accommodate
Musharraf and suggested that the COAS alone was not
responsible for the Kargil debacle. And yet, just a month
earlier, a senior US official had warned about a possible
coup in Pakistan—a warning against the return of days of
interrupted democracy.

When asked at his press conference whether he
regarded Musharraf as the 'architect' of Kargil, Milam
responded:

I am concerned this has been rooted about, but you
know my information and I am pretty knowledgeable
on this—is that Kargil was a collective failure on all
parts of government. Yes, of course, it was an army
operation, so Gen. Musharraf obviously had a part
in the decision. But—don't kid yourself—that
operation was agreed to by the civilian government
completely. So, 'arhitect of Kargil' is, perhaps, a bit
strong...it certainly has a connotation that I think is
misleading. Whether that reputation is going to last
despite the facts, whether this will get in the way of

resumption of the [India–Pakistan] dialogue, I don't know. I hope it doesn't.

Milam also took issue with the view that Musharraf was an extremist or presided over a rogue army. According to the ambassador, the general was a 'moderate' who had acted out of 'patriotic motivations'.

After having miserably failed to read the tea leaves in Pakistan, the Americans were now engaged in damage-control. Washington has always engaged with anybody in power in Pakistan. Issues like democracy or military rule have never come in the way of 'engagement'.

General Musharraf's rule was a fait accompli and both the Americans and the Indians had to deal with him. That was the message Milam was sending out to New Delhi. The last thing that the Americans wanted was another flare-up between India and Pakistan.

India, however, was on a different track. Its entire diplomatic effort was aimed at ensuring that Musharraf didn't gain any international legitimacy. On 12 November, Pakistan was suspended from the councils of the Commonwealth at the Commonwealth Heads of Government Meeting in Durban.

Harish Khare, *The Hindu*'s New Delhi bureau chief, wrote in his dispatch from Durban on 13 November:

> Making a brief intervention almost at the beginning of the first executive session, the Prime Minister, Atal Behari Vajpayee, did not leave the assembled delegates in any doubt that India would want the Millbrook Action Programme [to deal with interruptions of democracy in Commonwealth member states] to be applied to Pakistan, both in letter and in spirit. Much of Indian diplomatic effort has been directed—almost obsessively—at ensuring that the Commonwealth

decreed a timetable for restoration of democracy in Pakistan.

The Prime Minister also told journalists on board his special aircraft flying him from Durban back to New Delhi: 'When we were discussing the fate of Mr Nawaz Sharif, I told the other [Commonwealth] leaders that if there is no timely international intervention, then Mr Nawaz Sharif might end up meeting the [Zulfiqar Ali] Bhutto fate.'

Clearly, this was the wrong thing to say. Vajpayee should have kept his counsel to himself, rather than express publicly his fear that Sharif could be executed by the military, as Bhutto was on 4 April 1979, at a time when India and Pakistan were at loggerheads with each other.[4] It could only have the effect of hardening Musharraf's approach to Sharif. And it did.

As Sharif's formal arrest and trial commenced, all hell broke loose in Islamabad on 12 November. The quiet city was turned upside down. In coordinated attacks, at least six rockets were fired from improvised, twin-barrelled launchers at the US Information Centre on Jinnah Avenue and the US Embassy.

The target of some rockets was unclear, landing as they did outside the offices of the World Food Programme and the UN headquarters buildings. Luckily, only one person was injured in the attack which, in the end, appeared more symbolic than serious.

These attacks were a sign of the terrorist outfits' growing comfort-level with the Musharraf regime. In the post-Kargil scenario, these groups felt that Musharraf would back them. They had been emboldened by the military takeover.

To me, it appeared that the Harkat-ul-Mujahideen (HuM) was responsible for the attacks even though no formal claim to responsibility was made. Soon after the terrorist strikes at American Embassies in Tanzania and Kenya, the United States launched cruise missile attacks through Pakistani airspace on terrorist training camps in Afghanistan.

Ostensibly targetted at Osama bin Laden and Co., the 20 August 1998 missile attack ended up killing at least nine HuM 'trainees'. Soon after, HuM leader Fazlur Rehman Khalil warned that his group would exact 'revenge' for the deaths.

Days after the coup, Musharraf appointed X Corps Commander Mahmud Ahmed as the new chief of the ISI Directorate, in place of Ziauddin, whose whereabouts then were not known. Chief of General Staff Aziz Khan was appointed a corps commander.

Both Ahmed and Khan had played key roles in ensuring Musharraf's survival. The third key man had been the bearded Karachi corps commander Muzaffar Hussain Usmani. They greatly influenced Musharraf.

The Indians, meanwhile, were taking a 'no-contact, no-dialogue' position with Musharraf. The Indian High Commission in Islamabad was ordered that there should be no meetings with Musharraf, his Cabinet ministers or governors. Only contact with permanent officials—such as chief secretaries—was deemed allowed.

Given the troubled nature of relations between India and Pakistan, a distinction between contact and dialogue is essential. For instance, after the 24 December 1999 hijacking of Indian Airlines flight IC-814 to Amritsar, Lahore, Dubai and then Kandahar, India was forced to have contact with Pakistan for overflight permission. Non-contact was not a viable policy, as the BJP-led government would soon discover.

On the evening of that 24 December, my wife and I

were preparing to hold a farewell for our PTI friend, Shahid Khan, who was preparing to leave Pakistan for home in Kolkata. A number of our Pakistani friends, mostly journalists, were invited.

Then I received a call from Shahid early in the evening. 'My Delhi office just called me. An Indian Airlines flight from Kathmandu to New Delhi has been hijacked and is headed towards Lahore. Do you know anything about it?'

This was the first I'd heard of it. All thoughts of dinner vanished. What had happened? And then, began the long night that lasted till the end of the hijacking on New Year's Eve—31 December.

It was the most frustrating time for me as a reporter in Pakistan. United Nations flights were going from Islamabad to Kandahar and the press could hitch a ride. But that was not for me—I was Indian. The Government of Pakistan did not allow resident Indian reporters to 'exit' to Afghanistan. But, sitting in Islamabad, with the telephone handy, it wasn't impossible to get accounts of what was happening.

The hijacked aircraft, which entered Pakistani airspace around 6 p.m. (PST) on 24 December, was refused permission to land at Lahore airport and had to then make an emergency landing at Rajasansi airport in Amritsar.

The hijackers had had no intention of landing in Amritsar—Pakistan or Afghanistan were preferred destinations—they were forced to agree to land there since Lahore airport was initially closed by the Pakistanis to the hijacked aircraft.

Just as it appeared that the hostage drama would play itself out in Amritsar, the scene again shifted to Lahore. The Airbus A-300 aircraft narrowly escaped a major mishap while landing in Lahore since the runaway lights had been turned off.

'All the lights had been switched off at the [Lahore] airport as a precautionary measure but the passenger plane landed on the dark airport perilously averting a crash,' the Associated Press of Pakistan reported.

With the Government of India unable to prevent the hijacked plane with 189 passengers on board from leaving Amritsar, a major crisis was on hand. It was a Christmas Eve that these passengers would not forget.

The same evening Indian External Affairs Minister Jaswant Singh telephoned his Pakistani counterpart Abdul Sattar—the first such call since the military takeover. Singh claimed that Sattar had given a personal assurance that they would take all possible steps for the safety of the passengers.

Apart from the initial failure to engage with the hijackers in Amritsar, the BJP-led government thought it could substitute bluster for policy. In a statement, Prime Minister Vajpayee said on Christmas Day:

> It [the hijacking] has brought home with full impact the horror of terrorism that the country faces. We have to face this challenge with determination and self-confidence. *My government will not bend before such a show of terror* (emphasis added).

The Vajpayee government seemed to be suffering from the hangover of its own propaganda that it unleashed following the handling, by the V.P. Singh government, of the December 1989 kidnapping in Srinagar of Rubiya Sayeed, daughter of India's Home Minister Mufti Mohammed Sayeed.

The BJP and its associates had pointed to the weakness shown by Prime Minister V.P. Singh's government in releasing several Jammu & Kashmir Liberation Front (JKLF) activists in return for the freedom of Rubiya Sayeed. The party made it a major political issue in the country, adding, for effect, the fact that the BJP, as a strong party, would not have bent in the face of demands from the terrorists.

The party was also sharply critical of the Narasimha Rao government for its handing of the September 1993 siege of the Hazratbal shrine in Srinagar. As part of the deal with Kashmiri militants holed up inside, which would end the month-long siege, the Rao government allowed those inside the shrine safe passage into Pakistan-controlled Kashmir.

Using colourful language, the BJP said at the time that the Congress party was feeding 'biryani' to the terrorists holed up in the Hazratbal shrine, revered by millions of Kashmiris.

The BJP had accused previous governments of being weak-kneed and bending before the terrorists both during the handling of the Hazratbal siege and the release of the militants to secure the freedom of Rubiya Sayeed.

An act of terrorism has to be dealt with by the government of the day; in the absence of a no-negotiating-with-terrorists position, Vajpayee did himself and his government a disservice by taking an unbending position during Kandahar. Because bend he finally did.

Information is all, in a hostage situation. For two days, the Government of India did nothing—it did not even send a junior-level diplomat from Islamabad to Kandahar to talk directly to the hijackers.

For decisions to be taken, you need information. Just how tough a bargain are the hostage-takers driving, who they are: these are the questions that the government should have been asking. When you weigh the pros and the cons of such a situation, how does it look on balance?

In a country like India, where airline passengers make more news than, say, the kidnapping of a bus-load of peasants in a remote village, no government can choose to ignore 'live television'. It's a reality all governments—irrespective of their political hue—have to live with.

When Erick de Mul, United Nations Coordinator for Afghanistan, took off in a UN plane for Kandahar on 26 December, diplomats of four Western nations—who had nationals on board—accompanied him. There was no Indian diplomat.

Finally, on 27 December, an apprehensive commercial counsellor, A.R. Ghanashyam from the Indian mission in Islamabad, flew to Kandahar just in time to beat a 1.40 p.m. (IST) deadline that had been set by the hijackers. As I wrote in *Frontline* (21 January 2000):

> Shortly before Ghanashyam landed, the hijackers took two foreign passengers into the Club Class area [of the aircraft] and tied them up; they threatened that they would kill them if India did not immediately open negotiations. The diplomat managed to convince the hijackers that a team of negotiators was on its way from Delhi. The desperadoes then suspended their deadline...
>
> An Airbus A-320, with fifty-two persons on board, including a seven-member negotiating team headed by Ajit Doval, a senior intelligence officer, arrived that evening and opened negotiations with the hijackers...some National Security Guard (NSG) commandoes [India's 'crack' anti-hijacking force] were on board the Airbus A-320, ready to storm the hijacked aircraft if the Taliban gave permission.

Given the fact that the Indian press was absent from Kandahar, the government had a field day in New Delhi, feeding all kinds of 'stories' to the press corps. The Taliban, it was put out, were close to giving permission to the Indians to take out the hijackers.

Yes, contact with the Taliban had been established in Islamabad by the Indian High Commission, but they would hardly be amenable to giving permission to India to launch a commando operation against the hijackers.

Such situations always have a political context, which New Delhi seemed to have absurdly forgotten. Much before UN-mandated sanctions against the Taliban took effect on 14 November 1999, India stopped the Amritsar–Kabul flight. Making common cause with anti-Taliban forces, like the Northern Alliance, and later the United States, was part and parcel of India's Afghan policy.

A Pakistani correspondent, Ayaz Gul, who was among the first journalists to reach Kandahar on 25 December, has provided a brilliant account of what he saw there. In an eyewitness account published in the now-defunct weekly *Asiaweek*, Gul wrote:

> We were unsure how Afghanistan's ruling Taliban would receive us. The hardline Islamic movement had never been friendly toward international journalists. Photography of living things was called un-Islamic and banned. After our plane landed, to our surprise, we taxied and parked just fifty metres from the hijacked aircraft. Taliban officials not only gave us a warm welcome but also told us to do whatever we wanted, including take pictures.
>
> Soon, UN official Eric de Mul began negotiations with the hijackers, after a request by India for mediation. I was the only journalist present as de Mul spoke, via radio, with the chief hijacker. The militant identified himself as the brother of Masood Azhar, an ideologue of a Pakistan-based militant

group that changed its name from Harkat-ul-Ansar to Harkat-ul-Mujahideen after the United States branded it a terrorist group several years ago. The man de Mul spoke to was referred to only as 'Chief' by his comrades, said hostages later. I heard the hijacker responding in Urdu, with a smattering of English, to de Mul's appeals. 'Chief' appeared in full control inside the plane. 'Mr de Mul,' he said in calm, measured tones, 'it is useless talking to you. We want direct contact with the Indians. Otherwise, we will kill the hostages.' He also told the UN official there could be more hijackings. That way, he said, 'we will resolve the Kashmir issue quickly'.

On 27 December...de Mul persuaded India to fly in a team that evening....Even as the Indians were negotiating, it seemed what they had in mind was a commando strike. On 29 December, the Taliban convinced the hijackers to give up their demands for a $200-million ransom and the remains of Sajjad Afghani, a Harkat-ul-Ansar leader killed in Kashmir. Afghanistan's rulers called such demands 'un-Islamic'. Then the Taliban began to put pressure on India. Later that evening, they apparently became aware of reports about Indian commandos on the plane from New Delhi. Taliban leaders held a *shoora*, or ruling council meeting. They decided that no foreign power (read India) would be allowed to launch any military operation to free the hostages.

The next day, the Taliban dispatched crack troops, armed with multi-barrelled rocket-launchers, and two tanks, to the airport tarmac. But they targeted not the hijackers but the Indian negotiators' plane, which contained the commandos. That had a decisive impact on the talks. The Indians made a deal with the hijackers after the Taliban deployments convinced them a rescue operation was out of the question.

The hijackers held all the cards. They were in full control of the situation and the Taliban were not inclined to act against them. As far as the Taliban were concerned, they only wanted the hijacking crisis to end—and end quickly.

On the other hand, the hijackers themselves were describing their action as the 'millennium flight'. They seemed to be in no hurry to end their hold on the hostages or the plane. Negotiators were told that their hijacking would stretch across the entire millennium.

It was evident from the nature of their demands that the hijacking was Kashmir-related. However, the hijackers were not Kashmiris themselves; had that been the case they would have taken advantage of the international media's presence to bash India.

Actually, the hijacking was all about one man: Masood Azhar, who was arrested in Srinagar in February 1994 while travelling under a false Portuguese passport in the name of Essa Bin Adam.

The hijacking was the third attempt to spring Azhar from jail. Two previous attempts were made to get him out in June 1994 and July 1995—when foreign tourists were kidnapped in Kashmir. On both occasions, there was a demand made for the release of Azhar.

Azhar himself fancied himself as a journalist. Even while in an Indian jail he was contributing to the Harkat's Karachi-based jehadi journal, *Sada-e-Mujahid*, a paper he founded. How he was able to send his contributions all the way to Karachi is a question, as I said earlier, only authorities in the Jammu jail, where he was lodged, can answer.

Soon after the hijacking got underway, Taliban Foreign Minister Wakil Ahmed Mutawakkil named Ibrahim Azhar, brother of Masood Azhar, as one of the hijackers. In fact, he was the spokesman and leader of the group.

Later, at a press conference on 6 January 2000, in New Delhi, Indian Home Minister L.K. Advani gave Ibrahim Azhar's name as 'Ibrahim Athar' from Bahwalpur, Pakistan. He gave the names of the other hijackers as Shahid Akhtar Syed, Sunny Ahmed Qazi, Mistri Zahoor Ibrahim and Shakir—all of them said to be Pakistani nationals.

Masood Azhar was a rabble-rouser and ideologue of the Harkat. There had been considerable pressure for his release with even leading media associations in Pakistan passing resolutions for his release. His fiery pamphlets, exhorting people to join the 'jehad' were seen everywhere.

During a family shopping exercise at the upmarket Jinnah Super market in Islamabad, I came across a Harkat 'stall' which was selling, among other things, Masood Azhar's recorded speeches. There were scores of these audio cassettes available. The man was, clearly, an important propagandist and preacher.

As described in Chapter 2, there was a personal element in the whole affair. I had been warned after the May 1998 nuclear tests that the Harkat-ul-Ansar was planning to kidnap an Indian journalist. In the event, the Harkat had to go for far bigger fish than me to get one of their major leaders out of jail.

That it was the Harkat behind the hijacking was gradually becoming clear to me. On 31 December, I spoke to its top leader Fazlur Rehman Khaleel, just as the hijacking drama was winding down. 'It is a major defeat for the Government of India,' Khaleel told me.

At the time I spoke to him, about 4 p.m. Pakistan Standard Time, the identity of the third terrorist to be released was not clear. (The second man freed by India was Mushtaq Ahmed Zargar.) However, Khaleel knew his name: Ahmed Omar (Saeed Sheikh). Khaleel also had little hesitation in sharing this information with me.

It was evident that the Harkat-ul-Mujahideen leader had more information than ordinary mortals, since his group was directly linked to the hijacking.

After this conversation with Khaleel, my reporter's antenna was up. By the end of New Year's Day, I was able to get confirmation that it was, indeed, the Harkat-ul-Mujahideen, previously known as the Harkat-ul-Ansar, which was behind the hijacking of IC-814—a report on which was carried prominently in *The Hindu* of 3 January 2000.

As the time came for the terrorists-for-hostages trade-off on 31 December, Jaswant Singh personally escorted in the three terrorists: Masood Azhar, Ahmed Omar Saeed Sheikh and Mushtaq Ahmed Zargar alias 'Latram', a man whom I knew was associated with his own group called Al-Umar Mujahideen that operated in downtown Srinagar from the time that I reported in Kashmir. Singh flew into Kandahar with the three terrorists on a special Boeing 737 aircraft.

The Taliban, meanwhile, proved that whatever be their medieval notions of governance, they were no novices at diplomacy. Jaswant Singh was the one who announced that the hijackers had been given ten hours to leave Afghanistan. My 21 January 2000 report in *Frontline* said:

> Significantly, Jaswant Singh, flanked by [Taliban foreign minister] Wakil Ahmed Mutawakkil, announced that the hijackers had been given ten hours to leave Afghanistan. The Taliban put pressure on Jaswant Singh to make this announcement in order to ensure that India did not accuse the Taliban of agreeing to give the hijackers safe passage.

Jaswant Singh, however, told the Indian Parliament on 13 March 2000:

The Taliban had been told by us that as they exercised jurisdiction in Kandahar, the released terrorists would be brought to the Kandahar Airport, whereafter they would be under Taliban control but not that of the hijackers. It was also explicitly conveyed to the Taliban that we expected that both the hijackers and the released terrorists, would be treated as criminals in conformity with law. The decision taken by the Taliban to allow the hijackers and the released terrorists ten hours to leave Afghanistan was theirs alone.

And, what did Mr Vajpayee have to say after telling the people of India on 25 December that the Government of India would not bend? On the last day of the millennium, the Prime Minister said the action of his government in releasing the three terrorists was guided by two concerns: 'the safety of the passengers and the crew; and the long-term overall interests of the country'.

Not only did Mr Vajpayee bend, his government capitulated before the terrorists. In all fairness, however, it can be legitimately argued that the government had little choice when the lives of so many of its nationals were placed in jeopardy.

Rather than taking a rigid position on the hijacking, the government should have told the people that it was a difficult situation that would involve difficult decisions before it could be resolved.

In retrospect, it's evident that the release of Masood Azhar and Ahmed Omar Saeed Sheikh, a Pakistan-born British national, was a major disaster and a fillip to the jehad against India.

Azhar lost little time in surfacing in Pakistan and began hurling vile threats about at both India and the United States. Sheikh, of course, is in a Pakistani jail for the brutal murder of American journalist Daniel Pearl. Azhar split the Harkat-ul-Mujahideen and formed his own Jaish-e-Mohammad. While he was forced by Pakistani intelligence agencies to tone down his rhetoric against the US, Azhar was permitted to launch and build his own jehadi group, which claimed responsibility for several major attacks in Jammu & Kashmir in the post-2000 period. Azhar also sharpened the sectarian divide in Pakistan—and put to use a number of cadres belonging to the Sunni extremist outfit Sipah-e-Sahaba.

Not surprisingly, the week-long hijacking saw a resurfacing of a war of words between India and Pakistan. While Pakistan blared its propaganda about India's external intelligence agency, R&AW, as having stage-managed the whole affair, India cried itself hoarse about the role of the ISI Directorate.

While the R&AW theory is too absurd to be taken seriously since India had nothing to gain from stage-managing the hijack, reports from Kandahar spoke of ISI personnel hanging in and around the airport. They were also seen using their communication equipment.

The fact that Pakistan twice refused permission to IC-814 to land in Lahore would indicate that some part of the establishment did not want to deal with the hijacking on Pakistani soil.

But there's little doubt in my mind that the end to the hijacking took place on terms that Pakistan and its intelligence agencies desired and dictated. It's possible that a section of Pakistan's myriad intelligence agencies was aware of the hijacking.

On the other hand, they didn't want the hijacked Indian Airlines aircraft to land at any Pakistani airport; Afghanistan was a much safer destination. At the time of the hijacking, Islamabad had a consulate in Kandahar and the telephone codes for the few numbers that operated in

Mullah Omar's headquarters were the same as that of Quetta in Pakistan.

Clearly, the hijacking was a professional job and conducted by terrorists who vanished into Pakistan. The operation could have been plotted and planned by the Harkat-ul-Mujahideen itself, in their desire to secure the release of their chief rabble-rouser Masood Azhar.

There was never any possibility that the Taliban would have acted against the interests of the hijackers. Remember, the Harkat had a major presence in Afghanistan and their 'jehad' was similar to that of the Taliban.

In that sense, the Vajpayee government's efforts to suggest that the Taliban would be amenable to armed action to secure the release of the hijackers was simply a case of whistling in the dark.

The Afghan base for a global jehad had been used effectively even before 11 September 2001, by the Harkat. The Kandahar hijacking represented the growing strength, capabilities and sophistication of anti-India jehadis, for whom Pakistan and Afghanistan presented vast territory in which to train and plot.

At the end of the hijacking and as the new millennium began, I understood that a new and dangerous phase had commenced in India–Pakistan relations.

Each time one felt that India–Pakistan relations had hit rock bottom, Islamabad and New Delhi showed that 'rock-bottom' was a perpetually shifting level for the two countries. The hijacking was the latest example.

I said in my report published in *The Hindu* on 31 December 1999, that yet another round of vicious media propaganda could have grave implications for bilateral relations:

> India, having engaged with Pakistan during the [hijack] crisis, must realize that the Musharraf

government is the reality in Pakistan. There is no option but to engage with it diplomatically. No one is suggesting rushing into dialogue, but the norms of civilized engagement must not be lost sight of.

The Indian case of Pakistan aiding, abetting, supporting and training militants is a very strong one. At every opportunity, India must remind Pakistan and the rest of the world about this fact.

But that should not prompt a propaganda campaign that could have unforeseen implications in relations between the two countries. The people of India and Pakistan deserve better as they enter the new millennium.

11

Can Musharraf Reverse the Zia Legacy?

AFGHANISTAN WAS NOT just a failed state in the latter half of the 1990s. It was a forgotten state. Forgotten by the rest of the world after the mujahideen did their job—evicted the last Soviet soldier from Afghanistan in 1989.

The world would have to pay a price for this induced amnesia. Afghanistan would become a base for Islamist terrorism in the name of an internationalist Islam. Afghanistan, under the Taliban, would be the host nation to Islamist brigades, honed to perfection by Osama bin Laden and his associates in Afghanistan, without let or hindrance.

What happened *after* the victory over the Soviet 'infidels' hadn't interested the United States and its allies. After having fought a long battle, the CIA then wanted to extricate itself from Afghanistan and the ISI—it had probably begun to apprehend what impact its actions might have on their own future. Suddenly, there were concerns about Pakistan's nuclear weapons programme.

When the Soviets had been the enemy, all means were justified—including the international 'jehad' that was launched under the eyes of the CIA in Afghanistan. After all, it was only a question of supplying money and arms to the mujahideen through the Pakistani ISI Directorate so that they could take on the Soviets in Afghanistan.

From funnelling arms to the sale of narcotics, ISI-led activities went on untrammelled in Afghanistan, with ripple effects in Pakistan. Secure in his alliance with the Americans, Chief Martial Law Administrator Zia-ul-Haq had presided over the future course not just of Pakistan, but events in Afghanistan as well.

What Zia had done was to bind Pakistan to Afghanistan. A lot of the money and weaponry that was to flow to Afghanistan remained in Pakistan. In reverse, narcotics began to enter Pakistan in huge quantities. The illegal trade in weapons became rampant.

In his fascinating book *A Journey to Disillusionment*, one of Pakistan's boldest politicians, Baloch chief Sherbaz Khan Mazari, is scathing about the corruption that prevailed during Zia's tenure.

Mazari, who was living in retirement in Karachi when I met him, spoke of a September 1987 meeting he had had with US ambassador to Pakistan, Arnold Raphel, who was to perish along with Zia in that C-130 crash of 17 August 1988.

Referring to the discussions he had entered into on Afghanistan, Mazari quoted Raphel as having said that Washington was upset that a significant portion of weaponry being supplied to the Afghan mujahideen was finding its way into foreign hands.

Later, Mazari said he heard that, with Zia-ul-Haq's consent, ISI chief Akhtar Abdul Rehman, the man appointed by the late dictator to oversee Afghan policy, had been selling large amounts of weaponry destined for the mujahideen to clandestine customers.

Mazari, a rare Pakistani politician with both principle and guts, said that Zia, in his twelve-year tenure, had eradicated what Bhutto had left of Pakistan's national institutions. The Supreme Court had been rendered inffectual, the press bludgeoned by threats or by means of the chequebook and businesspersons had found that they could influence policy by leaving suitcases full of cash at government ministries.

Apart from letting loose the hordes of the Jamaat-e-Islami's youth wing on secular students, Zia had introduced norms that would fundamentally alter the way in which ordinary Pakistanis went about their normal lives.

In his *Civil-Military Relations*, Saeed Shafqat says that Zia's military regime introduced symbolic regulations, including one that dictated that people must say their ritual prayers even during working hours. A new office culture had been introduced by Zia.

For criminal offences, Islamic punishments like amputation of hands and feet for theft, stoning to death for adultery and flogging for consuming alcohol were introduced and imposed selectively, Shafqat writes. In his view, this de-politicized a highly political people and put in place new standards of compliance.

Another unwelcome legacy from the Zia era was militant sectarianism. According to one estimate, about 4,000 persons have been killed in sectarian violence in Pakistan during the last two decades. There are also substantiated links between Sunni extremist groups like the Lashkar-e-Jhangvi and jehadi groups that operate in Pakistan, Afghanistan and Kashmir.

When one looks back, what are ten years in the life of a nation? Not much at one level; but a lot at another. The seeds of Islamist extremism had been firmly planted in the Pakistani body politic by Zia-ul-Haq.

So, when the sanctioned jehad ended in Afghanistan in 1989, the tens of thousands of jehadis collected from all parts of the world began their own private jehad—one which gained a 'political cause' after the Americans stationed their troops in Saudi Arabia in the early 1990s.

Much has been written about this period, but something which hasn't received the attention it deserves is the attitude and approach of the United States to a Taliban gaining in both strength and resources during 1996–7.

At that time, the US had been wooing the Taliban for its own ends; in the mistaken notion that a Sunni Afghanistan would serve as a bulwark against Shia Iran. How mistaken the notion would prove to be.

In a now declassified cable from the US State Department in Washington to the American Embassy in Islamabad (which handled Afghanistan at the time), specific instructions were issued on 28 September 1996, soon after the Taliban took control of Kabul, about how Americans were to deal with these turbaned 'students'.

Islamabad-based diplomats, according to the cable, were instructed to:

- demonstrate to the Taliban, US government willingness to deal with them 'as the new authorities in Kabul',
- seek information about their plans, programmes and policies, and
- express US government views on areas of key concern—stability, human rights, narcotics and terrorism.

'We have Embassy property in Kabul, for which we seek your protection. We would like to re-open our Embassy here [in Kabul], when security permits. We are considering when we could take this step. In the meantime, we would like to make frequent trips to Kabul to stay in contact with your Government,' American diplomats in Islamabad were instructed to say to the authorities in Afghanistan.

At the same time, the US government would inform the Taliban that it was moving to address their publicly stated concerns about the security of their missions in the US.

The US State Department cable reveals that Washington had wanted to do business with the Taliban, who were the new masters of Kabul and key parts of Afghanistan. Soon, the interests of Unocal, an American oil company, in setting up a Turkmenistan–Afghanistan–Pakistan gas pipeline would become clear. American diplomats would facilitate Unocal's efforts for the pipeline.

Pakistan, meanwhile, had begun its intervention in Jammu & Kashmir. By now, it had sufficient experience from Afghanistan on how a low-cost operation could be run. An insurgency, with devastating consequences for the people of Kashmir, already suffering at the hands of an insensitive Indian government, was now in play.

The Al-Qaeda and Osama bin Laden now turned their attention to the United States. In this larger game, the Taliban and their Amir-ul-Momineen, Mullah Mohammad Omar, a product of the Binori seminary in Karachi, were to play a critical role.

Osama needed a sanctuary after quitting Sudan, and Afghanistan provided the best alternative. The Saudi-born Al-Qaeda chief returned to Afghanistan in May 1996, months before the Taliban took Kabul. Here, you could train all you wanted; there was going to be little or no interference in the anti-American jehad that was being plotted.

With the Taliban marching through most of Afghanistan and a friendly government in Kabul, the international jehadis had little trouble in setting up a network that would eventually lead to the terrorist attacks of 11 September 2001 in the US.

It was a seamless sequence of movements. The borders between Afghanistan and Pakistan were irrelevant—the jehadis could come and go as they pleased. While Afghanistan afforded them the perfect base, Pakistan was the means of communication to the outside world. The solid support of the religious right in Pakistan, especially the Jamiat-Ulema-e-Islam (JUI) of Maulana Fazlur Rehman, to the Taliban and their associates, was critical.

To secure a mythical 'strategic depth', the Pakistani state propped up the Taliban and was the first country to recognize the hardline Islamist cabal, which proclaimed itself to be a government in May 1997.

Groups like the Harkat-ul-Mujahideen were encouraged and abetted by Pakistan's permanent establishment to train their cadres in Afghanistan to fight the jehad in Kashmir.

In his book *Taliban*, Ahmed Rashid states that the Kashmir issue was the driving force behind Islamabad's Afghan policy. According to the writer, the Taliban used this advantage cleverly, aware that Pakistan could refuse them nothing as long as they provided training centres for Kashmiri and Pakistani terrorists.

Rashid also provides clinching evidence of Pakistani state support to the Taliban. In the last days of June 1998, there was a flurry of activity in Pakistan's finance and foreign ministries to provide funds for the Taliban. On 28

June 1998, Pakistan's finance ministry authorized the release of Pakistani Rs 300 million to pay the salaries of Afghanistan's government officials and bureaucracy. This amount would cover those salaries for the next six months.

Writing in *The Hindu* on 22 August 1999, two years before the events of 11 September 2001, I pointed to the possible costs that the international community might have to incur for abandoning Afghanistan:

> Clearly, Osama [bin Laden] is a symptom of the larger disease caused by the Afghan jehad. Today's larger 'Islamic jehad' is potentially destabilizing to a large number of governments in Central Asia and beyond. If the US is serious about getting Osama and keeping Afghanistan free of 'jehadi elements', the Taliban regime will be an obvious target. A Taliban-dominated Afghanistan, which has nothing to do with democracy, is always capable of producing Osamas....
>
> If terrorism is to be countered, the Taliban will have to be weakened. A representative, multi-ethnic, pluralistic government in Kabul is the minimum requirement to attain this objective. *The primitive 'system' being operated by the Taliban is a constant threat to the well-being of the Afghans, but also the rest of the world* (emphasis added).

At the time I was in Pakistan, the religious right saw Osama and the Taliban as heroes and role models. I wrote in my August article:

> For the religious right, Osama is a bulwark against American 'hegemony', an expression of Islamic defiance of a 'satanic enemy'. Given the vast numbers of 'jehadi madrasas' in Pakistan, which provide recruits for all kinds of perceived 'Islamic causes', religious groups see Osama as a 'natural ally'.

To my mind, the jehadi infrastructure propped up and sustained by the military-intelligence complex in Pakistan was strategically seen as a low-cost operation to bleed India in Kashmir.

Using the Afghan model, produced in collaboration with the United States, the Pakistani state ran the Kashmiri jehad, always careful not to get its fingers directly burnt in what was happening; keeping the option of denial always available to itself.

The favourite word used by Pakistani officialdom was 'indigenous'. Spokesmen, ministers, army chiefs, prime ministers and Presidents, all said the same thing: whatever was happening in Kashmir was 'indigenous'.

But to an Indian journalist it was clear that Pakistan was culpable for what went on in Kashmir. Whether it was the Harkat-ul-Mujahideen, the Hizb-ul-Mujahideen or the Lashkar-e-Taiba—all of them maintained offices across Pakistan.

Their spokesmen were issuing statements; they were available for comment and would regularly hold press conferences in the 'good old days' before 11 September 2001.

You could walk into any market in Islamabad and purchase Islamist literature and tapes. Newspapers were full of reports from different parts of Pakistan that parents were offering their children to fight the jehad in Kashmir.

For all his efforts to be friendly with India, Nawaz Sharif could do nothing about the jehad industry directed at India. For the army, the young boys going from the Frontier Province and the Punjab to their deaths in India meant that they didn't have to risk the lives of their own men.

Every Bakri Id, Islamabad was full of animal hide collection centres set up by the jehadi organizations.

There was, in fact, competition among the groups over the funds that could be generated through sales and the levels of collections made.

Spokesmen for these jehadi groups had offices, and quoted bank account numbers to which contributions for the jehad could be sent. Obviously, the Pakistani state felt that there was nothing wrong in all this. The groups' publications were freely available.

In his book *Jihad-e-Kashmir and Afghanistan*, Mohammad Amir Rana (Masha'l Books, Lahore) reveals that Maulana Sadruddin, Amir of the Jamaat-e-Islami in Jammu & Kashmir, had met the then Pakistani President, Zia-ul-Haq, in Pakistan in 1983, over plans to begin an armed struggle in Kashmir. He had stopped over in Pakistan while returning to India from Haj, Rana writes. The plan for the struggle had reportedly even been given its final touches at this meeting.

Rana quotes Syed Salim Gardezi, a Jamaat leader on the Pakistani side of Kashmir, as saying that Jamaat boys from Jammu & Kashmir were sent for training to Afghanistan. In 1984, a two-member delegation led by Ghulam Hasan had crossed the Line of Control for training and then proceeded to Afghanistan.

In December 1989, as a young reporter, I had been asked by my paper to proceed from New Delhi for Srinagar to cover the kidnapping (referred to in the previous chapter) of Rubiya Sayeed, daughter of India's home minister Mufti Mohammad Sayeed. A medical student in Srinagar, Rubiya Sayeed had, like most people, used public transport when she moved around town.

Later, the Jammu & Kashmir Liberation Front (JKLF)—with young leaders like Yaseen Malik, Hamid Sheikh and Ashfaq Majid in the lead—had announced that it was responsible for the kidnapping that eventually happened. (Both Hamid Sheikh and Ashaq Majid were killed by security forces in the 1990s.)

Already, the boycott of the 1989 parliamentary elections in the Kashmir Valley had highlighted the distrust with which the Kashmiris viewed New Delhi. Suddenly, the kidnapping of Rubiya Sayeed thrust Kashmir into the international limelight. Kashmir became a global story and the Indian government, rightly, was pilloried for its many violations of the civil and democratic rights of the Kashmiri people.

Rubiya Sayeed was released after long and tortuous negotiations in downtown Srinagar by her JKLF captors. Several militants being held by the government were released in exchange.

Rubiya, a Pakistani source told me, had been taken across the LoC by her JKLF captors—something of which she may not have been aware. According to the information that I received, senior officers of the Pakistan Army were in the know of the kidnapping and were later seen doling huge sums of cash to the militants to continue their activities in the Kashmir Valley.

Clearly, the idea was to manipulate the kidnapping directly by bringing Ruibya to Pakistani-controlled Kashmir. I have been able to ascertain, from at least two Pakistani sources over the years, that Rubiya was in fact taken across the Line—a detail that has hitherto never been reported.

Mercifully, this nugget of information has surfaced years after the actual event was over. Had it come to light earlier, it would have lent an altogether different colour to the kidnapping episode—in which the role of Pakistan would have taken centre stage.

Interestingly, and to the best of my knowledge, Rubiya Sayeed has never spoken in public or given any interviews about her experience. Her sister, Mehbooba Mufti, is an active leader of the People's Democratic Party (PDP) in Jammu & Kashmir.

By the early part of 1990, it had become clear to Pakistan's permanent establishment that the JKLF had a mind of its own—so they created the Hizbul Mujahideen.

Down the line, the Harkat-ul-Ansar, later known as the Harkat-ul-Mujahideen, the Lashkar-e-Taiba and the Jaish-e-Muhammad of Masood Azhar, which split from the Harkat, would receive the patronage of Pakistan's permanent establishment.

In any case, the idea of an independent Kashmir is anathema to the Pakistani state structure; there is no way in which Islamabad is going to promote the JKLF's notions of an independent Kashmir.

During my stint in Islamabad, I could also see that while the Pakistani establishment backed boys and men to join the Kashmir and Afghan jehads (later against the Northern Alliance led by Ahmad Shah Masud), the list of 'martyrs' in Kashmir, regularly published by groups like the Lashkar, never contained the names of sons of Pakistani generals or the elite.

It was the poor Pakistani that went on jehad, in the hope that the *tanzeem* (jehadi outfit) that launched him would take care of his family. Martyrdom was essentially for the poor; the rich escaped these religious duties.

The only exception to this rule, I learnt after leaving Pakistan, was the son of a top Pakistani official, who was recovered from a terrorist training camp in Muzaffarabad.

My information suggests that the son went missing from home and was later recovered from a 'jehadi' camp in Muzaffarabad. No harm came to the son; he never actually participated in any 'jehadi' action.

However, the story suggests that the sons of the rich

and influential could also be persuaded by the 'jehadis' to sign up for the cause of Kashmir. In an environment where Islamist extremism received official support, such examples pointed to the widening appeal of militant Islam.

On the subject of official sanction to the jehadi cause, I was shocked to see that the Pakistani establishment, possibly under pressure after Kargil, was becoming more and more open in its support to the jehadi groups.

Even earlier, during the tenure of Pervez Musharraf, banners of the Harkat-ul-Ansar could be seen outside key buildings in Islamabad, including the now-defunct Parliament. There was no way these banners could have been put up without the consent of the Pakistani establishment. That was the extent of support that the Pakistani establishment was prepared to extend to the jehadis.

'Islam does not preach terrorism...Islam believes in jehad, a fight in the path of God. Wherever Muslims are being victimized or killed, Islam asks all Muslims to come to their aid,' Musharraf was reported as saying in *The Washington Post* on 4 February 2000.

The jehad that had begun in Afghanistan with international support, Musahrraf said, had now shifted to Kashmir. 'It is a freedom struggle. To call those activities terrorism is not correct.' The general was justifying the killings of civilians. He was saying loud and clear that there was no terrorism in Jammu & Kashmir—it was simply a freedom struggle.

I wrote in *The Hindu* at the time:

The 'jehad is not terrorism' statement made by Pakistan's Chief Executive...must have been greeted with cheers in Kandahar, headquarters of the Taliban Amir-ul-Momineen, Mullah Mohammad Omar.

> Ironically, it appears that rather than Pakistan having a moderating influence on the Taliban, the militia's agenda and position has been publicly justified by none other than Pakistan's supreme leader. The permission granted to 'Chechnya' to open an embassy in Kabul is a clear indication that the Taliban remains a firm supporter of an 'international jehad'....
>
> Even today, Pakistan has not publicly asked that Osama bin Laden, named the most wanted terrorist by the United States, be expelled from territory controlled by the Taliban. In fact, the Taliban foreign minister, Wakil Ahmed Mutawakkil, made it clear during a visit to Islamabad in January that Osama's return could not be demanded by Pakistan for the simple reason that he was not a Pakistani.[1]

On their part, the Taliban were cocking a snook at Pakistan. Given that the Taliban had very few diplomatic dealings with the rest of the world, apart from the Pakistanis and the Saudis, it fell to Islamabad to defend the Taliban's medieval policies in international fora. This didn't help Pakistan's image any.

The Pakistani state, on its part, was miffed that the US had abandoned Afghanistan after 1989. The supply of arms and money had dried up. Pakistan was no longer important to America. No one knew that the events of 11 September 2001 would change all this around.

In November 1997, this Pakistani perception—of being abandoned by America—was forcefully expressed by Foreign Minister Gohar Ayub Khan during a joint press conference with visiting US Secretary of State Madeleine Albright in Islamabad.

If the Americans had abandoned Pakistan, they also came to understand that Islamabad was on the wrong path. Kargil had convinced Washington that Pakistan was an adventurist state. There was a need to take corrective measures.

There was long and sustained debate within the Clinton administration on whether or not the President should add Pakistan to his itinerary during his visit to India in March 2000.

The best piece of advice to Pakistan came in a speech US President Bill Clinton delivered live on Pakistan Television. Clinton's visit was pre-negotiated. The President would be permitted a live address on Pakistan Television to speak his mind to the people of Pakistan. No pictures were to be shown shaking hands with Musharraf.

It was all tightly regulated. The Americans went to the extent of saying that if the military government was not amenable to these conditions, there would be no visit at all. Musharraf and Co. acquiesced.

As I watched what I thought was his arrival live on PTV, the commentator announced that Clinton had arrived. But that was only a decoy aircraft, with a Clinton look-alike alighting at the Chaklala air base near Islamabad. The real Clinton would arrive soon after.

Such unprecedented security precautions were a statement on what the Clinton administration thought of the Musharraf regime and the threats that the US President might face during his brief stay in Islamabad.

To Clinton's credit, he used his PTV speech to deliver a blunt message to Pakistan on 25 March:

> Like all key moments in human history, this one poses some hard choices, for this era does not reward people who struggle in vain to redraw borders with blood [read as a reference to Kargil]. It belongs to those with the vision to look beyond borders, for partners and commerce and trade...I believe Pakistan can make its way through the trouble, and build a

future worthy of the vision of its founders: a stable, prosperous, democratic Pakistan, secure in its borders, friendly with its neighbours, confident in its future.

Calling for respect for the Line of Control by both India and Pakistan, Clinton suggested revisiting the February 1999 Lahore process:

> I have listened carefully to General Musharraf and others. I understand your concerns about Kashmir. I share your conviction that human rights of all its people must be respected. But a stark truth must also be faced. There is no military solution to Kashmir. International sympathy, support and intervention cannot be won by provoking a larger, bloodier conflict. On the contrary, sympathy and support will be lost. And no matter how great the grievance, it is wrong to support attacks against civilians across the Line of Control.

Those who bombed bus stations, targetted embassies or killed those who uphold the law were not heroes, they were common enemies of Pakistan and the US, Clinton said, adding that Islamabad needed to intensify efforts against those who inflict terror.

He didn't spare Pakistan's military regime either:

> We share your disappointment that previous democratic governments in Pakistan did not do better for their citizens. But one thing is certain: democracy cannot develop if it is constantly uprooted before it has a chance to firmly take hold. Successful democratic government takes time and patience and hard work. The answer to flawed democracy is not to end democracy, but to improve it.

The President's advice was like water off a duck's back. Musharraf wasn't buying any of this. He had his own ideas. Soon after Clinton left Pakistan, a tough-talking Chief Executive held a press conference.

Asked whether the Government of Pakistan had given any sort of assurance to stop the infiltration of militants into Indian Kashmir, Musharraf replied:

> There was no assurance because there was no question. Whatever is happening in Kashmir is indigenous...I did say [to Clinton] there is a requirement of reciprocal activities to reduce tensions, which means that they [the Indians] need to stop human rights' violations there [in Kashmir]...and then we could also use our influence to moderate the activity of freedom fighters.

To a question on the existence of terrorist training camps in Muzaffarabad and other parts of Pakistan-controlled territory, the General was equally unrelenting:

> This is something which also came up during our discussions with President Clinton...there is people's involvement with Kashmir. It started with the masses' uprising in Indian-held Kashmir and then the people of AJK [Azad Jammu & Kashmir] and Pakistan living here and abroad got involved in it...it is not government-sponsored...nobody is allowed to cross the Line of Control...so we are trying our best and not allowing anybody to go across. Despite that, if some people are infiltrating across, it is not with our knowledge.

So, what was the general saying here? He was admitting that Pakistan had 'influence' over the freedom fighters or the 'jehadis'—if India stopped human rights' violations, Pakistan could use its influence to 'moderate' the activities of the jehadis. There was no promise to 'end' the activities of the freedom fighters, only to moderate them. It was clear that Musharraf had no intention of stopping anybody from crossing the Line of Control—business was to go on as usual.

It was a pity that Pakistan didn't heed the suggestions made by Clinton. But then, institutional aggressiveness against India, which was linked to sponsoring the jehadis in both Pakistan and Afghanistan, was something that the permanent establishment was not prepared to abandon. And, long used to American doles and arms supplies, the generals in Pakistan were annoyed that Washington had not come out in open support of the military takeover by the faujis.

It would take the events of 11 September 2001 for Pakistan to partly reverse course and once again become a beneficiary of American aid—yet again given for very selfish reasons by the George W. Bush administration.

Deposing before the 9/11 Commission in March 2004, US Secretary of State Colin Powell spoke in some detail of the ultimatum that he had given Musharraf after the September attacks: you are either with us or against us. He went on to say:

> I just might point out that with respect to Pakistan, consistent with the decisions that we had made in early September, after 9/11, within two days, [Deputy Secretary of State] Mr [Richard] Armitage had contacted the Pakistani intelligence chiefs who...happened to be in the United States, and laid out what we now needed from Pakistan. The time for diplomacy and discussions was over; we needed immediate action. And Mr Armitage laid out seven specific steps for Pakistan to take to join us in this effort. We gave them twenty-four to forty-eight hours to consider it, and then I called President Musharraf

and said, 'We need your answer now. We need you as part of this campaign, this crusade.' And President Musharraf made a historic and strategic decision that evening when I spoke to him, changed his policy and became a partner in this effort as opposed to a hindrance to the effort.

On 23 October 2001, Musharraf was asked by Larry King of CNN: 'You had previously supported the Taliban, Mr President. What prompted you to change that policy?' The general's reply was candid:

> Well, the environment changed. As I have always been saying, policies are made in accordance with the environment that is prevailing. After the 11th of September, however, the environment changed drastically. Therefore, the requirement for adjusting the policies in accordance with the ground realities.

Musharraf was admitting that the change in policy had been made under pressure; the United States was no longer going to tolerate any support for the Taliban from Pakistan.

However, reversing Zia's legacy was quite another matter.

In April 2000, Musharraf announced that first information reports would be registered in blasphemy cases only after a preliminary inquiry by a deputy commissioner and that honour killings would be treated as murder.

Within days, the general had to eat his own words and withdraw his own directions. Obviously, he had been prevailed upon that such moves would not go down well in the Pakistani body politic.

To my mind, Musharraf lacks the vision and the ability to mobilize people's support in favour of a moderate

Pakistan, which he never tires of advocating. After the events of 9/11, Musharraf has repeatedly advocated to international audiences the benefits that would flow from a moderate Pakistan. But liberal credentials of individuals or even generals don't matter in Pakistan. Western three-piece suits may have gained popularity in Musharraf's tenure as opposed to the shalwar–kameez in Zia's and Nawaz Sharif's time. But the changes are cosmetic.

While there has been some change for the better, liberalism is unlikely to trickle down from the top in Pakistan. A society which has been sabotaged from within by its ruling elite, will need much more than the personal liberalism of a general, to rid itself of the cancers of Islamist extremism, cronyism and feudal practices.

In a country where the mullahs reign supreme, Musharraf's liberal-sounding words are a refreshing change from the Islamist rhetoric that substituted for governance in Pakistan. But Musharraf's words haven't checked the ever-growing strength of Islamist forces in Pakistan.

Speeches and pronouncements are not going to alter the situation on the ground. The general's addresses on television, interesting as they may seem, cannot create opinion in favour of moderation and rejection of Islamist groups.

Musharraf's own person was threatened by the jehadis twice in December 2003. It was the first time such attempts had been made on the life of a Pakistani army chief. It showed the extent of anger in some circles against Musharraf's U-turn on both Afghanistan and the support to the jehadis.

The respected Pakistani monthly, *Newsline*, published a report on Amjad Farooqui, the man responsible for the December 2003 assassination attempts on Musharraf, in its June 2004 issue:

A senior police investigator claims that the recent [terrorist] attacks in Karachi may have been planned by Amjad Farooqui, believed to be the mastermind behind the two assassination bids on Musharraf's life in December last year, with the help of low-ranking air force and military personnel and fellow jihadis. The thirty-year-old Farooqui [killed in an encounter in September 2004] hails from Toba Tek Singh in the Punjab, and belongs to a Sunni extremist group, the Harkat-e-Jihad Islami. Believed to have close links with the Al-Qaeda leadership, he is an absconder in the kidnapping and murder case of the *Wall Street Journal* reporter, Daniel Pearl.

The Harkat-e-Jihad Islami, an internationalist Islamist outfit in origin, has a long history of sending jehadis into Kashmir. Its leaders have been closely associated with the parent 'Harkat' and have worked in association with the faction led by Fazlur Rehman Khalil.

During the abortive bid for power by Major-General Zaheer-ul-Islam Abbasi in 1995, the Harkat-e-Jehadi Islami had been closely associated with this effort. Its Amir (chief), Qari Saifullah Akhtar, later became a government witness in the case against Abbasi, who at one time worked as Pakistan's military advisor in New Delhi.

Zahid Hussein (*Newsline*, August 2004) provided an account of the growing influence of the jehadi groups:

> ...Some of these new terrorist groups have penetrated into the ranks of the military, police and intelligence agencies. Several military personnel were arrested earlier this year for their involvement in the attack on President Musharraf and on suspicion of having links with pro Al-Qaeda Islamic militant groups. Some analysts maintain that the influence of the Islamic militants is now extremely deep-rooted, particularly among the soldiers and junior officers.

The growing influence of militant groups within the police force has also got alarm bells ringing. At least three policemen acted as suicide bombers in the attacks on Shiite mosques in Karachi and Quetta, which have also been hit by the spate of sectarian violence. A security officer posted at the Punjab chief minister's house has also been arrested for his links with Al-Qaeda.

In a poorly developed, seriously under-educated society with a burgeoning population of young people looking for gainful employment, which the state and private sector cannot provide, recruits for the jehad are not difficult to find.

My larger point is that the battle against extremism is a political one, a battle Musharraf cannot fight alone, or even with the support of his corps commanders and a co-opted prime minister.

This battle has to be fought in the villages and towns of Pakistan by a force that believes the country should be governed by the rule of law. Young people loitering around the mosques of Pakistan, or being fed by the madrassas, must see education, development and jobs as a real option; not simply as a carrot to wean them away from Islamist extremism.

Such a battle can only be fought politically. It's a tall order in a country where the military is free to tinker with the levers of power even as a civilian dispensation looks to it for advice and guidance.

Musharraf's record in addressing the problems of Pakistan, especially that of religious extremism, is poor. It has been a case of one step forward, two steps back.

The religious right in Pakistan continues to enjoy veto power over government policy. No government or general can, for instance, repeal the Hudood laws; a long-standing demand of Pakistan civil society. Including that of General Musharraf, who amended the Hudood laws in December 2006, through the Women's Protection Bill, but could not find the courage to repeal the laws.

On more than one occasion, sections of the religious right, such as the Jamaat-e-Islami, have chosen to shy away from the electoral path. But their stormtroopers are always available to scuttle a marathon run in which women participate or meetings of civil society groups who protest against fundamentalism and orthodoxy.

The veto-power, in a sense, flows from sheer street-power.

As far as General Musharraf is concerned, he looks smart and speaks well, but he, too, has shown himself to be the victim of the same forces that he had promised to tackle. The general, who entered into tactical alliances with the religious right to legitimize his rule, is on record to state that he cannot open several fronts at the same time.

Everyone knows that the reversal of policy on Afghanistan and the partial cut-down of support to the 'Kashmiri' cause is a result of American pressure. This complicates the matter even further for Pakistan and Musharraf.

Like in most parts of the world, in Pakistan the Americans are growing unpopular by the day. The people view Americans as an evil empire, composed of people who used them and moved on.

Implementing an American agenda can only undermine the prestige of a Pakistani leader. And President Musharraf is no exception. His popularity is at an ebb. The general may have consolidated his rule, but siding with the Americans has made him a target of his own people.

All the signs emanating from Pakistan suggest that

religious forces are consolidating their strength. Islamist militants aren't averse to targetting the Pakistani state or individuals who, they believe, have sold themselves to the Americans.

In the final analysis, General Musharaf has failed to put Pakistan on the road to becoming a more tolerant, moderate society. He hasn't been able to undo the wrongs of Zia-ul-Haq's pernicious legacy.

Ending the veto-power of the religious right will need more than the professed personal liberalism of a military general in Pakistan. It will need a political party that can mobilize the people to uphold the rule of law, create jobs and educate the masses.

12

India and Pakistan: Looking to the Future

Prime Minister Vajpayee said that in order to take forward and sustain the dialogue process, violence, hostility and terrorism must be prevented. President Musharraf reassured Prime Minister Vajpayee that he will not permit any territory under Pakistan's control to be used to support terrorism in any manner.

—Excerpt from the India–Pakistan joint press statement issued on 6 January 2004, in Islamabad

Conscious of the historic opportunity created by the improved environment in relations, and the overwhelming desire of the peoples of the two countries for durable peace and recognizing their responsibility to continue to move forward towards

*that objective, the two leaders had substantive talks
on all issues. They determined that the peace process
was now irreversible.*

—Pervez Musharraf and Manmohan Singh
in their joint statement issued on 18 April 2005

IT'S DIFFERENT AND it's working. Islamabad and New
Delhi have finally placed their relationship on a new
footing after Prime Minister Vajpayee's April 2003 'hand
of friendship' offer in Srinagar, which was followed by a
series of contacts leading to the 6 January 2004 joint
statement between the two countries.

Since 2003–4, India and Pakistan have managed to
put a lid on their differences; though their dramatic
progress on the bilateral front has slowed, measures like
the Srinagar–Muzaffarabad bus service in April 2005 are
a sign that the rapprochement process is for real.

After the October 1999 coup, India, in any case, had
opted to isolate the Musharraf regime internationally, and
stated publicly that it would not hold talks with a military
government that sponsored terrorism in India.

Musharraf, who had assumed the office of President
in June 2001, was, simultaneously, under tremendous
pressure from the United States to halt support to extremist
groups and crack down on Al-Qaeda and its offshoots in
Pakistan.

The army chief assumed the office of President *after*
he received an invitation in May 2001 from Prime Minister
Vajpayee to visit India at his convenience. The action
showed that the Pakistani leader wanted to be received
with full protocol in India—he wanted to be given the
honour accorded to a head of state and not merely to that
of his title of a Chief Executive.

After months of trying to isolate the Musharraf regime, the invitation to the Pakistani leader marked a dramatic reversal of the BJP-led government's untenable policy of having no contact with Pakistan till cross-border terrorism ended.

Musharraf's visit to Agra in July 2001 yielded precious little results, except to add to the atmosphere of tension and escalate the verbal war between the two countries. A senior Pakistani official told me later that Islamabad actually suspected a 'trap' when the invitation was extended to Musharraf.

Soon after, the events of 11 September and the attack on India's Parliament on 13 December 2001 would alter the situation to the Pakistani leader's disadvantage in the region. Afghanistan would have to be abandoned as the Americans sounded a strong note of warning to Pakistan on that score.

In the wake of the attack on India's Parliament, it seemed that the two countries were on the brink of war. A simultaneous strategy of military and diplomatic pressure on Pakistan was then mounted by New Delhi.

Tens of thousands of troops were mobilized by India in December. Typically, Pakistan responded in kind. Troops on both sides, eyeball-to-eyeball, remained mobilized till October 2002, when India announced a sudden and unilateral pullback or what it called 'redeployment'.

A series of diplomatic measures, which essentially hurt ordinary people on both sides of the border, were also taken by India. On 21 December 2001, India recalled its high commissioner from Pakistan and announced the suspension of the Attari–Lahore Samjhauta Express and the Delhi–Lahore bus service from 1 January 2002.

The Vajpayee government, which had switched to panic mode and being run by the hawks, announced further measures on 27 December. These were:

- suspension of over-flight facilities to Pakistan and Pakistan Airlines operations into India from 1 January 2002
- a 50-per-cent reduction in the strength of the Pakistani high commission in India
- restriction on the movement of Pakistan high commission staffers and their families to the municipal limits of New Delhi

Pakistan reciprocated in kind. And on 31 December, India handed over to Pakistan a list of twenty fugitives, demanding that these persons, who enjoyed safe haven in Pakistan, should be apprehended and extradited to India.

The pressure on Musharraf was growing. As India declared its full support for George W. Bush's 'war on terrorism' after 9/11, Musharraf found the need to make changes in both rhetoric and public posture.

I suspect that the Americans, whatever they might have said in public, were not terribly unhappy at the pressure India began mounting on Pakistan after the attack on Parliament.

As part of his tango with the United States, Musharraf announced a ban on the Jaish-e-Muhammad and the Lashkar-e-Taiba on 12 January 2002, in a televised address. But what the 'ban' meant was far from clear. It still isn't clear.

During the speech, which received wide publicity, the President promised that Pakistan would not allow its territory to be used for any terrorist activity anywhere in the world:

No organization will be allowed to indulge in terrorism in the name of Kashmir. We condemn the terrorist acts of 11 September ... and 13 December.

> Anyone found involved in any terrorist act would be
> dealt with sternly. Strict action will be taken against
> any Pakistani individual, group or organization
> involved in terrorism within or outside the country.

The general also had a clear message for Vajpayee. While
calling for a dialogue to resolve the Kashmir issue, the
President said, in his capacity as commander of the armed
forces of Pakistan:

> The armed forces are fully prepared and deployed to
> meet any challenge...let there be no attempt at crossing
> the border in any sector as it will be met with full
> force. Do not entertain any illusions on this account.

With India, the tensions after the attack on Parliament
would abate only when Prime Minister Vajpayee,
apparently out of the blue, offered to make peace with
Pakistan in the course of an address in Srinagar in April
2003.

Vajpayee's offer to smoke the peace pipe with Pakistan
again was as dramatic as his government's decision to
mobilize India's forces after the terrorist attack on its
Parliament.

The offer was well received in Pakistan, and other
parts of the world, and appeared part of an American-
choreographed attempt to end a prolonged period of
hostility between India and Pakistan. A telephone call
from Pakistani Prime Minister Mir Zafarullah Khan Jamali
to Vajpayee followed the Indian leader's speech in Srinagar.

Just four days before his about-turn speech in Srinagar
on 18 April 2003, Prime Minister Vajpayee had declared
in Sikkim that talks with Pakistan would only take place
after Pakistan ended cross-border terrorism.[1]

There's little doubt that the speech stood the Vajpayee

government's previous Pakistan policy on its head. After four years of bitter rhetorical exchanges, and of threatening the Pakistanis with war, the Prime Minister had backed off.

Flip-flops in India's Pakistan policy was a feature of the Vajpayee government. However, the Srinagar speech bailed out India from continuing with its disastrous policy of having no direct contact with Pakistan, opting instead to activate a channel through the Americans.

From 1 January 2004, India and Pakistan resumed over-flights and the Samjhauta Express began rolling from 15 January. The Lahore–Delhi bus service had already become operational on 11 July 2003. It was also decided to restore the full strength of the respective high commissions in New Delhi and Islamabad.

To me, the first sign that Pakistan was trying to chip away at its 'support jehad' policies came in October 2001, when Musharraf sacked his ISI chief and old pal, Mahmud Ahmed, and appointed Ehsan-ul-Haq in his place. Mahmud, who was widely believed to be supportive of jehad in Afghanistan and Kashmir, was given his marching orders by his chief.

Like another senior general, Muzaffar Hussain Usmani, who was sidelined, Mahmud chose to retire. Another close Musharraf aide during the Kargil war, Aziz Khan, was kicked upstairs as chairman, Joint Chiefs of Staff Committee.

Musharraf had broken away from the three generals who had ensured that he returned safely to Pakistan on 12 October 1999, after Nawaz Sharif tried to divert his civilian aircraft on a regular flight from Colombo to Karachi. These three generals, Musharraf felt, were a liability in the new situation where Americans were increasingly involved in Pakistan–Afghanistan affairs.

At the same time, the Pakistani leader felt comfortable enough to remove from positions of importance three key players without whom he could not have dealt with Nawaz Sharif.

After the events of 9/11, the United States became a direct player in the politics of the region. No longer was it content to stay on the sidelines; its involvement in Afghanistan and the strategic objective of rooting out Islamist terrorism meant that Washington would now demand the compliance of Musharraf and Co. in its 'war' against terrorism.

American interest lay in ensuring that Musharraf not be sidetracked from the principal task Washington had allocated him: to break the back of the Al-Qaeda in Pakistan and provide information about the Al-Qaeda network in Afghanistan.

The Americans also had significant stakes in relations between India and Pakistan. From preparing the ground for the Lahore Summit in 1999 to the Pakistani suggestion of a 'strategic restraint regime' to India in 1998, the Americans had been smack in the middle of the India–Pakistan process.

Conscious of the Government of India's sensibilities that there should be no hint of any mediation, each time an American official came visiting, he would state louder than the last that there was no question of Washington mediating between India and Pakistan.

Deputy Secretary of State Richard Armitage was a regular visitor to Islamabad and New Delhi in 2002; Defence Secretary Donald Rumsfeld, too, travelled to the region in the same period.

In fact, a June 2002 visit to the region by Armitage was key to the lowering of the general tension. After meeting the Pakistani leader in Islamabad, Armitage flew to New Delhi and informed Vajpayee on 7 June that Musharraf had pledged to 'stop cross-border infiltration permanently'.

On the same day, External Affairs Minister Jaswant Singh told reporters that if Musharraf's pledge was 'converted on the ground into action...India will reciprocate in a manner that is befitting'.

The Armitage visit brought immediate results. In the first departure from its hard-line stance, New Delhi unilaterally announced on 10 June that it would lift the ban on Pakistani aircraft using Indian air space.

On 13 June, Indian Defence Minister George Fernandes said, after a meeting with US Secretary of Defence Donald Rumsfeld in New Delhi, that some 'understandings' had been reached between India and the US that could lead to the creation of a better atmosphere in South Asia. Rumsfeld, after his meeting with Indian leaders, left for Pakistan.[2]

All this would lead to a ceasefire between India and Pakistan in November 2003—one of the most successful measures towards détente ever taken by the two sides. At the time the ceasefire took effect, no one was aware that Brajesh Mishra, Vajpayee's confidante and national security adviser, and Tariq Aziz, Musharraf's point-man and secretary, National Security Council, had met secretly to choreograph the ceasefire announcement.

All this would also lead to the successful summit meeting between Musharraf and Vajpayee in Islamabad in 2004. While India and Pakistan were keen to stress their 'bilateral' engagement, the reality lay elsewhere.

US Secretary of State Colin Powell publicly took credit for the rapprochement process between India and Pakistan. On 10 January 2004, Powell told the *US News and World Report*:

We've been working with the Indians and Pakistanis
for almost two years, from a period of, 'we're going
to nuclear war this weekend,' to, you know, this
historic change. And so I think that a lot of the seeds
that were planted are now germinating and you'll
[see] us harvesting the crops.

A few days earlier, on 7 January, Powell had told the ABC
Nightline programme:

And as we enter 2004, I think we've got quite a few
things we can point to where our foreign policy has
been successful, whether it's helping the Indians and
the Pakistanis get out of a crisis that was almost on
the verge of nuclear war—you remember how scared
everybody was about that just eighteen months ago.
We've worked closely with them and we saw success.

Some months later, in October 2004, Powell would go
further and reveal the extent of American involvement in
pushing the India–Pakistan dialogue forward. No longer
hesitant to take the credit, he told *USA Today* in an
interview:

And I'll never forget the day that President Musharraf,
in one of our conversations, as the conversation was
ending and the crisis had started to abate about then,
said to me, 'Do you think if my Prime Minister, the
Pakistani Prime Minister, were to call the Indian
Prime Minister, he would take the call?

I said, 'I'll call you back in a little while.' And we
set it up, the call was made. We also arranged for the
call to be 'How are you?' 'Fine. How are you?'
'Fine.'—just to begin this dialogue.

And now the dialogue has paid off with the
return of diplomatic relations, travel between the two
countries, and the ministers are meeting and talking

about the major outstanding issues that are still there between the two countries....

And many people were telling me all week long, there's going to be a war this weekend and it might go nuclear....It didn't happen, and it didn't happen because a lot of people worked on it over an extended period of time; the United States, United Kingdom, China. A lot of my colleagues and I spent an enormous amount of time on this and found a way to stop that mobilization or at least freeze it until we could get it moving in the other direction....

I think you have to keep engaged with these nations and with the personalities in these nations. And you also have to keep some perspective about where they were and where they are now and where they may be, where you hope they are heading in the future.

So, what Powell was saying that it was not the leaderships of India and Pakistan that scripted the breakthrough in their tense relationship, but the US, acting in concert, not just with Britain, but China as well. Analysts should be grateful to Mr Powell for what he revealed.

The Bush administration official was taking credit for scripting the 28 April 2003 telephone call that Prime Minister Jamali made to Vajpayee, during which the two leaders agreed to reappoint high commissioners and resume civil aviation links.

And, not only was the call 'fixed', Powell also engineered what was going to be said by the two prime ministers for starters. Not only did it reflect poorly on the Pakistani leadership, it revealed that the Vajpayee government was more than willing to be led by the Americans.

On 6 January 2004, soon after the Vajpayee–

Musharraf meeting in Islamabad, Pakistan conceded for the first time ever in an official, bilateral document with India that terrorism was an issue that it had to address. And, what was more important, there was no crowing on India's part after the ink dried on that statement.

Having moved to New Delhi as *The Hindu*'s diplomatic correspondent in July 2002, I returned to Islamabad to report this historic sideline meeting between Vajpayee and Pakistan President Pervez Musharraf.

I asked Brajesh Mishra, who had been negotiating the draft with the Pakistanis since 1 January, at a press conference in Islamabad, if this meant that India and Pakistan could now cooperate on tackling terrorism together.

Mishra responded:

> Amit...as we proceed along the lines of this...statement, and there is normalization of relations between our two countries, and the dialogue process moves forward, there is certainly the possibility, indeed the likelihood, of cooperation between the two countries to fight terrorism together. I am sure the [external affairs] minister [Yashwant Sinha] would have said it but I think I should say [it]. Please don't look at this document as a victory for one side or the other. It is a victory for peace and prosperity, for the people of India and Pakistan, and South Asia...in my view...it's a win-win situation for all of us.

I was in Pakistan for the January SAARC summit, and saw the joint statement that was produced. I was puzzled over the change in Musharraf's stance. Several Pakistani friends asked me when I was there: has Musharraf given in to Indian demands? I could not provide a coherent answer.

Matters, however, would become clear in the next few weeks. Even as Musharraf agreed to the joint statement with Vajpayee, there was a bigger crisis that had taken hold of him—the scientist Abdul Qadeer Khan affair—which would hit the headlines in less than a month.

Pakistan's national hero had been branded as the biggest-ever proliferator and profiteer from the sale of nuclear weapons technology to North Korea, Libya and Iran. The Americans had been working on his case for long and had now confronted Musharraf with proof.

In my understanding, Musharraf was aware that he couldn't fight on two fronts: deal with the fallout of the Qadeer Khan affair *and* tackle an aggressive India at the same time.

The re-initiation of the peace process with India at the time, therefore, made complete strategic sense. He wanted to keep the India front quiet while he dealt with the fallout from the Qadeer Khan scam.

A report in *The News* by well-informed Pakistani correspondent Kamran Khan stated that Richard Armitage had confronted Musharraf in Islamabad with evidence of the Qadeer Khan smuggling-ring during a meeting in October 2003.[3]

It had, the report said, been followed up with a letter from the International Atomic Energy Agency to Pakistan, which endorsed the American intelligence findings.

Musharraf may have been genuine in his promise to accommodate Indian concerns on the issue of terrorism, but he was pragmatic enough to realize that New Delhi would have the ultimate stick—the accusation that Pakistan was a proliferator state—to beat him with.

In a departure from the hammer-Pakistan-at-every-instance stance of the BJP, which had been visible in the past couple of years, the Vajpayee government also adopted an uncharacteristically low-key approach to the Qadeer Khan affair.

More than anything else, this case had the potential of pointing out to the world that India's worst-case fears of Pakistan were true: the country was leaking nuclear weapons technology. If there ever was a case for a definition of Pakistan as a pariah state, this was it. But, India would not exercise this option.

India's silence was only broken when External Affairs Minister Yashwant Sinha finally reacted to the Khan affair at a press conference with British Foreign Secretary Jack Straw, following a pointed question on 6 February 2004:

> Obviously, it appears to me, that things [the Khan affair] will not stop here because it is not merely an internal matter of Pakistan. It is a matter which concerns the entire international community.
>
> Pakistan itself is not a signatory to the Nuclear Non-proliferation Treaty but as Jack Straw said, Libya and Iran are. There are issues which will have to be debated by the IAEA [International Atomic Energy Agency] and elsewhere and resolved so that we have more responsible behaviour from countries which have nuclear capability.

It was a tame reaction from a party that was used to going for Pakistan's jugular. With a major agreement under its belt, India didn't want to be seen polluting the improved bilateral environment with any rhetoric against Pakistan.

Also, India was aware that President Bush himself wasn't going after the Pakistani army, which had backed and supported the clandestine nuclear programme all those years. The blame was basically being placed at the door of a single individual—Abdul Qadeer Khan.

Anyone with elementary knowledge of the Pakistani state structure was aware that the army intelligence establishment had had to have known of Khan's activities. The Pakistani state is a most suspicious creature and its myriad intelligence agencies are always watching every one who counts.

The Americans, whose single point focus in Pakistan at the time was getting to the Al-Qaeda leadership, had made a determination that they didn't want to rock Musharraf's boat.

So, they went along with the Pakistani contention that it was an individual, and not the military as an institution, that was responsible for the world's largest nuclear smuggling-ring ever.

The Government of India, too, fell in line—anxious not to disturb the Americans—since Washington and New Delhi were new-found allies whose strategic interests were in congruence.

India never took a public position that would have led to an investigation by the International Atomic Energy Agency into the Khan affair.

After the former national hero Qadeer Khan went on television and apologized for his sins, Musharraf pardoned him, and Khan now lives under house arrest in Islamabad. So ended the career of a man who was central to creating Pakistan's nuclear deterrent.

I believe that this context helped in clinching the January 2004 joint statement between the two countries, which generated a new momentum in India–Pakistan relations. General Musharraf believed that it would be politic not to have to deal with an aggressive India and the staggering blow from the Khan affair at the same time.

In an interview to BBC's *Hard Talk* programme in April 2005, national security adviser Brajesh Mishra provided a glimpse into his seven-month-long contacts with his Pakistani counterpart, Tariq Aziz, and the fact that Musharraf desperately wanted an agreement in Islamabad in 2004:

> Those discussions were extremely critical and, in fact, without them the 6 January statement of last year would not have come about. We had three meetings outside India and Pakistan and in those three meetings we were able to hammer out the differences on how to proceed to initiate or re-initiate the composite dialogue...the critical period was when I went to Islamabad, two days in advance of the SAARC Summit, and had four or five rounds with Tariq Aziz to hammer out the statement of 6 January 2004.
>
> ...He [Musharraf] made a commitment in writing on not permitting terrorism from Pakistani-controlled territory in any manner. Now this is a commitment given by a head of state to a head of government from India and I think we should take it seriously. We took it seriously at that time....It was not a question of trust or distrust. It was a question of assessing what were his compulsions.
>
> He [Musharraf] desperately needed a joint statement when we were in Islamabad. And he made it very clear. We were prepared to come away without a statement. Having gone there for a SAARC summit, having made our contribution there, we were quite satisfied. We could have come back without a statement. But he was extremely keen to have a joint statement with Prime Minister Vajpayee which he could not get in Agra.

Apart from the return to the composite dialogue that had collapsed on account of Kargil, people-to-people contacts between India and Pakistan have now resumed in a big way. Any excuse is good enough for people to be travelling—whether it is for reasons of cricket matches, business, seminars or conferences.

As part of the composite dialogue, home secretaries, defence secretaries, culture secretaries, foreign secretaries, joint secretaries and directors from India and Pakistan are regularly crossing the border to meet and discuss points of difference.

Every meeting cannot produce a breakthrough, but the fact is that there is no danger of the eight-agenda-point composite dialogue process collapsing. As late as 1997, Pakistan interrupted this very same process when it claimed that India was not keen on discussing the Kashmir issue seriously.

After initial hiccups, the Pakistanis and the new Congress-led United Progressive Alliance (UPA) government, which took power in May 2004, has settled down to a normal relationship of dialogue and discussion with Pakistan on a range of issues, including Kashmir.

As a reporter used to following details about the India–Pakistan relationship, I believe details of individual meetings, while important, no longer provide a complete picture of the emerging entente between New Delhi and Islamabad.

It was this focus on the big picture that led to the first crossing by bus of the LoC on 7 April 2005. A long battle between the two countries on the kind of travel documents to be used by passengers using the Srinagar–Muzaffarabad bus had been clinched in February 2005, during the visit of External Affairs Minister Natwar Singh to Islamabad.

And, then, the unimaginable happened between Pakistan and India. President Musharraf and Prime Minister Manmohan Singh 'determined' in April 2005 that the peace process between the two countries was 'now irreversible'.

It's a big statement from Indian and Pakistani leaders, never before used or heard of in the history of their troubled relationship in an official document. It's also a major commitment to the people of India and Pakistan—that the leaderships have to deliver on their agreement.

The people, hitherto voiceless in the peace process, finally seem to matter in the suspicious and abusive nature of Pakistan–India relations. They will have to keep reminding Messrs Musharraf and Manmohan Singh of the need to keep the peace process irreversible.

Yes, the issue of terrorism remains on the agenda; Musharraf has, so far, been unable or willing to tackle three men and their groups around whom Indian concerns should revolve: Masood Azhar (Jaish-e-Muhammad), Hafiz Saeed (Lashkar-e-Taiba) and Fazlur Rehman Khalil (Harkat-ul-Mujahideen).

All three of these men are Pakistanis; all three of them have claimed responsibility for terrorist actions in India; all three of them have been picked up, 'detained' and then released by the Pakistani state on more than one occasion.

These men may have been picked up from time to time, but appear free to get on with their activities. Their jehadi groups, meanwhile, continue the mayhem in Kashmir, in other parts of India, and in Pakistan.

To me, the litmus test of Musharraf's sincerity will be what is done with Azhar, Saeed and Khalil and their groups. So far, it would appear that a serious crackdown on these outfits hasn't been attempted by the Pakistani establishment.

It would be in India's interest to have a quiet dialogue on Pakistan's attitude towards these three men and what New Delhi feels needs to be done with them. There's little doubt that tackling these men and their terrorist outfits will remain the benchmark for the Pakistani permanent establishment's attitude towards anti-India terrorism. Terror tactics have the potential of undermining what otherwise appears to be a solidly-rooted peace process.

Kashmir, the major stumbling block between India and Pakistan, remains central to the agenda for the Pakistanis. Of late, there are signs of some flexibility in Pakistan's and India's positions; the 2005 visit of Hurriyat leaders and the cross-LoC bus service are two indications of a new approach.

It would be naive to assume that Pakistan and Musharraf have given up their position on Kashmir. They have not. In his 16 April 2005 banquet speech in New Delhi, an otherwise bullish Musharraf reminded India that brushing disputes under the carpet was 'no more an answer' because these 'always come out of the carpet and bedevil relations'. The reference to Kashmir and Musharraf wanting a final settlement was obvious.

In fact, the broad principles of a possible settlement have been listed by Musharraf himself: India saying there could be no change in boundaries, Pakistan stressing that the LoC was not acceptable as a border and both holding that boundaries should be made irrelevant.

The challenge for Indian and Pakistani leaders and negotiators has been defined very clearly. For a change, the Musharraf formulation correctly reflects the Indian position as well.

But the key question remains, are India and Pakistan up to it? Predicting what might happen between India and Pakistan is a job that many astrologers would reject as too difficult; for analysts and writers it is the overall direction of the relationship that is important.

But the trends of the moment, for the next several

years at least, indicate that India and Pakistan will move closer to each other. Their rigid establishments will align with the people's mood and, little by little, dismantle the barriers that have subverted free contact.

The third player—and referee—the United States of America, is also watching the two sides. If, at any time, the Indian and Pakistani governments don't stick to the rules of the game, Washington remains ready to blow the whistle.

A growing religious right in Pakistan and Hindu fundamentalist forces in India remain the principal threats to the peace process.

Notes

1. Great People, Paranoid State

1. The US State Department's 1998 report on human rights provided the context for the Bishop's action. It said, 'Ayub Masih (detained since October 1996), was convicted of blasphemy under Section 295(c) [of the Pakistan Penal Code] for making favorable comments about author Salman Rushdie and was sentenced to death on 27 April [1998]. Ayub's family and thirteen other landless Christian families were forced from his village in 1996 following the charges. Although the case was pending appeal before the Lahore High Court, Ayub's principal defender, Faisalabad Roman Catholic Bishop and human rights activist John Joseph, committed suicide on May 6 with a handgun outside the Sahiwal court where Ayub had been convicted, to protest the conviction.'

2. The changes introduced by Zia-ul-Haq in the blasphemy laws, are best described in the US State Department report: 'Section 295(a), the blasphemy provision of the Penal Code, originally stipulated a maximum two-year sentence for insulting the religion of any class of citizens. This sentence was increased to ten years in 1991. In 1982 Section 295(b) was added, which stipulated a sentence of

life imprisonment for 'whoever wilfully defiles, damages, or desecrates a copy of the holy Koran.' In 1986 another amendment, Section 295(c), established the death penalty or life imprisonment for directly or indirectly defiling 'the sacred name of the holy Prophet Mohammed'. In 1991 a court struck down the option of life imprisonment. These laws, especially Section 295(c), have been used by rivals and authorities to threaten, punish, or intimidate Ahmadis, Christians, and even orthodox Muslims.

2. India and Pakistan—Talking At Each Other

1. Quoted in *Frontline*, 19 June 1998.
2. I have repeatedly referred to this framework as a 'two-plus-six' agreement in my despatches to *The Hindu*.
3. *Frontline*, 25 July 1997.
4. *Frontline*, 4–7 October 1997.
5. *Frontline*, 15–28 August 1998.
6. See *Asiaweek*, 14 August 1998.
7. *Frontline*, 20 November 1998.
8. *Frontline*, 20 November 1998.
9. See Amit Baruah, 'Rising Expectations' *The Hindu*, 11 December 2003.

4. Sharif, Karamat and Musharraf

1. One kanal of land equals one-eighth of an acre.
2. After dismissing Benazir Bhutto in 1996, President Farooq Leghari had come up with his own version of a National Security Council, where the President, the army chief and the prime minister were all present—but the idea never really took off. Nawaz Sharif, in his second term as prime minister, ensured that Leghari's idea was stillborn.
3. The Mangla corps, stationed in the Punjab, is a strike formation of the Pakistan Army.
4. Hakim Said headed the Pakistani Hamdard, a branch of the Hamdard dawakhana set up by his father, Hakim

Hafiz Abdul Majeed in Delhi in 1906. At the time of partition in 1947, Hakim Said, then 29, migrated to Pakistan to set up the Pakistani branch of the dawakhana in Karachi, turning it into a major producer of herbal products and medicines. Chowk.com, a leading Pakistani website, had this to say about Hakim Said's murder:

'Hakim, social reformer, educationalist and philanthrophist, Hakim Said was murdered outside his clinic at 6:00 am on Saturday, October 17. The 78 year old head of the Hamdard Foundation and Chancellor of Hamdard University had arrived as per custom at his Clinic in Arambagh, Karachi after morning prayers at 6:00 am. As soon as he alighted from his car he was fired upon by assailants in a Mazda Hilux Pickup. Hakim Said sustained three bullet wounds in the head, face and neck. He was brought dead to Civil Hospital twenty minutes later. His assistant Hakim Qadir Qureshi and peon Wali Mohammed were also killed in the assault. Three others were also injured in the firing. The assailants continued firing from their Kalashnikovs even after Hakim Said had been fatally struck, before speeding away unhindered. The Hilux pickup was later found abandoned at Eleandor Road. The police and local authorities are clueless as to the identity of the assailants and the motivation of this senseles murder of a respected citizen, philanthrophist and patriot. Hakim Said, who was fasting at the time of his death was laid to rest later that day at Madinatul Hikmat. His legacy of social work and service to the country live on as a nation mourns the murder of a well-loved citizen.'

5. Going Nuclear

1. *The Hindu*, 19 May 1998.
2. An informal method of money transfer, which originated in South Asia, that operates parallel to the formal banking system.

6. Vajpayee in Lahore

1. There were a number of stories around the banquet. The best one I heard was that the Pearl Continental Hotel never got paid for laying on the spread at the Lahore Fort. There were delays in payment and, lo and behold, General Musharraf had come to power. So, the Hotel, I was told, couldn't press its case with the military government and till the time I was there, at least, never was paid for the lavish hospitality shown to Vajpayee!
2. The Jamaat protesters used a frightening weapon to smash windscreens: a lathi with spikes. It was used with telling effect and scared the daylights out of the dignitaries, who had been especially invited by Prime Minister Sharif to attend the banquet in honour of Vajpayee. Many of them told me that they had a nightmarish experience.
3. It wasn't insignificant that all this was kept a big secret by the Indian and Pakistani establishments. However, word has a way of getting out and soon after the Lahore bus yatra I was told about these new proposals.
4. It's another matter that Jammat-e-Islami activists washed the site after Vajpayee's visit!

7. From Lahore to Kargil

1. The AP report was carried by *The News* on 18 May 1999.
2. The Line of Control (LoC) was bilaterally agreed upon by India and Pakistan after the 1971 war. The 1972 Simla Agreement, signed between Prime Ministers Indira Gandhi and Zulfiqar Ali Bhutto, agreed to settle their differences through peaceful means.

3. *Time* magazine, 12 July 1999.
4. Flight Lieutenant Nachiketa was released from Pakistani custody on 3 June 1999, following an announcement by Nawaz Sharif. There was some drama relating to his release—with the Pakistanis wanting to make a big, public show about his handing over in front of the international press.

   Fortunately, the International Committee of the Red Cross was invited to supervise the release and Nachiketa was released with his dignity intact.

   Later, on 4 June, just before he crossed the border into India, I asked Nachiketa how he had been treated in Pakistani custody. Realizing that he wasn't going to say anything, I gently asked him how much sleep he had been able to catch while in custody.

   'Last night, I slept for about two hours,' Nachiketa, who spent the night of 3 June at the Indian air adviser's residence in Islamabad said. And, then the tall, lightly built young man changed the subject. 'How's life as an Indian journalist in Pakistan?' he asked. That was the end of our conversation.
5. See *The News*, 31 May 1999.
6. *The Nation*, 1 July 1999.
7. Nasim Zehra, a Pakistani journalist, often given ringside views of what goes on within the establishment, gave this account of the impact of the Zinni visit and pressure mounted by the Americans in *Arab News* (31 July 2004):

   > Throughout Kargil the Washington angle acquired special significance especially against the backdrop of Pakistan's weak and fractured decision-making apparatus. The Clinton-Sharif exchanges and the Zinni trip created further divisions and distrust.
   >
   > He [Sharif] was greatly affected by his June 24 meeting with Zinni. After the visit, during a Islamabad-Lahore flight with the prime minister in his special plane, Sharif explained

to the author [Zehra] how 'India would initiate electronic warfare, jam all military installations and how all that could lead to a nuclear war.' He feared that the Kargil operation could spiral into a bigger and dangerous war.

The scale of Indian military retaliation and the international response to Kargil had surprised the Pakistanis. Sharif's foreign office team, his kitchen Cabinet and the DCC [Defence Committee of the Cabinet] increasingly worked at odds. Its final manifestation was the prime minister's sudden dash to Washington in the early hours of July 4.

On July 2 the army chief had given a detailed military briefing to the DCC. Musharraf's conclusion was that India would never take the war beyond Kargil and Pakistan could hold its positions. The DCC ended inconclusively to reconvene on the afternoon of July 5. Instead on July 3 at 10 p.m. the prime minister instructed his key aides to prepare for the Washington departure.

The kitchen Cabinet had decided to seek an 'honourable exit' from Kargil via the Washington route. Musharraf too was instructed to arrive at the airport. He merely told the prime minister to 'get the best deal.'

Zehra's account goes to show that Sharif's panic level was beginning to mount and he wanted out of the situation. And that the Pakistani Prime Minister was 'greatly affected' by whatever the big, burly Zinni had told him.

8. *The Hindu*, 27 June 1999.
9. Ritu Sarin reported in *The Indian Express* (24 October 1999):

And by June 4, India had taken the audacious step of delivering the Musharraf tapes, along with a written transcript to Pakistan's Prime Minister Nawaz Sharif himself.... Those in the know say that Mishra's appointment with Nawaz Sharif was fixed by a senior member of the Prime Minister's Office (PMO) for the breakfast hour the following morning. Mishra went alone at about 8:30 am, handed over the tape and transcript and apparently made it known that this was just a sample of the 'evidence' of military involvement in possession of New Delhi ... a worried-looking premier said he would look into the contents and act accordingly.

10. About a month later, Nasim Zehra revealed in *The News*, 28 July 1999, in rich detail of how the bilateral deal between India and Pakistan was being negotiated and how it fell through:

It was on the afternoon of June 27 that it all appeared to have been finalised. On his way to Beijing Nawaz Sharif would fly over Indian territory. While doing so he would send a message of goodwill to his Indian counterpart. In response to the Pakistani Prime Minister's message, Vajpayee would invite him to visit Delhi, to make a technical stop. Responding to Vajpayee's invitation, Nawaz Sharif would stop in Delhi on his way back from China. In Delhi the two Prime Minsters were to sign the four-point finalised agreement.

Zehra's piece, quoted extensively by A.G. Noorani in *Frontline* (10 September 1999), continued:

Agreement was reached on four points: appropriate steps to be taken by both sides to mutually respect the LoC determined under the Simla Agreement of 1972; immediate resumption of the composite dialogue initiated under the Lahore process; Islamabad to use its influence on the Mujahideen to request them to disengage; find an expeditious solution to the Kashmir dispute within a specified time-frame. It was also agreed that following the agreement, Pak-India dialogue would resume involving the Foreign Ministers. For immediate military de-escalation, the Directors-General Military Operations of the two countries were to hold a meeting.

The agreement on the text was evolved during the five R.K. Mishra's Pakistan trips (sic). Mishra would carry back and forth amendments in a draft form in which amendments were made based on input from both sides. As a special envoy of the Indian Prime Minister, the businessman R.K. Mishra met with the Pakistani Prime Minister during all his trips to Pakistan.'

On 27 June, around 5 p.m., the text of the proposed 'goodwill message' from Sharif was faxed from Islamabad to New Delhi, Noorani's article said. Zehra wrote:

The return message was coming in later than expected. The Indians were requested to fax the message at the Prime Minister's Model Town residence. The message came at around 10 p.m. And like a bombshell, Vajpayee was not inviting Nawaz Sharif to visit Delhi. Instead he was asking to 'withdraw' the intruders from Kargil so that bilateral dialogue could be resumed. Telephone contacts with the Indians at the highest level did not help. India's principal interlocutor blamed Delhi's going back on a 'done deal' first on some misunderstanding on what had been agreed but subsequently conceded that the hawks in the Indian establishment had won out. There was a sudden panic amongst those who were the principal actors of Pakistan's back-channel diplomacy. The trip to China had still to go ahead. However, a decision was taken to cut it short.

Zehra's is a fly-on-the-wall account. To the best of my knowledge, the Government of India never denied this account.

Later, when General Musharraf would take charge of Pakistan's destiny, Zehra would emerge as a 'messenger girl' for the Government of Pakistan—staying for a considerable length of time in days when India wasn't issuing visas to any Pakistanis. At a time of eyeball-to-eyeball military confrontation between India and Pakistan in 2002, Zehra was in Delhi. She was reportedly given access to the top echelons of the Vajpayee government, including the powerful National Security Adviser Brajesh Mishra.

Just before Vajpayee travelled to Islamabad for the landmark South Asian Association for Regional Cooperation (SAARC) summit in January 2004, he granted an exclusive interview to Zehra for state-run Pakistan Television.

Zehra is believed to be close to General Musharraf and her writings reflect the thinking process in the Pakistani establishment.

11. Aitazaz Ahsan also addressed a press conference in Islamabad on 11 August 1999. He raised 101 questions about the Kargil war—demanding answers from the government.
12. *The Nation*, 1 August 1999.

8. The Fallout from Kargil

1. *The News*, 27 June 1999.
2. *The News*, 12 July 1999.

3. *The News*, 9 July 1999.
4. *The News*, 18 July 1999.
5. My report in *The Hindu*, 26 July 1999.
6. See *Frontline*, 30 July 1999.
7. See my report in *The Hindu*, 15 August 1999.

10. Musharraf, India and Kandahar

1. *The Hindu*, 13 October 1999.
2. *The Hindu*, 15 October 1999.
3. *The Hindu*, 22 October 1999.
4. It's worth recalling that none other than Vajpayee was Morarji's foreign minister at the time when Bhutto was executed after a dubious trial. However, Vajpayee took a diametrically opposite view in the case of Sharif. Mercifully, Sharif despite being convicted in the 12 October hijacking case, went into exile in Saudi Arabia on 10 December 2000, following a deal with Musharraf. Morarji Desai was awarded Pakistan's highest civilian honour—the Nishan-e-Pakistan by Zia—the only reason behind it I can think off is gratitude on the military dictator's part for the Indian prime minister's position on Bhutto's execution. India believed at the time that the Bhutto case was an internal affair of Pakistan and, consequently, New Delhi did not join other countries in making an appeal for clemency.

11. Can Musharraf Reverse the Zia Legacy?

1. *The Hindu*, 20 February 2000.

12. India and Pakistan: Looking to the Future

1. *The Hindu*, 15 April 2003.
2. *The Hindu*, 14 June 2002.
3. *The News*, 8 February 2004.